United States
S D0831933

Published for the United States Postal Service by Scott Publishing Co.

Editor	Harvey R. Warm
Associate Editors	William W. Cummings
	Lilly B. Freed
	William W. Wylie
Editorial Staff	Barbara A. Bullied
	Leslie A. Wolf
	Steven C. Frumkin
Art Director	Leo Lesser
Editorial Consultant	Irving Koslow
Stories (1975)	Lynne S. Warm

Cover Illustration by
Jim Sharpe

Stamp quotations from
the 1975 Scott Catalogue.
James B. Hatcher
Editor-in-Chief

For previous contributors see page 228

Library of Congress Catalogue Card Number 74-15135

Printed in the United States of America.

HOW TO USE
STAMPS & STORIES

On this unique journey through the pages of our history, postage stamps are your guide. Illustrated stories of the famous people and events shown on stamps recreate the building of a nation from its founding to the present day.

The book also includes a color catalogue of postage stamps of the United States, its territories and former possessions, and United Nations stamps. This illustrated catalogue lists current market values and gives useful information that will help you to identify your stamps. Every stamp is listed chronologically by Scott catalogue number and each listing contains the following:

The catalogue also lists philatelic details such as watermarks, perforations, and years of issue. These will aid you in identifying stamps of similar design. Watermarks (Wmk.) are designs incorporated in the paper on which certain stamps are printed. Perforations are the number of small holes in a two centimeter space on the edge of a stamp. A stamp which has 12 such holes is listed as Perf. 12 (perforated 12), while a stamp with no perforations is listed as Imperf. (imperforate). Coil stamps are perforated on two sides only, either horizontally or vertically. **When a perforation, year of issue, or watermark is mentioned the description applies to all succeeding issues until a change is noted.**

All philatelic terms mentioned in the text are defined in the glossary. In addition, the book includes information about different types of early stamp designs. This material provides an interesting avenue of exploration for those who like the challenge of a mental puzzler.

"Sia" Numbers

Some of the stamps catalogued in this book are not shown. The illustrations on such stamps are identified by a "sia" number (sia — same illustration as). For example, in the listings which appear below Scott No. 247 has the same illustration as Scott No. 246.

246	3.50	.85	1c Franklin
247	5.50	.45	1c blue Franklin, sia 246

How to Order Stamps

When ordering stamps from a dealer, identify items wanted by country of issue, Scott No., and condition (unused or used). Please note that Scott Publishing Co. does not sell stamps.

Condition is an important factor of price. Unused prices are for stamps in fine condition. Off center, heavily cancelled, faded, or stained stamps usually sell at large discounts. Values in italics indicate latest auction prices, infrequent sales, or fluctuating market values. Dealers' handling costs are not included in price quotations. Expect to pay more for inexpensive stamps.

TABLE OF CONTENTS

The Magic Stamp World Goes From

A

Australia to Zanzibar

Animals to Zoology

How to Be a Happy Stamp Collector

At first glance stamp collecting may seem like a maze of colors, shapes, and mystifying symbols; but look a little closer and you'll see that...

Anything and almost everything you like is found on stamps, from animals to astronauts... from famous works of art to sports ...from safaris to far-off lands to music and flowers.

Above all stamps capture the spirit and preserve the history of famous people, places, things... To look at them is to take a journey into the far-distant and near-distant past... to relive the exciting days of chivalry and buccaneers, explorers and kings... man's first landing on the moon.

Regardless of what type of stamps you choose to collect, *you* will find that stamps are educational, inspiring, enjoyable, and entertaining. From *Australia* and *architecture* all the way to *Zambia* and *zebras,* stamps offer you a fun-filled way to utilize your leisure time.

How to Start
Your First Collection

Select a subject you like — anything! Perhaps you'd like to collect the stamps you've just seen in this book...or fashion...theater ...dogs...wildlife...sports...Canada...It can be any country — any topic — you have the world to choose from!

Now start to save stamps from mail delivered to your home. (Here's a special tip: to remove bits of envelope from the stamp, soak it in cold water for fifteen minutes, or until the water has softened the gum on the back of the stamp. Take one edge of the attached paper, bend it back, and peel it away!)

If you're fortunate enough to travel in countries other than your own, be sure to obtain that nation's latest issues before you leave. Frequent your post office and buy the new issues at actual face value. Ask friends and relatives to save stamps for you ...Barter with other collectors...Join a stamp club . . . Look in your telephone directory for the name and address of a stamp dealer in your area.

Austria to Zululand

Brazil

Mr. Zip used with permission of U.S.P.S.

5

Make Your Own Magic World

Canada

China

Children

Cards

Do's and Don'ts of Mounting Stamps

Don't paste stamps on album pages... they are fragile!

Do use the best peelable hinges you can find. Follow these directions:

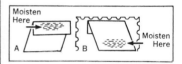

In diagram A we have folded a hinge, gummed side out, one quarter from the end and lightly moistened it as shown. Fasten the gum side to the back of the stamp near the top just below the perforation as shown in diagram B. Then moisten the tip of the hinge and fasten squarely in position on the album page.

Now that you've put your first stamps in your first album (easy, wasn't it) you've probably discovered that stamp collecting

Dominican Republic

Dance

Explorers

is ... *Educational and enjoyable* — a marvelous way to explore the world ... to thrill to the wonders of nature. Stamps also offer you a chance to make new *friends*. As you collect and exchange stamps you will meet new people, and develop lasting friendships that will grow over the years.

How to Identify Stamps

Your first stamps will probably be modern commemoratives. These stamps, issued to honor famous people and events, are easy to identify and catalogue.

First, pick up your stamp with *stamp tongs*. These handy gadgets, shaped like tweezers, keep fingerprints off your stamps.

Examine the stamp. Look at its year and place of issue, its color and denomination.

Now flip through your stamp catalogue to locate the year and country in question. Search the listings for a stamp that looks like yours ... is the same color, has the same design, and shows the same denomination. Look for the Scott number that appears with this listing. Once you've found it you have catalogued your stamp!

Education

Flags

Ecuador

France

Flowers

Gambia

Geography

Greece

Germany

How Postage Stamps Originated

Long ago, before the postage stamp was invented, the recipient of a letter — not the sender — had to pay for its transportation from one mail station (post) to another. The charges that he paid were referred to as postage. The letters themselves were sealed with wax and then stamped with a seal or ring design to identify the sender.

In England, this practice came to an end in 1840 when a British educator named Rowland Hill convinced Parliament to adopt a sweeping postal reform. This reform lowered British postal rates and provided for the prepayment of mail through the use of postage stamps.

The reform of 1840 revolutionized postal history. It produced the world's first postage stamp, the "Penny Black", and made it possible for anyone to send a letter anywhere in Britain for a penny. As a result, the number of letters mailed in Britain

Italy

Heroes

doubled in a year. More importantly, other nations followed Britain's lead in lowering their rates and issuing postage stamps.

How Stamp Collecting Started

One year following the appearance of the "Penny Black", a young woman advertised in the *London Times* for cancelled stamps. Destined to be remembered as the first collector, she wished to use the stamps to paper her bedroom walls. Then, in 1865 a Frenchman named M. Herpin coined the word philately, a term often used interchangeably with stamp collecting. Taken from the Greek, it means "the love of tax-free things" and refers to the use of stamps to deliver mail "tax-free" to the recipient.

Whether called philately or stamp collecting the hobby is today the most popular in the world. In the United States alone, an estimated sixteen million people are collectors.

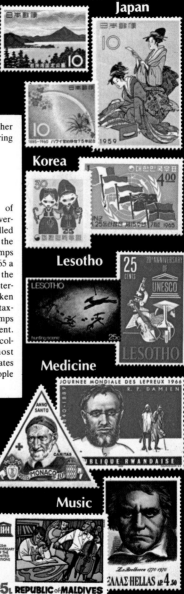

Napoleon

Norway

REPUBLIQUE DU DAHOMEY

Olympics

Oldenburg

Postal History

U.S. Postal History

In pre-Revolutionary America the mails were the domain of private enterprise or the colonies. But after the United States achieved its independence, the U.S. Post Office became a branch of the federal government in Washington, D.C.

In the first half of the nineteenth century two developments brought about drastic changes in the postal service. In 1845 rates were lowered, and in 1847 the United States became the fourth country in the world to issue postage stamps. The first U.S. stamp, issued on July 1, portrayed Benjamin Franklin who was Deputy Postmaster General for the American colonies in the years before the Revolutionary War.

As the country grew, new demands were placed on the postal service. The Overland Mail Service, formed in 1858, helped speed letters to the pioneers, and the Pony Express, operational from 1860-61, carried mail from East to West in the days before the Civil War.

After the Civil War, the rails replaced the horse as the chief means of moving mail. During the twentieth century, however, an even faster form of transportation—the airplane—was invented. The first regularly

Paintings

scheduled air mail service was inaugurated on May 15, 1918, and by 1924 the United States had 24-hour transcontinental air mail service.

With increased speed came increased service. In 1855 registered mail service was introduced. Free city mail service followed in 1863, and ten years later rural free delivery was established. In 1885 special delivery stamps made their appearance, and in 1913 parcel post service was begun.

Modernization of the mail service culminated on July 1, 1971, when the U.S. Post Office became the United States Postal Service, a quasi-independent public utility. On that day the new U.S.P.S. issued its first stamp, which shows the Service's streamlined emblem.

Building a U.S. Collection

For the beginning collector of United States stamps, issues of the twentieth century are an interesting place to start. Most of these stamps are easy to obtain, colorful, and inexpensive, and they also offer you an opportunity to become familiar with United States philately. It would be wise to complete a collection of these stamps before moving to more specialized and classic areas.

Panama

Poland

Qatar

Queens

Quixote

Romance

Religion

POSTA ROMANA

Romania

Sports

Stamp Condition

When buying stamps, it is wise to look for well-centered copies, which means that the margins form a perfect frame around the stamp design. At the same time, check the color of the stamp and the gum condition. Richly colored stamps with most of their original gum intact are more highly prized than faded stamps, or stamps lacking their original gum.

If you collect used stamps, it is advisable to look for lightly cancelled copies, as these are generally more valuable than those with heavy cancellations.

Coil stamps are often collected in pairs. If you obtain a coil pair you may want to leave it intact. Also, pairs or blocks of stamps containing different designs (i.e., stamps issued se-tenant) should be kept intact, as they are sometimes more desirable in that state.

Remember that well-cared for stamps are always the most valuable.

Scouting

Spain

Tchad

Rarities

The world's rarest and most valuable stamp was issued by British Guiana in 1856. Only one copy of this stamp is known to exist, and it recently sold at auction for the fantastic price of $280,000.

Sometimes luck pays off and collectors find rare stamps by accident. W. T. Robey did. In 1918 Robey, a clerk in a Washington brokerage house, bought a sheet of U.S. air mail stamps for $24.00, and then discovered that the centers of the stamps were printed upside down. In 1971 a single stamp from this unusual sheet sold at a New York auction for $36,000.

Unusual Types of Stamps

Everyone is familiar with air mail stamps and stamps used to post letters, but did you know that stamps have been used to tax potatoes, wine, and beer? That the English Stamp Act helped bring about the American Revolutionary War?

Varieties of Stamps

Sometimes two stamps look almost alike but are not. They are different varieties. Experienced collectors learn to tell such varieties apart by measuring the number of perforations in a length of 20 millimeters...

Theater

United Kingdom

United Nations

U.S.S.R.

Vatican

Writers

Wallis and Futuna

by finding out if the stamp was printed by rotary press or flat press (stamps printed by rotary press are longer or wider than stamps printed by flat press).

Watermarks

Watermarks are formed in the paper making process of a stamp. They are the design, lettering, or overall pattern created in the paper fibers, and can often be seen if you hold a stamp up to bright light. Sometimes the only way to distinguish between two stamps is to find out which one has a watermark.

Learning More About Stamps

The more you explore the magic world of stamps, the more you will find there is to learn about them. Local libraries can supply you with a wealth of interesting information about stamps — their history and lore. So can philatelic societies, magazines and newspapers, books and catalogues. For your reference, a list of major United States philatelic societies and publications is included in the appendix at the back of this book.

STAMP COLOR GUIDE

Stamp colors shown in this book include (clockwise from upper left):

bistre brown (bis. brn.)
black (blk.)
blue (bl.)
blue green (bl. grn.)
bright blue (brt. bl.)
brown
carmine (car.)
deep blue (dp. bl.)
gray
green (grn.)
henna brown
lake
light green (lt. grn.)
lilac
olive
olive bistre
olive green
orange (org.)
purple
red
rose
sepia
turquoise
ultramarine (ultra.)
vermilion (verm.)
violet (vio.)
yellow (yel.)
yellow green (yel. grn.)

NOTE: In this book, all stamps are reproduced in color at about 70% of actual size to conform to government regulations. This may diminish the beauty of the originals. Color fidelity is not guaranteed.

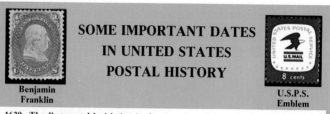

SOME IMPORTANT DATES IN UNITED STATES POSTAL HISTORY

Benjamin Franklin

U.S.P.S. Emblem

1639: The first postal legislation in the American colonies, a Massachusetts act regulating overseas communication, is passed.

1707: Postal service in the colonies becomes a function of the British Crown, which appoints deputy postmasters general to manage the mail. Benjamin Franklin, the most important person to hold this position (1753-74), greatly improves postal finances and mail service to and from major cities.

1787: The U.S. Constitution authorizes Congress to "establish Post Offices."

1842: Postage stamps are introduced in the United States by a private firm, Greig's City Despatch Post of New York.

1845: Some United States postmasters begin to provide special stamps of local origin to show prepayment of mail. These stamps are called postmasters' provisionals and are usually very rare.

1847: The U.S. government issues its first postage stamps (Scott Nos. 1 and 2).

1855: Registered mail is introduced to provide postal patrons with greater security for valuable mail and insurance in case of loss.

1864: Money order service is introduced to allow people to send the equivalent of cash through the mails without danger of loss or theft.

1885: Special delivery service is inaugurated.

1896: At the request of farmers, rural free delivery is established.

1913: Parcel post and C.O.D. (cash on delivery) service is introduced.

1918: Air mail service is begun. By 1924 the United States has 24-hour transcontinental air mail service.

1971: The United States Postal Service, a quasi-public utility, assumes operation of the United States Post Office Department.

Postmasters' Provisional

Air Mail

Registered Mail

Colonial Postrider

Special Delivery

Parcel Post

THE UNITED STATES

GOVT. — Republic.
AREA — 3,615,211 sq. mi.
POP. — 203,184,772 (1970).
CAPITAL — Washington, D. C.
100 Cents — 1 Dollar
In addition to the 50 States and the District of Columbia, the Republic includes Guam, the

Commonwealth of Puerto Rico, the Virgin Islands, American Samoa, Wake, Midway and a number of small islands in the Pacific Ocean, all of which use stamps of the United States.
Included also is the Panama Canal Zone which issues its own stamps.

1   2   3   4

Issues of 1847 to 1894 are Unmarked
Issue of 1847, Imperf.

1	500.00	120.00	5c Benjamin Franklin Jul. 1
2	3000.00	350.00	10c George Washington Jul. 1

Actually, official imitations made from new plates by order of the Post Office Department, issued without gum.

Issue of 1875, Reproductions of 1 & 2

3	285.00	5c Franklin
4	400.00	10c Washington

Reproductions. The letters R. W. H. & E. at the bottom of each stamp are less distinct on the reproductions than on the originals.

5c. On the originals the left side of the white shirt frill touches the oval on a level with the top of the "F" of "Five." On the reproductions it touches the oval about on a level with the top of the figure "5."

10c. On the reproductions, line of coat at left points to right tip of "X" and line of coat at right points to center of "S" of CENTS. On the originals, line of coat points to "T" of TEN and between "T" and "S" of CENTS. On the reproductions the eyes have a sleepy look, the line of the mouth is straighter, and in the curl of hair near the left cheek is a strong black dot, while the originals have only a faint one.

GEORGE WASHINGTON (1732-99)

Let me now . . . warn you in the most solemn manner against the baneful effects of the spirit of party. Farewell Address, 1796

Following a triumphant procession from Mount Vernon, George Washington arrived in New York City on April 30, 1789 for his inauguration as the first president of the United States. Standing on the balcony of Federal Hall, the man who had led the Continental Army to victory in the Revolution took the oath of office and the crowd lining Wall Street broke into cheers of confidence and approval.

Washington's two terms in office (1789-97) justified the faith of his countrymen. Despite his fears that he faced "an ocean of difficulties without that competency of political skill, abilities, and inclinations which is necessary to manage the helm," he proved an able executive. Ignoring the antagonism that existed between Thomas Jefferson and Alexander Hamilton he made Jefferson secretary of state, Hamilton secretary of the treasury, and then utilized both men's talents to the fullest. His administration saw the establishment of national credit, the setting up of an effective working government where none had been before, and a new era of strength for the nation he served so well in war and peace.

Portraits of George Washington have consistently appeared on U. S. stamps from 1847 to the present.

Haiti Scott No. C11.

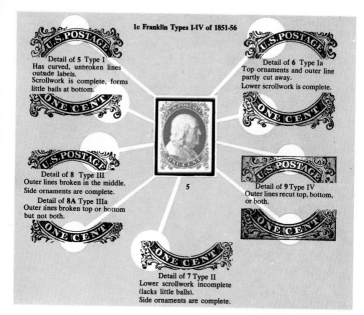

1c Franklin Types I-IV of 1851-56

Detail of 5 Type I
Has curved, unbroken lines outside labels.
Scrollwork is complete, forms little balls at bottom.

Detail of 6 Type Ia
Top ornaments and outer line partly cut away.
Lower scrollwork is complete.

Detail of 8 Type III
Outer lines broken in the middle.
Side ornaments are complete.

Detail of 8A Type IIIa
Outer lines broken top or bottom but not both.

5

Detail of 9 Type IV
Outer lines recut top, bottom, or both.

Detail of 7 Type II
Lower scrollwork incomplete (lacks little balls).
Side ornaments are complete.

BENJAMIN FRANKLIN (1706-90)

Do not squander time, for that is the stuff life is made of. Poor Richard's Almanac, 1757.

Benjamin Franklin served his country for fifty years as inventor, philosopher, statesman, diplomat, author, and scientist. As a statesman he helped draft the Declaration of Independence and was one of its signers. As a diplomat he served for many years as the American representative to France, where he enlisted financial and military support for the American Revolutionary cause.

A Bostonian by birth and a Philadelphian by choice, Franklin was also an accomplished printer. He helped develop the first circulating library and the first post office; invented the Franklin stove, the lightning rod, and bifocal glasses; organized police and fire departments; wrote *Poor Richard's Almanac* and his famous *Autobiography*.

The "father" of the U. S. Postal Service, Franklin has appeared on more U. S. stamps than any other public figure except Washington.

U.S.S.R. Scott No. 1875

18

Issue of 1851-56, Imperf.

5	*20,000.00*	*7000.00*	1c Franklin, type I
5A	*2000.00*	650.00	1c Same, type Ib

Nos. 6–9: Franklin, sia 5

6	*2,650.00*	850.00	1c dark blue, type Ia
7	150.00	30.00	1c blue, type II
8	*1400.00*	450.00	1c blue, type III
8A	475.00	225.00	1c pale blue, type IIIa
9	90.00	26.50	1c blue, type IV

10	275.00	16.50	3c orange brown Washington, type I, sia 11
11	30.00	2.00	3c Washington, type I
12	*1650.00*	225.00	5c Jefferson, type I
13	*1850.00*	250.00	10c green Washington, type I, sia 15

Detail of **11**
THREE CENTS.
  Type I. There is an outer frame line at top and bottom.

Detail of **12**
FIVE CENTS.
  Type I. There are projections on all four sides.

10c Washington Types I-IV of 1855

Detail of **13**
  Type I. The "shells" at the lower corners are practically complete. The outer line below the label is very nearly complete. The outer lines are broken above the middle of the top label and the "X" in each upper corner.

Detail of **14**
  Type II. The design is complete at the top. The outer line at the bottom is broken in the middle. The shells are partly cut away.

15

Detail of **15**
  Type III. The outer lines are broken above the top label and the "X" numerals. The outer line at the bottom and the shells are partly cut away, as in Type II.

Detail of **16**
  Type IV. The outer lines have been recut at top or bottom or both.
  Types I, II, III and IV have complete ornaments at the sides of the stamps and three pearls at each outer edge of the bottom panel.

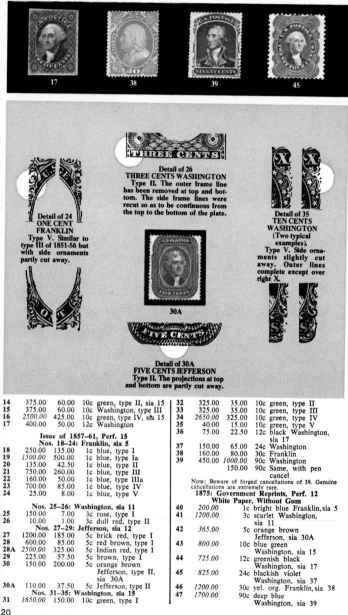

17   38   39   45

Detail of 26
THREE CENTS WASHINGTON
Type II. The outer frame line
has been removed at top and bottom. The side frame lines were
recut so as to be continuous from
the top to the bottom of the plate.

Detail of 24
ONE CENT
FRANKLIN
Type V. Similar to
type III of 1851-56 but
with side ornaments
partly cut away.

Detail of 35
TEN CENTS
WASHINGTON
(Two typical
examples).
Type V. Side orna-
ments slightly cut
away. Outer lines
complete except over
right X.

30A

Detail of 30A
FIVE CENTS JEFFERSON
Type II. The projections at top
and bottom are partly cut away.

14	375.00	60.00	10c green, type II, sia 15
15	375.00	60.00	10c Washington, type III
16	2500.00	425.00	10c green, type IV, sia 15
17	400.00	50.00	12c Washington

Issue of 1857-61, Perf. 15
Nos. 18-24: Franklin, sia 5

18	250.00	135.00	1c blue, type I
19	1500.00	500.00	1c blue, type Ia
20	135.00	42.50	1c blue, type II
21	750.00	260.00	1c blue, type III
22	160.00	50.00	1c blue, type IIIa
23	700.00	85.00	1c blue, type IV
24	25.00	8.00	1c blue, type V

Nos. 25-26: Washington, sia 11

25	150.00	7.00	3c rose, type I
26	10.00	1.00	3c dull red, type II

Nos. 27-29: Jefferson, sia 12

27	1200.00	185.00	5c brick red, type I
28	600.00	85.00	5c red brown, type I
28A	2500.00	325.00	5c Indian red, type I
29	225.00	57.50	5c brown, type I
30	150.00	200.00	5c orange brown Jefferson, type II, sia 30A
30A	110.00	37.50	5c Jefferson, type II

Nos. 31-35: Washington, sia 15

31	1650.00	150.00	10c green, type I
32	325.00	35.00	10c green, type II
33	325.00	35.00	10c green, type III
34	2650.00	325.00	10c green, type IV
35	40.00	15.00	10c green, type V
36	75.00	22.50	12c black Washington, sia 17
37	150.00	65.00	24c Washington
38	160.00	80.00	30c Franklin
39	450.00	1000.00	90c Washington
		150.00	90c Same, with pen cancel

Note: Beware of forged cancellations of 39. Genuine
cancellations are extremely rare.

1875: Government Reprints, Perf. 12
White Paper, Without Gum

40	200.00		1c bright blue Franklin, sia 5
41	1200.00		3c scarlet Washington, sia 11
42	365.00		5c orange brown Jefferson, sia 30A
43	800.00		10c blue green Washington, sia 15
44	725.00		12c greenish black Washington, sia 17
45	825.00		24c blackish violet Washington, sia 37
46	1200.00		30c yel. org. Franklin, sia 38
47	1700.00		90c deep blue Washington, sia 39

THOMAS JEFFERSON (1743-1826)

Third President of the United States, legislator, diplomat, and author; scientist, musician, and inventor; architect, philosopher, and planter, Thomas Jefferson was a Renaissance man born into the Age of Reason.

The son of a well-to-do Virginia planter, Jefferson attended the College of William and Mary and received his law degree before serving in the legislature of Virginia. By the time the Second Continental Congress met in Philadelphia he was well-known as a politician, as a firm, outspoken advocate of Locke's philosophy of man's inherent right to liberty, as a gifted writer, and as a strong supporter of the rebels' cause in the Revolution. It was only natural that he became a member of the five-man committee charged with drafting the Declaration of Independence.

The Declaration, adopted by the Continental Congress on July 4, 1776, was largely the work of Jefferson, then thirty-three. It was for this accomplishment, for the drafting of Virginia's Statute for Religious Freedom and for founding the University of Virginia that the "Sage of Monticello" wished to be remembered.

Americans today also remember that he designed and built Monticello, his Virginia home, that he authorized the Louisiana Purchase, and that he believed in an agrarian nation in which all men would share in the choice of government.

See Scott No. 12, 30A , 1318

Scott No. 1318 shows the Jefferson Memorial in Washington, D. C.

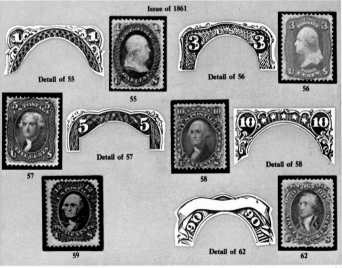

Issue of 1861

Detail of 55

55

Detail of 56

56

Detail of 57

57

58

Detail of 58

59

Detail of 62

62

Issue of 1861-62

63

1c. A dash has been added under the tip of the ornament at right of the numeral in upper left corner.

64

3c. Ornaments at corners have been enlarged and end in a small ball.

67

5c. A leaflet has been added to the foliated ornaments at each corner.

68

10c. A heavy curved line has been cut below the stars and an outer line has been added to the ornaments above them.

69

12c. Ovals and scrolls have been added to the corners.

Issue of 1861, Perf. 12

Following the outbreak of the Civil War, the U. S. government re-designed all postage stamps to prevent their usage by the South.

55	12,000.00	1c Franklin
56	300.00	3c Washington
57	7500.00	5c brown Jefferson,
58	1500.00	10c Washington
59	27,500.00	12c Washington
60	2000.00	24c dk. vio. Washington, sia 70
61	9000.00	30c red org. Franklin, sia 71
62	12,500.00	90c dull blue Washington, sia 72
62B	1500.00 225.00	10c dark green Washington, sia 58

Nos. 55-62 were not used for postage and do not exist in a cancelled state. The paper they were printed on is thin and semi-transparent, that of the following issues is more opaque.

Issue of 1861-62, Perf. 12

63	32.50	7.25	1c Franklin
64	875.00	100.00	3c Washington
65	10.00	.45	3c rose Washington, sia 64
66	650.00		3c lake Washington, sia 64
67	850.00	75.00	5c Jefferson
68	45.00	6.50	10c Washington
69	85.00	10.00	12c Washington
70	150.00	16.00	24c Washington
71	115.00	17.50	30c Franklin
72	325.00	60.00	90c Washington

Issue of 1861-66, Perf. 12

73	37.50	7.50	2c Andrew Jackson ("Black Jack")
74	1500.00		3c scarlet Washington, sia 67
75	265.00	42.50	5c red brown Jefferson, sia 67

72

90c. Parallel lines form an angle above the ribbon with "U. S. Postage"; between these lines a row of dashes has been added and a point of color to the apex of the lower pair.

Grill

70

71

73

77

76	62.50	12.00	5c brn. Jefferson, sia 67
77	150.00	20.00	15c Abraham Lincoln
78	55.00	13.50	24c lilac Washington, sia 70

No. 74 was not regularly issued

Grills on U. S. Stamps

Between 1867 and 1870, postage stamps were embossed with grills to prevent people from re-using cancelled stamps. The pyramid-shaped grills absorbed cancellation ink, making it virtually impossible to chemically remove a postmark.

Issue of 1867, With Grills, Perf. 12
Grills A, B, C: Points Up
A. Grill Covers Entire Stamp

79	900.00	250.00	3c rose Washington, sia 64
80	32,500.00		5c brn. Jefferson, sia 67
81		27,500.00	30c org. Franklin, sia 71

B. Grill about 18x15 mm

82		27,500.00	3c rose Washington, sia 64

C. Grill about 13x16 mm

83	400.00	75.00	3c rose Washington, sia 64

Grills, D, Z, E, F: Points Down
D. Grill about 12x14 mm.

84	800.00	250.00	2c blk. Jackson, sia 73
85	400.00	70.00	3c rose Washington, sia 64

Z. Grill about 11x14 mm.

85A		25,000.00	1c bl. Franklin, sia 63
85B	300.00	65.00	2c blk. Jackson, sia 73
85C	900.00	200.00	3c rose Washington, sia 64
85D		20,000.00	10c green Washington, sia 69
85E	500.00	125.00	12c black Washington, sia 69
85F		22,500.00	15c blk. Lincoln, sia 77

ANDREW JACKSON (1767-1845)

There are no necessary evils in government. Its evils exist only in its abuses. Message Vetoing the Bank Bill, July 10, 1832.

Andrew Jackson, founder of the Democratic party and hero of the Battle of New Orleans, was the first U.S. president not born of the Virginia or Massachusetts aristocracy. In 1828 the once-poor soldier hero of the War of 1812 defeated venerable John Quincy Adams for the presidency and the aspirations of the common man were given voice in Washington.

During "Old Hickory's" two terms in office (1829-36) the nation entered a new era of expansion under "Jacksonian Democracy". An enemy of "money power", the president vetoed the re-charter of the Bank of the United States in 1832. Under his policy of fiscal reform the public debt was paid for the first time. In 1837 Jackson, more popular than when elected, retired to the Hermitage, his home in Tennessee.

See Scott Stamp Nos. 73, 1037

E. Grill about 11x13 mm.

86	130.00	40.00	1c blue Franklin, sia 63
87	65.00	14.00	2c black Jackson, sia 73
88	30.00	1.85	3c rose Washington, sia 64
89	250.00	32.50	10c grn. Washington, sia 68
90	275.00	32.50	12c blk. Washington, sia 69
91	725.00	77.50	15c black Lincoln, sia 77

F. Grill about 9x13 mm.

92	70.00	17.50	1c blue Franklin, sia 63
93	35.00	8.00	2c black Jackson, sia 73
94	18.50	1.20	3c red Washington, sia 64
95	250.00	55.00	5c brown Jefferson, sia 67
96	100.00	17.50	10c yellow green Washington, sia 68
97	115.00	18.50	12c black Washington, sia 69
98	120.00	20.00	15c black Lincoln, sia 77
99	300.00	115.00	24c gray lilac Washington, sia 70

100	400.00	72.50	30c orange Franklin, sia 71
101	800.00	200.00	90c blue Washington, sia 72

Reissues of 1875, Without Grill, Perf. 12

102	*175.00*	100.00	1c blue Franklin, sia 63
103	*900.00*	500.00	2c black Jackson, sia 73
104	*1200.00*	600.00	3c brown red Washington, sia 64
105	*750.00*	425.00	5c brown Jefferson, sia 67
106	*950.00*	500.00	10c grn. Washington, sia 68
107	*1250.00*	500.00	12c blk. Washington, sia 69
108	*1100.00*	500.00	15c black Lincoln, sia 77
109	*1300.00*	500.00	24c deep violet Washington, sia 70
110	*1750.00*	650.00	30c brownish orange Franklin, sia 71
111	*2000.00*	750.00	90c blue Washington, sia 72

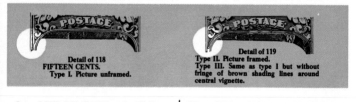

Detail of 118
FIFTEEN CENTS.
Type I. Picture unframed.

Detail of 119
Type II. Picture framed.
Type III. Same as type II but without fringe of brown shading lines around central vignette.

Issue of 1869, With Grill Measuring 9½x9 mm. Perf. 12

112	75.00	22.50	1c Franklin
113	45.00	8.50	2c Post Horse & Rider
114	27.50	1.75	3c Locomotive
115	175.00	27.50	6c Washington
116	185.00	30.00	10c Shield and Eagle
117	165.00	27.50	12c S.S. Adriatic
118	500.00	95.00	15c Columbus Landing, type I

119	200.00	35.00	15c brown and blue Columbus Landing, type II, sia 118
119b	*50,000.00*	7500.00	Center inverted
120	475.00	150.00	24c Declaration of Independence
120b	*30,000.00*	6000.00	Center inverted
121	500.00	67.50	30c Shield, Eagle and Flags
121b	*37,500.00*	22,500.00	Flags inverted
122	1400.00	350.00	90c Lincoln

FIRST PICTORIALS

Although the customary portraits of Franklin, Washington and Lincoln remained on three values of this series, the pictorial stamps represented a drastic change in United States stamp design. Three low values were used to publicize postal progress. At the time the first postal service was instituted in America in 1639 all mail was carried overland by postriders (2c) on horses usually supplied by the postmaster. 1864 marked the beginning of regular railway mail service and in 1869 the historic link between the East and West coasts was completed providing fast postal service across the country.

Transatlantic mail was carried by steamships like the Galway Line's S.S. Adriatic shown on the 12c stamp. (The vignette of the S.S. Adriatic had been used on the $10.00 bank note of the Citizen's Bank of Louisiana. These notes were called "Dix Notes," soon shortened to "Dixies" and the country along the southern Mississippi River became Dixieland.)

The higher denominations, the "Shield and Eagle," "Landing of Columbus," and "The Signing of the Declaration of Independence," were our first stamps produced in two colors. The 2c "Signing of the Declaration of Independence" with 42 persons engraved in a space 3/8 of an inch high by 13/16 of an inch wide is an outstanding example of the engraver's skill. The features of six of the principal figures taken from Trumbull's famous painting can be recognized when examined through a magnifying glass. The 30c was originally prepared with another Trumbull painting, the "Surrender of Burgoyne," but, so the story goes, it was not adopted lest it prove offensive to our English cousins.

Since these beautiful stamps have been among the favorites of collectors for many years, it is difficult to understand why they were so sharply criticized by the press at the time they were issued. The criticism was so strong another series of stamps in new designs had to be issued within a year.

See Scott Nos. 112-133

HIDDEN OPPORTUNITIES IN STAMP COLLECTING

For the beginning collector or the seasoned expert the chance discovery of a rare and valuable stamp can be the excitement of a lifetime. As is the case with most other collector's items, it is the desirability and the rarity of a stamp which can make it worth thousands of dollars. An interesting case in point concerns the first U. S. pictorial stamps, which were issued in 1869 and and were the forerunners of modern commemoratives. Due to a printing error, portions of the designs of three of these stamps were printed upside down. These inverted varieties of the 15c, 24c and 30c denominations are now among the most valuable of all U. S. stamps.

The inverts were discovered while the 1869 stamps were still in circulation, but they received no spectacular notice in the writings of the day. Long after, copies of the stamps started to turn up. During the 1930's a New York stamp dealer visiting in Portland, Oregon, stumbled onto a copy of the 30c with inverted flags. The stamp was included in a dealer's regular stock and had evidently been in several collections before that. None of its owners had noticed that the flags were upside-down! An unused copy of this stamp has a catalogue value of $37,500 and a used copy is valued at $22,500.

See Scott Nos. 112-122, 119b, 120b, 121b, 1474

120b

119b

121b

	Reissues of 1875, Without Grill Hard White Paper, Perf. 12						
				129	625.00	225.00	15c brown and blue Columbus Landing, type III, sia 118
123	115.00	75.00	1c buff, sia 112				
124	175.00	100.00	2c brown, sia 113				
125	900.00	500.00	3c blue, sia 114	130	525.00	200.00	24c grn. & vio., sia 120
126	350.00	175.00	6c blue, sia 115	131	775.00	325.00	30c bl. & blk., sia 121
127	525.00	200.00	10c yellow, sia 115	132	1300.00	600.00	90c car. & blk., sia 122
128	550.00	225.00	12c green, sia 117	**Reissues of 1880, Soft, Porous Paper, Perf. 12**			
				133	95.00	90.00	1c buff, sia 112

OLIVER HAZARD PERRY (1785-1819)

"We have met the enemy and they are ours: Two Ships, two Brigs, one Schooner & one Sloop."

Letter to General Harrison, dated
"United States Brig Niagara, Off the
Western Waters, Sept. 10, 1813, 4 P. M."

In the year 1812, America was ill-prepared to fight her "second War for Independence." When hostilities formally began on June 18, the U. S. Navy of a dozen ships effectively blockaded the coast of the United States.

In February, 1813, Oliver Hazard Perry, a handsome 27-year old Navy Lieutenant, was ordered to Erie, Pa. to supervise the completion of a naval fleet to defend the Great Lakes. As a mid-shipman, Perry had fought against the Barbary pirates when he was fifteen. From 1807 to 1809 he had been engaged in building and commanding coastal gunboats and at the outbreak of the war was in command of a gunboat flotilla.

Perry's nine-ship fleet was ready in August. He sailed up Lake Erie on board his flagship, the *Lawrence,* named for the heroic Captain of the *Chesapeake,* James Lawrence, who had died in battle a few months earlier uttering his historic words, "Don't give up the ship!"

Early on the morning of September 10th, Perry sighted Captain Robert Barclay's English fleet near Put-in-Bay on Lake Erie. Courageous and confident, Perry, according to his own report, "Made sail and directed the other vessels to follow, for the purpose of closing with the enemy." Shortly before noon, while still out of range of the American cannons, the British ship *Detroit* opened fire on the *Lawrence* with her long guns. Undaunted, Perry sailed closer and ten minutes later the Americans began to reply.

The British fire was more destructive than had been anticipated. Much of the *Lawrence's* rigging was soon shot away and she became unmanageable. Barclay brought up his flagship, *Queen Charlotte,* to support the *Detroit* in the hopes of capturing Perry's flagship. Although the *Lawrence* had been hopelessly disabled, Perry kept her colors flying until he transferred to her sister ship, the *Niagara,* to continue the fight.

The *Niagara* bore down on the *Detroit* which, while trying to avoid Perry's fire, fell foul of the *Queen Charlotte.* The Americans took advantage of the situation, bringing up the rear schooners to deliver a raking cannonade. Perry bravely brought the *Niagara* to within pistol shot of the *Detroit* and within minutes the *Detroit, Queen Charlotte,* and *Lady Prevost* surrendered, followed soon after by the whole of the British squadron. America had regained firm control of the Great Lakes and the way was clear for General Harrison's cavalry to recover Detroit. The Battle of Lake Erie was the first time the British had been forced to give up a naval squadron by surrender.

See Scott Nos. 144, 155, 166, 177, 191, 202, 218, 229, 261, 261A, 276, 276A

134   135   136   137   138   139   140   141   142   143   144

PATRICK HENRY (1736-99), "TONGUE OF THE REVOLUTION"

English poet Lord Byron called Patrick Henry the "Forest-born Demosthenes," an apt description of the best-known orator of the American Revolutionary War. Henry's forensic skill in the Virginia legislature helped spur colonial revolt in the South. His famous "Give me liberty or give me death!" speech was made to his state's assembly in 1775 in support of armed resistance to the British.

In addition to serving in the legislature, Henry also served as governor of Virginia several times. An Antifederalist, he refused election to the Constitutional Convention of 1787, but subsequently fought for the addition of the Bill of Rights. Throughout his life he was a hero of Virginia.

See Scott Stamp Nos. 1052, 1144

1873: Printed by the Continental Bank Note Co.
Designs of the 1870-71 Issue with secret marks on the values from 1c to 15c
as described and illustrated below.

156
1c. In the pearl at the left of the numeral
"1" there is a small crescent.

157
2c. Under the scroll at the left of "U. S." there
is a small diagonal line. This mark seldom shows
clearly. The stamp, No. 157, can be distinguished
by its color.

158
3c. The under part of the upper tail of the left
ribbon is heavily shaded.

159
6c. The first four vertical lines of the shading
in the lower part of the left ribbon have been
strengthened.

160
7c. Two small semi-circles are drawn around
the ends of the lines which outline the ball in the
lower right hand corner.

161
10c. There is a small semi-circle in the scroll
at the right end of the upper label.

162
12c. The balls of the figure "2" are crescent
shaped.

163
15c. In the lower part of the triangle in the
upper left corner two lines have been made
heavier forming a "V". This mark can be found
on some of the Continental and American (1879)
printings, but not all stamps show it.

Secret marks were added to the dies of the 24c,
30c and 90c but new plates were not made from
them. The various printings of these stamps can
be distinguished only by the shades and paper.

Issue of 1870–71
With Grill, White Wove Paper, Perf. 12

134	175.00	15.00	1c Franklin
135	90.00	10.00	2c Jackson
136	55.00	1.75	3c Washington
137	300.00	60.00	6c Lincoln
138	275.00	50.00	7c Edwin M. Stanton
139	425.00	100.00	10c Jefferson
140	5500.00	700.00	12c Henry Clay
141	450.00	150.00	15c Daniel Webster
142		5250.00	24c General Winfield Scott
143	1100.00	250.00	30c Alexander Hamilton
144	1650.00	185.00	90c Commodore O. H. Perry

Without Grill
White Wove Paper, Perf. 12

145	23.00	1.75	1c ultra. Franklin, sia 134
146	13.50	1.25	2c red brn. Jackson, sia 135
147	12.50	.15	3c green Washington, sia 136
148	60.00	3.50	6c carmine Lincoln, sia 137
149	90.00	13.50	7c verm. Stanton, sia 138
150	65.00	4.00	10c brown Jefferson, sia 139
151	150.00	14.00	12c dull violet Clay, sia 140
152	125.00	15.00	15c bright orange Webster, sia 141
153	100.00	16.50	24c purple W. Scott, sia 142
154	300.00	30.00	30c black Hamilton, sia 143
155	325.00	50.00	90c carmine Perry, sia 144

Issue of 1873, Without Grill, Perf. 12
White Wove Paper, Thin to Thick

156	13.50	.50	1c Franklin
157	30.00	1.50	2c Jackson
158	6.50	.08	3c Washington
159	55.00	2.00	6c Lincoln
160	100.00	15.00	7c Stanton
161	55.00	3.00	10c Jefferson
162	185.00	15.00	12c Clay
163	150.00	15.00	15c Webster
165	140.00	12.50	30c Hamilton, sia 143
166	300.00	50.00	90c Perry, sia 144

It is generally accepted as fact that the Continental Bank Note Co. printed and delivered a quantity of 24c stamps. They are impossible to distinguish from those printed by the National Bank Note Co.

Issue of 1875
Special Printing
Hard, White Wove Paper, Without Gum

167	3000.00		1c ultra. Franklin, sia 156
168	1700.00		2c dark brown Jackson, sia 157
169	4250.00	—	3c blue green Washington, sia 158
170	3750.00		6c dull rose Lincoln, sia 159
171	1350.00		7c reddish vermilion Stanton, sia 160
172	2800.00		10c pale brown Jefferson, sia 161
173	1500.00		12c dark violet Clay, sia 162
174	3000.00		15c bright orange Webster, sia 163
175	1350.00	—	24c dull purple W. Scott, sia 142
176	3250.00		30c greenish black Hamilton, sia 143
177	3500.00		90c violet car. Perry, sia 144

Although perforated, these stamps were usually cut apart with scissors. As a result, the perforations are often much mutilated and the design is frequently damaged.

Yellowish Wove Paper

178	50.00	1.25	2c vermilion Jackson, sia 157 Jun. 21
179	47.50	2.75	5c Zachary Taylor, Jun. 21

Special Printing
Hard, White Wove Paper, Without Gum

180	8000.00	2c carmine verm. Jackson, sia 157
181	11,000.00	5c bright blue Taylor, sia 179

Issue of 1879. Printed by the American Bank Note Company. Soft, porous paper, varying from thin to thick.

182	35.00	.55	1c dark ultramarine Franklin, sia 156
183	13.50	.50	2c vermilion Jackson, sia157
184	7.50	.08	3c green Washington, sia 158
185	40.00	2.00	5c blue Taylor, sia 179
186	150.00	3.00	6c pink Lincoln, sia 159
187	165.00	3.50	10c brown Jefferson, sia 139 (no secret mark)
188	77.50	3.00	10c brown Jefferson, sia 161 (with secret mark)
189	30.00	4.25	15c red orange Webster, sia 163
190	90.00	6.50	30c full black Hamilton, sia 143
191	300.00	45.00	90c carmine Perry, sia 144

Issue of 1880, Special Printing
Soft, Porous Paper, Without Gum

192	4250.00	1c dark ultramarine sia 156
193	2750.00	2c dark brown Jackson, sia 157
194	4750.00	3c blue green Washington, sia 158
195	3750.00	6c dull rose Lincoln, sia 159
196	1750.00	7c scarlet vermilion Stanton, sia 160
197	3750.00	10c deep brown Jefferson, sia 161
198	2750.00	12c blackish purple Clay, sia 162
199	3750.00	15c orange Webster, sia 163
200	1250.00	24c dark violet W. Scott, sia 142
201	3500.00	30c greenish black Hamilton, sia 143
202	3500.00	90c dull car. Perry, sia 144
203	7500.00	2c scarlet vermilion Jackson, sia 157
204	10,000.00	5c deep blue Taylor, sia 179

Detail of 206
1c. Upper vertical lines have been deepened, creating a solid effect in parts of background. Upper arabesques have lines of shading.

206

Detail of 207
3c. Shading at sides of central oval is half its previous width. A short horizontal dash has been cut below the "TS" of "CENTS"

207

Detail of 208
6c. Has three vertical lines instead of four between the edge of the panel and the outside of the stamp.

208

Detail of 209
10c. Has four vertical lines instead of five between left side of oval and edge of the shield. Horizontal lines in lower part of background have been strengthened.

209

179

205

210

211

212

		Issue of 1882	
205	25.00	1.75	5c James Garfield, Apr. 10

Special Printing. Soft, Porous Paper, Without Gum

205C	10,000.00		5c gray brown, sia 205

Issue of 1881–82, Designs of 1873 Re-engraved.

206	7.00	.30	1c Franklin
207	12.50	.08	3c Washington
208	75.00	15.00	6c Lincoln
209	15.00	1.00	10c Jefferson

Issue of 1883

210	4.25	.05	2c Washington, Oct. 1
211	20.00	2.00	4c Jackson, Oct. 1

Special Printing. Soft, Porous Paper.

211B	275.00		2c pale red brown Washington, sia 210
211D	7500.00		4c deep blue green Jackson, sia 211, no gum

Issue of 1887

212	12.50	.30	1c Franklin
213	2.75	.05	2c grn. Washington, sia 210
214	10.00	8.75	3c vermilion Washington, sia 207

Issue of 1888, Perf. 12

215	20.00	3.00	4c carmine Jackson, sia 211
216	17.50	1.50	5c indigo Garfield, sia 205
217	67.50	20.00	30c orange brown Hamilton, sia 143
218	190.00	45.00	90c purple Perry, sia 144

Issue of 1890–93, Perf. 12

219	4.25	.05	1c Franklin
219D	13.50	.20	2c Washington
220	3.25	.05	2c carmine sia 219D
221	14.00	1.35	3c Jackson
222	15.00	.50	4c Lincoln
223	16.50	.55	5c Ulysses S. Grant
224	14.00	4.00	6c Garfield
225	10.50	2.00	8c William T. Sherman
226	30.00	.50	10c Webster
227	42.50	5.00	15c Clay
228	57.50	6.75	30c Jefferson
229	100.00	30.00	90c Perry

Henry Clay began his law career at the age of fifteen. Before he was twenty-one he had his license to practise law. His natural eloquence made him exceptionally successful in the Courtroom and within a few years he became one of Kentucky's outstanding lawyers. Young Clay's career advanced rapidly. In 1799 he was a delegate to the State Constitution Convention and in 1803 he was elected to the Kentucky Legislature. On November 4, 1811 he was elected to his first of many terms as Speaker of the U. S. House of Representatives.

At the end of the War of 1812, Clay emerged as the voice of young America. He was one of the first to advocate better roads, canals and improved means of communication at Government expense. He raised his voice on behalf of every effort to help American manufacturers and to encourage an "American System" of internal improvements. Under his guidance, timidity and fear of England gave way to bold, well-defined, intensely American policy. Clay's outstanding oratory in the 1820 debate over the admission of Missouri as a slave state—in which he placed primary stress of the preservation of the Union—won him the title of "The Great Pacificator." The title was again justified in 1833 when he guided a compromise tariff through Congress. Although he was 73 years old and weary, he summoned up his old eloquence to fight for the enactment of the Compromise of 1850, and thus helped to hold the Union together for another decade.

A true patriot, Clay was loved and admired by thousands, but his conservatism caused him to be unsuccessful in his three bids for the presidency. Eloquent even in defeat, he said, "I'd rather be right than President."

HENRY CLAY (1777-1852)

See Scott. Nos. 140, 151, 162, 173, 198, 227, 259, 274, 284, 309, O6, O20, O30, O63, O78, O89, O101, O119

Columbian Exposition Issue, 1893, Perf. 12				**234**	23.50	2.50 5c Columbus Seeking Aid
230	7.00	.15	1c Columbus Sights Land	**235**	23.50	7.00 6c Columbus at Barcelona
231	6.25	.06	2c Landing of Columbus	**236**	14.00	2.65 8c Columbus Restored
232	14.00	6.00	3c The Santa Maria			to Favor
233	20.00	2.25	4c Fleet of Columbus, ultramarine	**237**	37.50	2.25 10c Columbus Presenting Indians
233a	4750.00	1800.00	4c blue (error), sia 233			

THE VOYAGES OF CHRISTOPHER COLUMBUS (1451?-1506)

Christopher Columbus found America by chance while looking for the Indies. Today Columbus is regarded as a great explorer; in his own time, he was often thought of as a dreamer and a fool.

When Columbus first decided that the riches of the Indies could be reached by sailing west from Europe, kings and princes scoffed at him. But the stubborn Columbus was not easily denied. He persisted in his dream until the Queen of Spain, Isabella, intervened to help him.

Outfitted by Isabella and King Ferdinand with a crew of ninety and a fleet of tiny ships—the *Nina, Pinta,* and *Santa Maria*—the intrepid navigator left Spain on August 3, 1492 on "the most important voyage in all history." On October 12, 1492

San Marino Scott No. 315

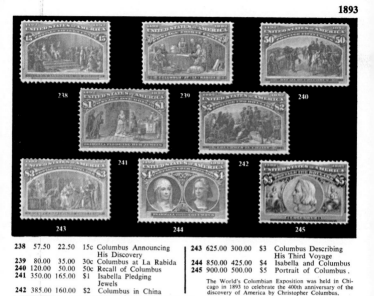

238	57.50	22.50	15c	Columbus Announcing His Discovery
239	80.00	35.00	30c	Columbus at La Rabida
240	120.00	50.00	50c	Recall of Columbus
241	350.00	165.00	$1	Isabella Pledging Jewels
242	385.00	160.00	$2	Columbus in China

243	625.00	300.00	$3	Columbus Describing His Third Voyage
244	850.00	425.00	$4	Isabella and Columbus
245	900.00	500.00	$5	Portrait of Columbus .

The World's Columbian Exposition was held in Chicago in 1893 to celebrate the 400th anniversary of the discovery of America by Christopher Columbus.

he landed on an island named San Salvador (in the Bahamas), where he was greeted by a group of peaceful Arawaks. Convinced that he had found the Indies, Columbus named these natives "Indians."

When Columbus and his crew returned to Spain they were greeted with a hero's welcome. But the glory of the journey did not last. Although three more voyages were made, the Indies failed to yield the riches Spain was looking for, the colonies Columbus tried to found were failures, and the government of Spain became convinced that his discoveries were worthless.

Nor did it listen when Columbus countered, "By...Divine Will I have placed under the sovereignty of the King and Queen an Other World, whereby Spain, which was reckoned poor, is to become the richest of all countries." Neglected and alone, Columbus died in poverty before his prophecy came true.

See Scott Stamp Nos. 230-245.

DANIEL WEBSTER (1782-1852)

I speak today for the preservation of the Union. Hear me for my cause.
Senate debate of the Clay Compromise, March 7, 1850

Twice secretary of state and twenty years a senator, Daniel Webster was an eloquent spokesman for the Union in the years before the Civil War. In 1832, when South Carolina challenged the exercise of federal laws within its boundaries, Webster supported his old enemy, President Andrew Jackson, against the states' righters. In 1850 the New England lawyer was again embroiled in the defense of the Union. In his last great Senate speech he rose to answer John C. Calhoun during a heated debate over the Clay Compromise. Webster's impassioned argument was instrumental in the passage of Henry Clay's brainchild, a stopgap solution to the slavery question that postponed the Civil War for eleven years.

Webster is also known for his successful argument of several landmark Supreme Court cases including the Dartmouth College Case of 1819, which held that a state cannot violate a contract.
See Scott Stamp Nos. 258, 259, 725, 1380, O31

O31

246

253

254

255

256

257

**2c Washington
Types I-III of 1894
Triangle of 248-250**
Type I. Horizontal lines of uniform thickness run across the triangle.

258

Triangle of 251
Type II. Horizontal lines cross the triangle, but are thinner within than without.

248

Triangle of 252
Type III. The horizontal lines do not cross the double frame lines of the triangle.

259   260   262   263

$1 Perry Types of 1894

Detail of 261
Type I. The circles enclosing $1 are broken.

261

Detail of 261 A
Type II. The circles enclosing $1 are complete.

Bureau Issues

Starting in 1894, the Bureau of Engraving and Printing at Washington has produced all U. S. postage stamps except Nos. 909-921 (Overrun Countries), 1335 (Eakins painting), 1355 (Disney), 1410-1413 (Anti-Pollution), and 1414-1418 (Christmas, 1970), Bureau-printed stamps are e n g r a v e d except Nos. 525-536, which are offset, and certain combinations of lithography and engraving, such as No. 1275.

Issue of 1894, Perf. 12 Unwmkd.

246	4.50	.85	1c Franklin
247	7.50	.45	1c blue Franklin, sia 246
248	3.25	.65	2c Washington, type I

Nos. 249–252: Washington, sia 248

249	18.50	.25	2c carmine lake, type I
250	4.25	.05	2c carmine, type I
251	45.00	.70	2c carmine, type II
252	16.50	1.00	2c carmine, type III
253	11.00	2.18	3c Jackson
254	13.50	.60	4c Lincoln
255	10.00	.85	5c Grant
256	15.00	3.50	6c Garfield
257	12.00	2.00	8c Sherman
258	30.00	1.50	10c Webster
259	52.50	12.50	15c Clay
260	62.50	22.50	50c Jefferson
261	175.00	70.00	$1 Commodore Perry, type I
261A	300.00	110.00	$1 black Perry, type II, sia 261
262	295.00	135.00	$2 James Madison
263	700.00	350.00	$5 John Marshall

JAMES MADISON (1751-1836)

I believe there are more instances of the abridgment of the freedom of the people by gradual and silent encroachments of those in power than by violent and sudden usurpations. Speech in the Virginia Convention, 1788

James Madison, fourth president of the United States, justly earned his title "Father of the Constitution", for he was the chief drafter of that document which is the bulwark of U. S. government. A co-author of the *Federalist Papers,* he also figured prominently in the drafting of the Bill of Rights, and was Jefferson's secretary of state from 1801 until 1809.

During Madison's administration (1809-17), the War of 1812 took place, the White House was burned, and Madison was forced to flee the capital, the only president to do so.

See Scott Stamp No. 262

TEN CENTS.

Type I. The tips of the foliate ornaments do not impinge on the white curved line below "TEN CENTS."

282C

283

Type II. The tips of the ornaments break the curved line below the "E" of "TEN" and the "T" of "CENTS."

Watermark 191

Wmkd. USPS (191)

Issue of 1895, Perf. 12

264	.75	.06	1c blue Franklin, sia 246

Nos. 265–267: Washington, sia 248

265	6.75	.20	2c carmine, type I

266	8.25	.75	2c carmine, type III
267	.65	.03	2c carmine, type III
268	7.25	.45	3c purple Jackson, sia 253
269	8.00	.45	4c dk. brown Lincoln, sia 254
270	6.75	.70	5c chocolate Grant, sia 255
271	15.00	1.25	6c dull brn. Garfield, sia 256
272	5.25	.40	8c vio. brn. Sherman, sia 257
272	11.50	.50	10c dk. green Webster, sia 258
274	38.50	2.25	15c dark blue Clay, sia 259
275	57.50	4.75	50c orange Jefferson, sia 260
276	150.00	16.00	$1 black Perry, type I, sia 261
276A	300.00	30.00	$1 blk. Perry, type II, sia 261
277	200.00	90.00	$2 brt. blue Madison, sia 262
278	425.00	100.00	$5 dk. grn. Marshall, sia 263

Issue of 1898, Perf 12

279	1.35	.06	1c dp. green Franklin, sia 246
279B	1.25	.05	2c red Washington, type III, sia 248
280	5.25	.35	4c rose brn. Lincoln, sia 254
281	5.00	.30	5c dark blue Grant, sia 255
282	8.25	.75	6c lake Garfield, sia 256
282C	30.00	.80	10c Webster, type I
283	22.50	.70	10c Webster, type II
284	30.00	2.25	15c olive green Clay, sia 259

Trans–Mississippi Exposition Issue, Jun. 17 Perf. 12

285	8.25	1.65	1c Marquette on Mississippi
286	7.25	.60	2c Farming in the West
287	37.50	7.75	4c Indian Hunting Buffalo
288	33.50	7.00	5c Frémont on the Rocky Mountains
289	47.50	12.00	8c Troops Guarding Train
290	60.00	7.75	10c Hardships of Emigration
291	225.00	35.00	50c Western Mining Prospector
292	500.00	200.00	$1 Western Cattle in Storm
293	725.00	250.00	$2 Mississippi River Bridge at St. Louis. Missouri

The Trans-Mississippi Exposition was held in Omaha, Nebraska from June 1 to Novelber 1, 1898. For this reason, t h e above stamps have been n i c k n a m e d "Omahas."

THE LEWIS AND CLARK EXPEDITION

On May 14, 1804 Meriwether Lewis (1744-1809), William Clark (1770-1838), thirty-two soldiers, and ten civilians climbed into a 55-foot keel boat and headed up the Missouri river on a perilous, 4,000 mile expedition through the vast Louisiana Territory. The goal of the expedition, which began at St. Louis, was to find a water route to the Pacific and to learn about the far West and its Indians.

After wintering among the Mandan Indians, Lewis and Clark were led across the Rockies by their Shoshone guide, Sacajawea (the Bird Woman). On November 15, 1805, when they canoed down the Columbia to the Pacific, a new route had been found to the Northwest and the United States was able to add Oregon to its western claims. This vast territory included the present states of Oregon, Washington, Idaho, and parts of Montana and Wyoming.

See Scott Stamp Nos. 323-327, 1020, 1063

285　　286　　287

288　　289　　290

291　　292　　293

JACQUES MARQUETTE (1637-1675)

"Indian corn, with some smoked meat constituted all our provisions—with these we embarked—Monsieur Jollyet and myself with five men—in two bark canoes, fully resolved to do and suffer anything for so glorious an undertaking."

Pere Marquette's Journal

While the Spanish and English explorers were looking for a waterway to China through the New World, the French were exploring Canada. At their settlements around the Great Lakes the Indians told them of a mighty river that flowed from the lakes to the sea. In the Spring of 1673 Jesuit Missionary Jacques Marquette and fur trader Louis Jolliet set out to discover the great river. They canoed westward on Lake Michigan to Green Bay and crossed Wisconsin by river and land. Just south of Prairie de Chien they entered the Mississippi River. For thirty days they fought heat, hunger and rapids as they paddled southward. They mapped the western coast of Illinois, passed the Missouri River and saw the wilderness around the bay at what is now St. Louis. They continued on past the present site of Memphis, charting the river as it zig-zagged along between Mississippi and Arkansas, until they reached the mouth of the Arkansas River.

Upon learning from the Arkansas Indians that the river continued south to the Gulf of Mexico and that Spaniards were on the lower river, they knew they had not found a passage to the Orient. Anxious not to fall into the hands of their Spanish rivals, they turned homeward.

See Scott Nos. 285, 1356

37

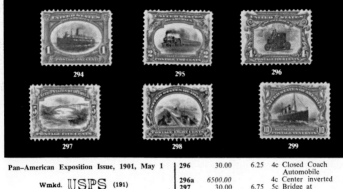

294 295 296

297 298 299

Pan–American Exposition Issue, 1901, May 1		
Wmkd. USPS (191)		
Perf. 12.		
294	5.25	1.35	1c Great Lakes Steamer
294a	3750.00	1500.00	1c Center inverted
295	5.25	.40	2c An Early Locomotive
295a	20,000.00	6500.00	2c Center inverted

296	30.00	6.25	4c Closed Coach Automobile
296a	6500.00		4c Center inverted
297	30.00	6.75	5c Bridge at Niagara Falls
298	42.50	15.00	8c Sault Ste. Marie Canal Locks
299	55.00	10.00	10c American Line Steamship

The Pan-American Exposition was held in Buffalo, New York in 1901. It stressed engineering progress in the Western hemisphere in the nineteenth century.

HENRY FORD

Henry Ford (1863-1947) was a Michigan farm boy whose vision changed a nation. He was not the first automobile manufacturer, nor was he the first to use mass production methods, but his idea that everyone could own an inexpensive automobile was revolutionary, as was his use of conveyor belts to speed assembly lines. The famous black 1909 Model T was the result.

Later Ford innovations were profit-sharing with employees and higher wages for shorter hours. When America took to the highways in Ford's Model T, a billion-dollar industry began to grow.

See Scott Stamp Nos. 296, 1286A

Monaco Scott No. 545

294a 295a 296a

300 — 301 — 302 — 303 — 304 — 305 — 306 — 307 — 308 — 309 — 310 — 311 — 312 — 313 — 319

	Regular Issue of 1902–03		
	Wmkd. **USPS** (191)		
	Perf. 12.		
300	1.35	.05	1c Franklin
300b	400.00	150.00	Booklet pane of six
301	1.50	.05	2c Washington
301c	325.00	125.00	Booklet pane of six
302	9.50	1.00	3c Jackson
303	9.50	.40	4c Grant
304	9.50	.35	5c Lincoln
305	12.00	.85	6c Garfield
306	6.50	.55	8c Martha Washington
307	14.00	.35	10c Webster
308	6.00	3.00	13c Benjamin Harrison
309	40.00	2.00	15c Clay
310	110.00	8.00	50c Jefferson
311	190.00	15.00	$1 David G. Farragut

312	275.00	60.00	$2 Madison
313	525.00	225.00	$5 Marshall

For listings of 312 and 313 with Perf. 10, see Nos. 479 and 480.

	Issues of 1906–08		
	Imperf.		
314	17.50	7.50	1c blue green Franklin, sia 300
314A	6000.00	3500.00	4c brown Grant, sia 303
315	225.00	150.00	5c blue Lincoln, sia 304

No. 314A was issued imperforate, but all copies were privately perforated with large oblong perforations at the sides. (Schermack type III).

	Coil Stamps		
	Perf. 12 Horizontally		
316	8500.00	——	1c blue green pair Franklin, sia 300
317	1650.00	——	5c blue pair Lincoln, sia 304

JOHN MARSHALL (1755-1835)

John Marshall, a man of extraordinary vision, opened a new age of jurisprudence in America. The fourth Chief Justice of the United States, he gave the Constitution its first, historic interpretation and established the right of the Supreme Court to review the constitutionality of state and Federal laws.

Born in Virginia of a frontier family, Marshall was a member of the Virginia convention which debated the ratification of the Constitution. He was appointed Chief Justice of the Supreme Court by President John Adams in 1801 and served in the post for thirty-four years.

See Scott Stamp No. 313

323 324 325 326 327 328 329 330

319g 40.00 10.00 Booklet pane of six
Issue of 1906
Nos. 320–322: Washington, sia 319
Imperf.
320 11.00 7.50 2c carmine, Oct. 2
Issue of 1908, Coil Stamps
Perf. 12 Horizontally
321 2c carmine pair
Perf. 12 Vertically
322 *1500.00* 2c carmine pair
Issue of 1904, Perf. 12

Wmkd. USPS (191)

Louisiana Purchase Exposition Issue, Apr. 30
323	10.00	2.25	1c Robert R. Livingston
324	9.00	.60	2c Thomas Jefferson
325	30.00	11.00	3c James Monroe
326	37.50	7.25	5c William McKinley
327	87.50	12.00	10c Map of Louisiana Purchase

The Louisiana Purchase Exposition was held in St. Louis in 1904 in conjunction with the World's Fair of that year. President William McKinley (1843-1901), who d i e d before the Exposition opened, authorized the Fair.

Issue of 1907, Perf. 12

Wmkd. USPS (191)

Jamestown Exposition Issue
328	5.50	1.75	1c Captain John Smith
329	7.00	1.00	2c Founding of Jamestown
330	40.00	10.00	5c Pocahontas

The first permanent English settlement in North America was established in 1607, at Jamestown, Virginia.

Perf. 12 Vertically
318 *1350.00* 1c bl. grn., pr. Franklin, sia 300
With this series the Post Office Department began issuing stamps in coils for use in vending and affixing machines. The stamps in coils are perforated on two sides only, either horizontally or vertically, and are imperforate on the other sides.
Collectors are warned that imperforate stamps are being fraudulently perforated to resemble coil stamps and part perforate varieties.
Issue of 1903, Perf. 12

Wmkd. USPS (191)

Shield–shaped Background
319 1.35 .04 2c Washington Nov.

THE GAINING OF A NEW FRONTIER

Intricate diplomacy and power politics lay behind the Louisiana Purchase which, in 1803, more than doubled the size of the young United States at a cost of only $15 million.

Upon hearing that Louisiana had been ceded to Napoleon, President Thomas Jefferson, fearful for the country's safety, sent James Monroe to France with orders to assist Robert Livingston in buying Florida and New Orleans for $10 million. When Napoleon announced his willingness to sell the entire tract for $5 million more, Jefferson set aside his doubts about the constitutionality of such a purchase and had the Senate ratify the treaty before Bonaparte could change his mind.

So it was that in 1803 Louisiana became U. S. land. From it, thirteen states were carved; into it, in 1804, went Meriwether Lewis and William Clark to pave the way for future pioneers.

See Scott Stamp Nos. 323-327, 1020, 1063

France Scott No. B263

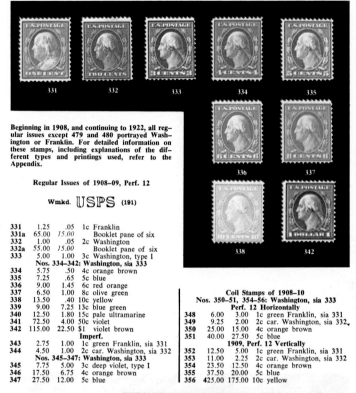

Beginning in 1908, and continuing to 1922, all regular issues except 479 and 480 portrayed Washington or Franklin. For detailed information on
these stamps, including explanations of the different types and printings used, refer to the
Appendix.

Regular Issues of 1908–09, Perf. 12

Wmkd. USPS (191)

331	1.25	.05	1c	Franklin
331a	65.00	15.00		Booklet pane of six
332	1.00	.05	2c	Washington
332a	55.00	15.00		Booklet pane of six
333	5.00	1.00	3c	Washington, type I

Nos. 334–342: Washington, sia 333

334	5.75	.50	4c	orange brown
335	7.25	.65	5c	blue
336	9.00	1.45	6c	red orange
337	6.50	1.00	8c	olive green
338	13.50	.40	10c	yellow
339	9.00	7.25	13c	blue green
340	12.50	1.80	15c	pale ultramarine
341	72.50	4.00	50c	violet
342	115.00	22.50	$1	violet brown

Imperf.

343	2.75	1.00	1c	green Franklin, sia 331
344	4.50	1.00	2c	car. Washington, sia 332

Nos. 345–347: Washington, sia 333

345	7.75	5.00	3c	deep violet, type I
346	17.50	6.75	4c	orange brown
347	27.50	12.00	5c	blue

Coil Stamps of 1908–10
Nos. 350–51, 354–56: Washington, sia 333
Perf. 12 Horizontally

348	6.00	3.00	1c	green Franklin, sia 331
349	9.25	2.00	2c	car. Washington, sia 332.
350	25.00	15.00	4c	orange brown
351	40.00	27.50	5c	blue

1909, Perf. 12 Vertically

352	12.50	5.00	1c	green Franklin, sia 331
353	11.00	2.25	2c	car. Washington, sia 332
354	23.50	12.50	4c	orange brown
355	37.50	20.00	5c	blue
356	425.00	175.00	10c	yellow

THE JAMESTOWN COLONY

Wee hope to build a nation where none before hath stood, Anonymous, 1610

On April 26, 1607 three small ships bearing some 120 English settlers arrived in
Virginia. On May 14 the colonists disembarked at Jamestown; on May 26 they were
attacked by Indians; within six months over fifty of them perished, victims of starvation and disease.

Despite this inauspicious start Jamestown survived, largely through the efforts
of Captain John Smith, who made friends with the Indian Powhatan and his daughter, Pocahontas. Soon tobacco was a thriving industry, a landed gentry had developed, and the little colony could boast the New World's first elected legislature,
the House of Burgesses.

See Scott Stamp Nos. 328-330

THE ALASKA PURCHASE

In 1867 President Andrew Johnson's secretary of state, William H. Seward, bought Alaska from the Russians at a cost of $7.2 million.

The purchase of the huge, northern land mass seemed at first a poor bargain. Not only was Alaska difficult to reach, but it was also hard to live in, and appeared to have no strategic value.

Soon, however, people changed their thinking about "Seward's Folly". In 1896 gold was found in the Klondike region and droves of people poured into the land, once inhabited mainly by Eskimos and Indians.

Since then, coal, oil, platinum, uranium, and other minerals have been discovered in Alaska, which also boasts a rich fur trade and a thriving fishing industry. In 1959 Alaska joined the Union as the forty-ninth state.

See Scott Nos. 370, 371, 800, 1454,
C53, C70

Issues of 1909, Bluish Paper Perf. 12
Nos. 359–366: Washington, sia 333

357	27.50	*17.50*	1c green Franklin, sia 331
358	25.00	*15.00*	2c car. Washington, sia 332
359	475.00	*350.00*	3c deep violet, type I
360	*6500.00*		4c orange brown
361	*1750.00*		5c blue
362	350.00	*250.00*	6c red orange
363	*6500.00*		8c olive green
364	400.00	*250.00*	10c yellow
365	850.00	*450.00*	15c blue green
366	325.00	*250.00*	15c pale ultramarine

Lincoln Memorial Issue, Feb. 12

Wmkd. USPS (191)

367	3.25	1.00	2c Lincoln, Perf. 12
368	18.50	10.00	2c Lincoln, Imperf.
369	87.50	55.00	2c Lincoln, Perf. 12, Bluish Paper

Issued on the 100th anniversary of the birth of Abraham Lincoln. The portrait on the stamps is from the statue by Saint-Gaudens.

Alaska–Yukon Exposition Issue

Wmkd. USPS (191)

370	3.75	.85	2c William Seward, Perf. 12
371	22.00	8.00	2c William Seward, Imperf.

William H. Seward (1801-72), Lincoln's Secretary of State, bought Alaska for the U. S., in 1867.

Hudson–Fulton Celebration Issue, Sep. 25

Wmkd. USPS (191)

372	3.75	1.25	2c Half Moon and Clermont, Perf. 12
373	23.00	9.50	2c Half Moon and Clermont, Imperf.

Henry Hudson discovered the New York River named for him in 1609. Robert Fulton's *Clermont* was the first commercially successful steamboat.

367   368   369   370

372   373   371

		Issues of 1910–13
		Perf. 12
		Nos. 376–82: Washington, sia 333
374	1.35	.06	1c green Franklin, sia 331
374a	65.00	20.00	Booklet pane of six
375	1.10	.03	2c car. Washington, sia 332
375a	55.00	15.00	Booklet pane of six
376	3.00	.60	3c deep violet, type I
377	5.25	.25	4c brown
378	5.25	.25	5c blue
379	9.50	.30	6c red orange
380	23.50	4.25	8c olive green
381	21.00	1.25	10c yellow
382	45.00	6.50	15c pale ultramarine

Imperf.

383	1.50	.75	1c green Franklin, sia 331
384	2.75	.50	2c car. Washington, sia 332

Coil Stamps

Perf. 12 Horizontally

385	7.00	4.25	1c green Franklin, sia 331
386	8.50	4.00	2c car. Washington, sia 332

Perf. 12 Vertically

387	11.50	7.50	1c green Franklin, sia 331
388	90.00	20.00	2c car. Washington, sia 332
389	7500.00	1650.00	3c dp. vio. Washington, type I, sia 333

Stamps sold as 388 are sometimes privately perforated copies of 384.

Perf. 8½ Horizontally

390	1.00	.75	1c green Franklin, sia 331
391	13.50	2.50	2c car. Washington, sia 332

Perf. 8½ Vertically

Nos. 394–396: Washington, sia 333

392	7.50	5.00	1c green Franklin, sia 331
393	16.00	1.25	2c car. Washington, sia 332
394	26.50	11.50	3c deep violet, type I
395	26.50	8.50	4c brown
396	26.50	11.00	5c blue

ROBERT FULTON (1765-1815)

To Robert Fulton nothing was impossible. The most original boy in the little town of Lancaster, Pennsylvania always seemed able to make some kind of marvelous contrivance to meet a need of his own, his mother's or his friends. While still in his teens he developed skyrockets to celebrate the second anniversary of the Declaration of Independence, became an expert gunsmith and made a paddle wheel boat to take himself and his friends on fishing trips.

He went to France to study painting and in his spare time built a torpedo boat that he tried to sell to Napoleon. Then he built a steamboat, but it sank to the bottom of the Seine.

Fulton had come home discouraged when his wealthy friend Robert Livingston urged him to build another steamboat on the Hudson. He put together an ugly little vessel described by Livingston as "exactly like a sawmill put on a scow and set on fire." On August 17, 1807 it was ready for its first trip up the river. The people of New York who had watched the building of the "Clermont" lined the shores expecting to see the end of "Fulton's Folly." Instead, with a mighty whistle and a huge cloud of black smoke she started upstream and made the 150-mile journey to Albany in 32 hours and the return trip in 30 hours. After this many steamboats were built. Americans by the thousands were able to travel our great rivers into the wilderness to build new homes and new states.

See Scott Nos. 372-373, 1270

VASCO NUNEZ de BALBOA (1475?-1519)

Many European nations established settlements in the New World, but Spain had a head start on all the others. The first European colony in the New World was established on the island of Haiti by some members of Columbus' expedition in 1492. Vasco Nunez de Balboa settled in Haiti in 1501, but grew restless after ten years of being a pioneer farmer. He sailed on a ship carrying supplies to a settlement on the coast of Columbia. They landed to find only 41 of the colonists had survived the heat and Indian attacks. Balboa helped the survivors move west to build a new colony near where the Panama Canal is now and he soon became their leader.

They made friends with the Indian Chief Comogre and his tribe who gave the Spaniards gifts of golden ornaments. When they saw how delighted the Spaniards were with the gold, Comogre's son told them of the great sea beyond the mountains which was "navigated by ships with sails and oars" and whose shores were lined with gold. Balboa was sure the body of water must be the legendary south sea—the route every Spanish explorer hoped to find to the Spice Islands.

Accompanied by Francisco Pizarro and a few guides, Balboa set out on the long journey over the rugged mountains. As they were nearing their goal, Balboa halted the men and went to the mountain top alone. There, in solitude, he looked down and saw a limitless body of sparkling blue water. What an awesome sight! He dropped to his knees and thanked God for the favor shown him and named the mighty ocean Mal de Sur, or the South Sea. He claimed it and all the shores it washed in the name of the Spanish Crown.

Balboa, like all Europeans of his time, believed the New World was all part of India and that there was only one ocean, the Atlantic, which he had crossed from Spain. The first white man to gaze upon the peaceful waters of the Pacific from America did not know he had discovered the greatest ocean in the world.

See Scott No. 397

Spanish explorer Vasco Nuñez de Balboa discovered the Pacific Ocean in 1513. The Panama Canal, which links the Pacific and Atlantic Ocean, was opened in 1914.

Panama Pacific Exposition Issue
1913, Perf. 12

Wmkd. USPS (190)

397	5.00	.80	1c Balboa
398	5.50	.30	2c Locks, Panama Canal
399	27.50	4.00	5c Golden Gate
400	50.00	6.00	10c Discovery of San Francisco Bay
400A	85.00	4.25	10c orange, sia 400

1914-15, Perf. 10

401	8.75	2.50	1c green Balboa, sia 397
402	25.00	.50	2c car. Canal Locks, sia 398
403	70.00	6.00	5c blue Golden Gate, sia 399
404	400.00	22.50	10c orange Discovery of San Francisco Bay, sia 400

Wmkd. USPS

in Single lined Capitals. (190)

Wmk. 190

Issues of 1912–14
Nos. 405–413: Washington, sia 333
Perf. 12

405	1.00	.06	1c green
405b	20.00	5.00	Booklet pane of six
406	.75	.03	2c carmine, type I
406a	30.00	10.00	Booklet pane of six
407	20.00	2.75	7c black

Imperf.

408	.30	.25	1c green
409	.35	.25	2c carmine, type I

Coil Stamps
Perf. 8½ Horizontally

410	1.50	1.00	1c green
411	2.25	1.00	2c carmine, type I

Perf. 8½ Vertically

412	5.00	1.50	1c green
413	13.00	.25	2c carmine, type I

Perf. 12

414	8.00	.50	8c Franklin

Nos. 415–21: Franklin, sia 414

415	10.50	5.00	9c salmon red
416	7.50	.10	10c orange yellow
417	4.50	1.50	12c claret brown
418	15.00	1.25	15c gray
419	30.00	5.50	20c ultramarine
420	25.00	5.25	30c orange red

421	125.00	6.00	50c violet

Nos. 422–423: Franklin, sia 414, Perf. 12
Wmkd. (191)

422	55.00	5.00	50c violet	Feb. 12
423	135.00	22.50	$1 violet brown	Feb. 12

Issues of 1914–15, Perf. 10
Wmkd. (190)
Nos. 424–430: Washington, sia 333

424	.90	.06	1c green
424d	2.75	.75	Booklet pane of six
425	.40	.04	2c rose red, type I
425e	6.50	2.00	Booklet pane of six
426	3.25	.60	3c deep violet, type I
427	9.00	.18	4c brown
428	5.50	.20	5c blue
429	8.75	.40	6c red orange
430	15.00	1.50	7c black

Nos. 431–440: Franklin, sia 414

431	9.00	.65	8c pale olive green
432	11.00	3.00	9c salmon red
433	7.75	.06	10c orange yellow
434	4.50	2.50	11c dark green
435	4.50	1.50	12c claret brown
437	28.50	2.75	15c gray
438	47.50	1.30	20c ultramarine
439	65.00	4.00	30c orange red
440	185.00	4.50	50c violet

HENRY HUDSON
(died c. 1611)

English explorer-navigator Henry Hudson had one great desire—to find a short way to the rich trade of China by way of the North Sea. In 1609 the Dutch gave him a small ship, the Half Moon, and twenty-four English and Dutch seamen. From Holland they sailed toward the north, but the little ship could not get through the heavy ice of the Berent Sea. Expecting to find a narrow isthmus like the Isthmus of Panama that would take them to the Pacific, they headed towards the New World.

They reached a magnificent bay surrounded by lush green forests and sailed up a broad, majestic river. In all their travels the men had never seen anything to resemble the splendor of the giant palisades on the west bank of the river. As they passed through beautiful valleys great crowds of friendly Indians came to stare at the strange ship. They welcomed the sailors and their gentle captain, happily exchanging splendid furs for bright colored ribbons and shiny beads. After surveying the country and trying the streams above what is now Albany, Hudson realized he had not found a waterway to the Orient. He sailed the Half Moon back down the river that now bears his name and claimed the whole valley for the Dutch. His reports about the fertile valley he had found and the possibility of a rich fur trade brought Dutch settlers to the area within a few years. They built a settlement at the mouth of the river and called it New Amsterdam. Today it is New York City.
See Scott Nos. 372, 373

Coil Stamps, 1914 Washington, sia 333
Perf. 10 Horizontally

441	.40	.20	1c green
442	4.75	2.25	2c carmine, type I

Perf. 10 Vertically

443	4.50	1.75	1c green
444	10.00	.50	2c carmine, type I
445	85.00	37.50	3c violet, type I
446	57.50	15.00	4c brown
447	22.50	6.50	5c blue

Coil Stamps, Washington, sia 333
1915-16, Perf. 10 Horizontally

448	2.00	1.00	1c green
449	550.00	45.00	2c red, type I
450	4.50	1.20	2c carmine, type III

1914-16, Perf. 10 Vertically

452	2.75	.60	1c green
453	57.50	2.75	2c red, type I
454	65.00	8.50	2c carmine, type II
455	5.50	.35	2c carmine, type III
456	95.00	30.00	3c violet, type I
457	8.75	5.00	4c brown
458	8.75	5.00	5c blue

Issue of 1914 Washington, sia 333, Imperf. Coil

459	135.00	125.00	2c carmine, type I Jun. 30

Issues of 1915, Perf. 10

Wmkd. USPS (191)

460	225.00	20.00	$1 violet black Franklin, sia 414 Feb. 8

Perf. 11

Wmkd. USPS (191)

461	20.00	18.50	2c pale carmine red, type I, Washington, sia 333 Jun. 17

Privately perforated copies of No. 409 have been made to resemble No. 461.

From 1916 to date all postage stamps (except Nos. 519 and 832b) are on unwatermarked paper.

Issues of 1916-17, Unwmkd. Perf. 10
Nos. 462-469: Washington, sia 333

462	1.50	.15	1c green
462a	4.00	1.00	Booklet pane of six
463	.75	.06	2c carmine, type I
463a	35.00	15.00	Booklet pane of six

464	18.50	4.25	3c violet, type I
465	9.25	.80	4c orange brown
466	17.50	.65	5c blue
467	220.00	200.00	5c car. (error in plate of 2c)
468	21.00	3.00	6c red orange
469	17.50	3.75	7c black

Nos. 470-78: Franklin, sia 414

470	15.00	2.50	8c olive green
471	11.50	5.00	9c salmon red
472	30.00	.50	10c orange yellow
473	6.50	5.50	11c dark green
474	10.00	2.00	12c claret brown
475	37.50	4.75	15c gray
476	50.00	4.50	20c light ultramarine
476A	——		30c orange red
477	275.00	27.50	50c light violet
478	225.00	7.00	$1 violet black

Issues of 1917, Perf. 10, Mar. 22

479	82.50	11.00	$2 dk. blue Madison, sia 312
480	62.50	13.00	$5 lgt. grn. Marshall, sia 313

Issues of 1916-17, Washington, sia 333, Imperf.

481	.35	.30	1c green
482	.60	.60	2c carmine, type I
482A	3750.00		2c carmine, type Ia
483	5.50	4.00	3c violet, type I
484	3.75	2.75	3c violet, type II
485	3750.00		5c car. (error in plate of 2c)

Coil Stamps, Washington, sia 333,
1916-19, Perf. 10 Horizontally

486	.25	.10	1c green
487	8.50	1.50	2c carmine, type II
488	.75	.50	2c carmine, type III
489	.85	.50	3c violet, type I

1916-22, Perf. 10 Vertically

490	.25	.08	1c green
491	600.00	75.00	2c carmine, type II
492	2.50	.08	2c carmine, type III
493	15.00	2.00	3c violet, type I
494	6.50	.35	3c violet, type II
495	4.00	1.60	4c orange brown
496	.80	.35	5c blue
497	6.00	3.75	10c orange yellow Franklin, sia 414

ALEXANDER HAMILTON (1757-1804)

In 1772 Alexander Hamilton left his birthplace in the West Indies and came to New York where he became an attorney and joined the struggle for American independence. After serving at the Constitutional Convention, he, James Madison, and John Jay wrote the *Federalist Papers,* which were instrumental in the ratification of the Constitution.

As Washington's secretary of the treasury, his organizational brilliancy and financial wizardry were invaluable to the new nation. He instituted a plan to pay the national debt, established the Bank of the United States, and began the mint. As a Federalist he believed in a strong centralized government composed of an aristocracy of landowners and industrialists which would lead the new country into an urban, industrialized future.

In 1804 Hamilton's political and personal rivalry with Aaron Burr ended in the tragic duel at Weehawken, N. J. in which Hamilton was killed at the height of his career. *See Scott Stamp No. 1086*

St. Kitts-Nevis Scott No. 157

THOMAS PAINE (1737-1809)

Armed with letters of introduction from Benjamin Franklin, this "ingenious worthy young man" left London in 1774 for Philadelphia where he edited the "Pennsylvania Magazine" and became a leading spokesman for the patriots. In January 1776 Thomas Paine anonymously published "Common Sense", a pamphlet in which he stated clearly the case of the colonies against the mother country. "Europe and not England is the parent country of America," he said and warned that a continent could not remain tied to an island. "'Tis time to part," he wrote, "for nothing but independence" would keep the New World as an "asylum for the persecuted lovers of civil and religious liberty from *every part* of Europe." The appeal of his argument added greatly to the movement towards independence.

Later, his new pamphlet, "The American Crises" opened with these stirring words, "These are the times that try men's souls: the summer soldier and the sunshine patriot will, in this crises, shrink from the service of his country; but he that stands it NOW, deserves the love and thanks of man and woman. Tyranny, like hell, is not easily conquered; yet we have this consolation with us, that the harder the conflict, the more glorious the triumph."

See Scott No. 1292

Issues of 1917–19, Perf. 11
Nos. 498–507: Washington, sia 333

498	.20	.04	1c green
498e	1.00	.35	Booklet pane of six
498f	300.00		Booklet pane of 30
499	.10	.03	2c rose, type I
499e	1.50	.50	Booklet pane of six
499f	2750.00		Booklet pane of 30
500	85.00	35.00	2c deep rose, type Ia
501	1.50	.08	3c light violet, type I
501b	35.00	10.00	Booklet pane of six
502	2.00	.15	3c dark violet, type II
502b	20.00	5.25	Booklet pane of six
503	3.00	.10	4c brown
504	1.25	.08	5c blue
505	150.00	120.00	5c rose (error in plate of 2c)
506	1.75	.12	6c red orange
507	6.00	.50	7c black

Nos. 508–518: Franklin, sia 414

508	4.00	.35	8c olive bistre
509	5.25	1.00	9c salmon red
510	3.25	.05	10c orange yellow
511	2.75	1.25	11c light green
512	1.50	.18	12c claret brown
513	3.50	2.25	13c apple green
514	9.00	.35	15c gray
515	6.50	.12	20c light ultramarine
516	7.75	.30	30c orange red
517	12.00	.25	50c red violet
518	15.00	.50	$1 violet brown

Issue of 1917, Perf. 11
Wmkd. USPS (191)

519	30.00	30.00	2c carmine Washington, sia 332 Oct. 10

Privately perforated copies of No. 344 have been made to resemble No. 519.

Issues of 1918, Unwmkd., Perf. 11

523	175.00	60.00	$2 orange red and black Franklin, sia 547 Aug. 19
524	72.50	9.00	$5 deep green and black Franklin, sia 547 Aug. 19

Issues of 1918–20, Washington, sia 333
Perf. 11

525	.75	.30	1c gray green
526	5.75	2.00	2c carmine, type IV
527	3.00	.60	2c carmine, type V
528	1.85	.15	2c carmine, type Va
528A	5.50	.45	2c carmine, type VI
528B	3.00	.08	2c carmine, type VII
529	.40	.10	3c violet, type III
530	.30	.06	3c purple, type IV

Imperf.

531	4.25	4.25	1c green
532	12.00	8.50	2c carmine rose, type IV
533	85.00	35.00	2c carmine, type V
534	5.50	4.00	2c carmine, type Va
534A	12.50	11.00	2c carmine, type VI
534B	750.00	235.00	2c carmine, type VII
535	4.00	4.00	3c violet, type IV

Issues of 1919
Perf. 12½

536	3.50	2.75	1c gray green Washington, sia 333 Aug. 15

Perf. 11

537	3.75	1.90	3c Allied Victory Mar. 3

The Armistice of Nov. 11, 1918 ended World War I on a note of triumph for the Allies.

Nos. 538–546: Washington, sia 333
1919, Perf. 11x10

538	2.50	2.50	1c green
539	675.00	225.00	2c carmine rose, type II
540	2.50	2.50	2c carmine rose, type III
541	9.50	9.50	3c violet, type II

1920, Perf. 10x11

542	1.50	.30	1c green May 26

1921, Perf. 10

543	.10	.06	1c green

1921, Perf. 11

544	4000.00	750.00	1c green, 19x22½mm.
545	35.00	25.00	1c grn., 19½–20mm.x22mm.
546	20.00	15.00	2c carmine rose, type III

Issues of 1920
Perf. 11

547	60.00	10.00	$2 Franklin

537   547

COMING OF THE PILGRIMS

Because they demanded the right to worship as they pleased, a group of Separatists from the Church of England had been driven from England. The "Saints" as they called themselves, had crossed to Holland where they enjoyed religious freedom, but they were afraid their children would grow up and forget their English ways. They looked towards the New World as a haven where they could have their own farms and keep their own traditions.

About forty Saints—named Pilgrims a century later because of their travels—returned to England. Financed by a London company of merchants and adventurers they secured a charter for a settlement. They sailed from Plymouth on the Mayflower. The 90-foot former wineship also carried many people the Saints called "Strangers" who were not seeking religious refuge, but a free land and a chance to make a decent living. All told there were 50 men, 20 women and 34 children on board. In the middle of November, 1620, the seasick colonists dropped anchor off the coast of Cape Cod.

Before disembarking, the Pilgrim leaders drew up America's first colonial legislation. Under the "Mayflower Compact," the Saints and Strangers constituted themselves a "civill body Politick" to be ruled by "just and equal laws . . . for ye general good of ye colonies." By this charter of freedom they created their own commonwealth and elected Deacon John Carver Governor, the first freely elected colonial official in America.

After a little exploring, the Mayflower deposited the settlers on the "stern and rockbound coast" of Plymouth on Christmas Day. Weather, scurvy and pnuemonia killed half the settlers that first winter. In the spring the Indians taught them how to plant corn, build fish traps and stalk game in the woods. Within three years, with the help of the Indians, the Pilgrims succeeded in establishing themselves in the wilderness and the first fertile seeds of democracy were firmly planted on our shores.

See Scott Nos. 548, 549, 550, 1420

Pilgrims 300th Anniv. Issue, Dec. 21

548	3.00	1.20	1c Mayflower
549	5.00	.80	2c Pilgrims Landing
550	20.00	8.50	5c Signing of Compact

In 1620 the Pilgrims landed in Massachusetts and drew up the Mayflower Compact.

548   549   550

Issues of 1922–25, Perf. 11

551	.06	.05	½c Nathan Hale
552	.60	.07	1c Franklin (19x22mm)
552a	1.50	.50	Booklet pane of six
553	1.20	.10	1½c Harding
554	.60	.03	2c Washington
554c	3.25	1.00	Booklet pane of six
555	6.00	.35	3c Lincoln
556	5.00	.08	4c Martha Washington
557	5.25	.06	5c Theodore Roosevelt
558	11.00	.25	6c Garfield
559	1.75	.25	7c McKinley
560	13.50	.25	8c Grant
561	3.25	.55	9c Jefferson
562	5.00	.06	10c Monroe
563	.60	.12	11c Rutherford B. Hayes
564	1.75	.08	12c Grover Cleveland

NATHAN HALE (1755-1776)

Nathan Hale, one of twelve children of parents prominent in public affairs, had gone to Yale when he was sixteen. His tall, blond good looks, his amazing wrestling and football feats, plus his literary and oratorical skills, had earned him great popularity among men and women. During one of the darkest hours of the American Revolution, even though he knew that spies were hanged if captured, twenty-one year old Nathan volunteered to go into the British camp and find out what they were planning. Dressed as a Tory schoolteacher, armed with his diploma as credentials, he entered the British camp on Long Island where he secretly made maps and learned all that Gen. Washington wished to know.

His mission completed, he returned to New York and had almost reached his own camp on Harlem Heights when, on the night of September 21st, he was recognized and arrested. The maps he had made were found in the soles of his shoes. Nathan knew his end had come, but he faced General Howe so bravely, the British General offered to spare his life if he would join the British army and fight the Americans. Nathan Hale refused. Without any form of trial, Howe sentenced him to be executed at daybreak. Nathan walked to the gallows with great calmness. As they put the rope around him he said "I only regret that I have but one life to lose for my country."

See Scott No. 551

565	1.35	.30	14c American Indian
566	4.50	.06	15c Statue of Liberty
567	5.50	.05	20c Golden Gate
568	5.00	.15	25c Niagara Falls
569	8.00	.15	30c Buffalo
570	15.00	.08	50c Arlington Amphitheater
571	10.00	.25	$1 Lincoln Memorial
572	35.00	3.25	$2 U.S. Capitol
573	75.00	4.75	$5 Head of Freedom, Capitol Dome

For listings of other perforated stamps of
issues 551-573 see:

Nos. 578 and 579	Perf. 11x10
Nos. 581 and 591	Perf. 10
Nos. 594 and 595	Perf. 11
Nos. 622 and 623	Perf. 11
Nos. 632 to 642, 653, 692 to 696	Perf. 11x10½
Nos. 697 to 701	Perf. 10½x11

Issues of 1923–25 Imperf.

575	2.50	1.90	1c green Franklin, sia 552
576	.75	.60	1½c yellow brown Harding, sia 553
577	.85	.75	2c carmine Washington, sia 554

Perf. 11x10

578	16.50	15.00	1c green Franklin, sia 552
579	8.25	8.25	2c carmine Washington, sia 554

Issues of 1923–26 Perf. 10

581	1.75	.40	1c green Franklin, sia 552
582	1.20	.30	1½c brown Harding, sia 553
583	.70	.05	2c carmine Washington, sia 554
583a	27.50	10.00	Booklet pane of six
584	9.00	.75	3c violet Lincoln, sia 555
585	4.75	.15	4c yellow brown M. Washington, sia 556
586	4.75	.09	5c blue T. Roosevelt, sia 557
587	1.80	.25	6c red orange Garfield, sia 558
588	2.50	1.85	7c black McKinley, sia 559
589	8.00	1.20	8c olive green Grant, sia 560
590	1.60	.90	9c rose Jefferson, sia 561
591	11.00	.06	10c orange Monroe, sia 562

Perf. 11

594	5000.00	1350.00	1c green Franklin, 19¾ x22¼ mm, sia 552
595	35.00	30.00	2c carmine Washington, 19¾ x22¼ mm, sia 554
596		10,000.00	1c green Franklin, 19¼ x22¾ mm, sia 552

Coil Stamps 1923–29, Perf. 10 Vertically

597		.14	.06	1c green Franklin, sia 552
598		.35	.08	1½c brown Harding, sia 553
599		.20	.04	2c carmine Washington, type I, sia 554
599A	67.50	3.75	2c carmine Washington, type II, sia 554
600	3.50	.08	3c violet Lincoln, sia 555
601	1.35	.20	4c yellow brown M. Washington, sia 556
602	.65	.10	5c dark blue T. Roosevelt, sia 557
603	1.10	.06	10c orange Monroe, sia 562

Coil Stamps 1923–25 Perf. 10 Horizontally

604	.10	.08	1c yellow green Franklin, sia 552
605	.20	.12	1½c yellow brown Harding, sia 553
606	.15	.10	2c carmine Washington, sia 554

Harding Memorial Issue, 1923
Flat Plate Printing

610	.35	.08	2c Harding, Perf. 11 Sep. 1
611	2.50	1.75	2c Harding, Imperf. Nov. 15

Rotary Press Printing

612	6.50	.50	2c black Perf. 10, sia 610 Sep. 12
613		7000.00	2c black Perf. 11, sia 610

Warren G. Harding (1865-1923) was the 28th President
of the United States (1921-23).

Huguenot–Walloon 300th Anniv. Issue
1924, May 1

614	2.50	1.50	1c New England
615	3.25	1.25	2c Landing at Fort Orange
616	17.50	10.00	5c Huguenot Monument, Florida

In the seventeenth century Dutch Walloons and French
Huguenots fled to America to escape religious per-
secution. The Walloons founded Albany, New York.

565

567

568

566

569

570

571

572   573   610   611

INDIANS OF NORTH AMERICA

When the first Europeans came to North America about 100,000 Indians were living on the land. The richly diverse culture of these people dated from a prehistoric time when their ancestors had crossed the Bering Strait and peopled the New World.

Around 1000 A. D. an ancient Pueblo tribe evolved the first-known etching process, probably by using acid from fermented cactus juice. Along the Northwest Coast the Haida, Kwaikutl, and other tribes had a highly advanced culture and economy that was based on fishing. By 1575 the powerful Five Nations of the Iroquois had a governmental system that would later serve as a model of confederation for no less a personage than Benjamin Franklin.

Czechoslovakia Scott No. 1406

Despite these accomplishments the Indians could not successfully defend themselves against the colonists who settled the United States and seized their lands. The different tribes, used to fighting one another, tried too late to unite against a common foe and were driven from their homes by settlers moving west. By the late nineteenth century even the great fighters of the Plains had been subdued and placed on reservations by the government. In the words of one chief, "We first thought he (the white man) came from the Light; but he comes like the dusk of evening now..."

Czechoslovakia Scott No. 1400

See Scott Stamp Nos. 565, 972, 1364, 1389

Czechoslovakia Scott No. 1404

614   615   616

617   618   619

THE THIRTEEN COLONIES REVOLT

*The Revolution was effected before the war commenced. The Revolution was in the minds and hearts of the people...*John Adams

The American War for Independence began on April 19, 1775 in Lexington and Concord, Massachusetts when British troops clashed with armed and angry Minutemen over weapons held by the Americans. On that day the "shots heard round the world" were fired and the military phase of the Revolution finally began.

One says finally because the Revolution had begun long before the Massachusetts skirmish. It began after the French and Indian War, when England barred her growing colonies from settling lands be-

yond the Allegheny Mountains. It began when Britain levied heavy taxes on her colonies but failed to seat their representatives in Parliament. It began when the Americans were forced to "quarter" English troops in their homes; when intellectuals like Franklin, Jefferson, and Adams became convinced that Britain had usurped many of their rights.

This mood—this rebellious spirit—was abetted by the Boston Massacre of 1770, by the Tea Act and the Boston Tea Party, and by the so-called Intolerable Acts, which were designed to punish radicals in Massachusetts but served in effect to unite the colonies against a common enemy.

Following the meeting of the First Continental Congress in Philadelphia on September 24, 1774 and the drafting of a strongly-worded resolution of their rights to rule themselves, the colonies were set on a collision course with England that resulted in the "shots heard round the world." *See Scott Stamp Nos. 617-619*

Monaco Scott No. 354

France Scott No. 814

THE DECLARATION OF INDEPENDENCE

When, in the course of human events, it becomes necessary for one people to dissolve the political bands which have connected them with another...The Declaration of Independence

The United States of America was born on July 4, 1776 when the Second Continental Congress ratified the Declaration of Independence. With this document the colonies renounced all ties with the British Crown and pledged their lives, their fortunes, and their sacred honor to the cause of building a new nation.

The Declaration was, however, far more than a formal statement of rebellion against the government of England and a list of grievances against King George III. It was also an affirmation of the right of every man to "Life, Liberty and the pursuit of Happiness."

Written with great eloquence and force by Thomas Jefferson, it affirmed the hopes and dreams of the founders of the United States and held forth the promise of a just and democratic government for all.

See Scott Stamp Nos. 120,627

Lexington–Concord Issue, 1925, Apr. 4

617	2.25	1.75	1c Washington at Cambridge
618	5.50	3.25	2c Birth of Liberty
619	15.00	8.75	5c Statue of Minute Man

Issued for the 150th anniversary of the Battle of Lexington and Concord.

Norse–American Issue, May 18

620	2.75	2.00	2c Sloop Restaurationen
621	12.00	9.00	5c Viking Ship

In 1825, the first Norwegian immigrants arrived in New York City on the Sloop *Restaurationen.*

Issues of 1925–26

622	3.75	.30	13c Benjamin Harrison
623	3.75	.20	17c Woodrow Wilson

Issues of 1926

627	1.75	.40	2c Independence, 150th Anniv.	May 10

The U.S. Declaration of Independence was written and signed in 1776. The stamp shows the Liberty Bell.

628	5.00	3.00	5c Ericsson Memorial	May 29

John Ericsson designed and built the Union Warship *Monitor.*

629	1.75	1.20	2c Battle of White Plains	Oct. 18

In 1776, Washington fought a brilliant battle at White Plains, N.Y., but was defeated. The stamp shows the battery of Alexander Hamilton, who also fought at White Plains.

631 633 643 644
645 646 648 649

International Philatelic Exhibition Issue, Oct. 18			
Souvenir Sheet			
630	185.00	150.00	2c car. rose, sheet of 25 with selvage inscription, sia 629
		Imperf.	
631	1.00	.90	1½c Harding Aug. 27 18½−19x22 mm.
	Issues of 1926−34, Perf. 11x10½		
632	.08	.03	1c green Franklin, sia 552
632a	.75	.25	Booklet pane of 6
633	.30	.08	1½c Harding
634	.10	.03	2c carmine Washington, type I, sia 554
634A	145.00	5.00	2c carmine Washington, type II, sia 554
635	.25	.04	3c violet Lincoln, sia 555

636	.60	.08	4c yellow brown M. Washington, sia 556
637	.60	.03	5c dark blue T. Roosevelt, sia 557
638	.60	.03	6c red org. Garfield, sia 558
639	.65	.08	7c black McKinley, sia 559
640	.65	.05	8c olive grn. Grant, sia 560
641	.70	.05	9c org. red Jefferson, sia 561
642	1.00	.03	10c orange Monroe, sia 562
		Issues of 1927, Perf. 11	
643	.80	.55	2c Vermont 150th Anniversary Aug. 3

Issued for the 150th anniversary of the Battle of Bennington.

644	1.90	1.40	2c Burgoyne Campaign Aug. 3

THE WAR FOR INDEPENDENCE — FROM BUNKER'S HILL...

When John Adams wrote, "We shall have a long, obstinate, and bloody war to go through," few people believed him. At the time (1776) both sides thought the war would be a short-lived thing; both were wrong.

The Battle of Bunker's Hill, fought at Breed's Hill, Massachusetts, was prophetic of the true course that the war would follow. In June, 1775 the British suffered heavy losses (1,054 killed or wounded) while capturing the famous hill from the Americans. As a result the Continentals claimed a "moral victory" and confidently thought that other victories would follow. Yet the war dragged on, through the Battle of White Plains (1776), and through Washington's retreat across New Jersey (1777). As these later conflicts proved, it took more than raw determination to defeat the British.

See Scott Stamp Nos. 629, 1034, 1361

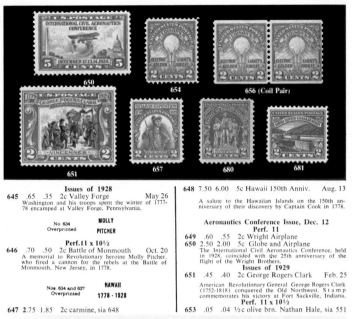

650 | 654 | 656 (Coil Pair)

651 | 657 | 680 | 681

Issues of 1928

645 .65 .35 2c Valley Forge May 26
Washington and his troops spent the winter of 1777-78 encamped at Valley Forge, Pennsylvania.

| No. 634 Overprinted | **MOLLY PITCHER** |

Perf.11 x 10½

646 .70 .50 2c Battle of Monmouth Oct. 20
A memorial to Revolutionary heroine Molly Pitcher, who fired a cannon for the rebels at the Battle of Monmouth, New Jersey, in 1778.

| Nos. 634 and 637 Overprinted | **HAWAII 1778 - 1928** |

647 2.75 1.85 2c carmine, sia 648

648 7.50 6.00 5c Hawaii 150th Anniv. Aug. 13

A salute to the Hawaiian Islands on the 150th anniversary of their discovery by Captain Cook in 1778.

Aeronautics Conference Issue, Dec. 12
Perf. 11

649 .60 .55 2c Wright Airplane
650 2.50 2.00 5c Globe and Airplane
The International Civil Aeronautics Conference, held in 1928, coincided with the 25th anniversary of the flight of the Wright Brothers.

Issues of 1929

651 .45 .40 2c George Rogers Clark Feb. 25

American Revolutionary General George Rogers Clark (1752-1818) conquered the Old Northwest. Stamp commemorates his victory at Fort Sackville, Indiana.

Perf. 11 x 10½

653 .05 .04 ½c olive brn. Nathan Hale, sia 551

... TO SARATOGA

The Battle of Saratoga, fought two years after Bunker's Hill, set in motion a chain of events which gave the Continental Army badly-needed help in its fight for independence.

In 1777 when General Burgoyne proposed to take New York and New England by way of the Hudson River and Lake Champlain, he failed to take Vermont's militia, the Green Mountain Boys, into account. This was a costly oversight, for when diversionary troops went to Vermont in search of food, they were soundly routed by the Green Mountain Boys at Bennington.

From Bennington Americans under Gates followed Burgoyne to New York, where they defeated him again, this time at Saratoga. The general's surrender of October 17 ended British hopes of conquering the North and helped persuade the French to ally themselves with the Americans.

See Scott Stamp Nos. 643, 644

After the Revolution, Britian violated the Treaty of Paris by refusing to withdraw from the valuable fur trading area around the Great Lakes. She used her troops to stir up Indian unrest in the region. Americans attempting to settle the land were driven off by Indians supplied with arms and ammunition from British traders and soldiers on American soil.

General Wayne, who had been given the name "Mad Anthony" because of his strict discipline, trained an army for two years before advancing north of the Ohio River where he built Fort Defiance on the Maumee River. The Indian tribes assembled near the present site of Toledo to prepare a full-scale attack on the fort. "Mad Anthony," instead of waiting for the attack, charged through the brush with his well-trained forces and in less than an hour completely crushed the Indian confederacy. Wayne's skill convinced the Indians of the hopelessness of their cause. At a meeting with over ninety Indian Chiefs at Greenville, a treaty was signed ending hostilities and the Indians agreed to surrender their rights to most of what is now Ohio.

See Scott. No. 680

ANTHONY WAYNE
(1745-1796)

Electric Light Jubilee Issue
Perf. 11

654	.50	.40	2c Edison's First Lamp

Perf. 11 x 10½

655	.40	.15	2c carmine rose, sia 654

Coil Stamp, Perf. 10 Vertically

656	13.50	.85	2c Edison's First Lamp

Thomas A. Edison invented the first practical incandescent electric light bulb on Oct. 21, 1879.

Perf. 11

657	.40	.30	2c Sullivan Expedition Jun. 17

In 1779, General Sullivan led a daring Revolutionary War raid against the Iroquois in New York State.

Regular Issue of 1926–27

Overprinted **Kans.**

Perf. 11 x 10½

658	.70	.70	1c green Franklin, sia 552
659	1.25	1.00	1½c brown Harding, sia 553
660	.90	.25	2c carmine Washington, sia 554
661	6.00	5.00	3c violet Lincoln, sia 555
662	5.00	3.00	4c yellow brown
			M. Washington, sia 556
663	4.25	3.75	5c dp. bl. T. Roosevelt, sia 557
664	8.50	6.50	6c red orange Garfield, sia 558
665	9.25	8.75	7c black McKinley, sia 559
666	26.50	23.00	8c olive green Grant, sia 560
667	3.85	3.75	9c light rose Jefferson, sia 561
668	7.50	3.50	10c org. yel. Monroe, sia 562

669	.65	.65	1c green Franklin, sia 552
670	.85	.80	1½c brown Harding, sia 553
671	.75	.30	2c carmine Washington, sia 554

672	4.00	3.50	3c violet Lincoln, sia 555
673	5.25	3.75	4c yellow brown
			M. Washington, sia 556
674	4.25	4.00	5c dp. bl. T. Roosevelt, sia 557
675	8.50	7.00	6c red orange Garfield, sia 558
676	6.50	6.00	7c black McKinley, sia 559
677	10.00	9.00	8c olive green Grant, sia 560
678	10.50	9.50	9c light rose Jefferson, sia 561
679	25.00	8.50	10c org. yel. Monroe, sia 562

W a r n i n g: Excellent forgeries of t h e Kansas and Nebraska overprints exist.

Perf. 11

680	.85	.60	2c Battle of Fallen Timbers
			Sep. 14

A memorial to General "M a d" Anthony Wayne (1745-1796), who fought in the Revolution.

681	.50	.40	2c Ohio River Canal Oct. 19

Issued to commemorate the completion of the Ohio River Canalization Project between Cairo, Illinois, and Pittsburgh, Pennsylvania.

Issues of 1930

682	.40	.25	2c Mass. Bay Colony Apr. 8

In 1630, English Puritans founded the Massachusetts Bay Colony. Stamp shows the seal of colony.

683	.80	.60	2c Carolina–Charleston Apr. 10

Issued for the 260th anniversary of the C a r o l i n a Province a n d t h e 250th anniversary of the city of Charleston, South Carolina.

Perf. 11 x 10½

684	.12	.03	1½c Warren G. Harding
685	.20	.04	4c William H. Taft

Coil Stamps, Perf. 10 Vertically

686	.35	.05	1½c brown Harding, sia 684
687	.50	.12	4c brown W. H. Taft, sia 685

Perf. 11

688	.70	.50	2c Braddock's Field Jul. 9

The Battle of Braddock's F i e l d, f o u g h t near Ft. Duquesne, Pennsylvania in the F r e n c h and Indian War, was a crushing defeat for the English.

682 683 684 685 688

KAZIMIERZ (CASIMIR) PULASKI (1747-1779)

His valiant leadership in Poland's battle against the Russian invasion of 1769 had made Count Casimir Pulaski a war hero by the time he was twenty-one. During the anti-Russian insurrection following Poland's defeat, one brother had been killed, another taken prisoner and young Casimir was falsely accused of attempting to assassinate King Stanislaus II. The family estates were confiscated and he fled the country penniless. While living in Paris he was presented to Benjamin Franklin who gave him a letter of introduction to George Washington and advanced him passage to America. Washington, who had had to contend with raw troops, welcomed the well-trained soldier. He gave Pulaski command of the cavalry during the battle of Brandywine. Immediately after, Congress commissioned him Brigadier-General and Chief of Cavalry of the Army. He fought in the battles of Germantown, Egg Harbor and others in the winter campaign of 1777-78. He bravely defended Charlestown with his "Pulaski Legion" in May 1779. While leading a cavalry charge in the allied attempt to recapture Savannah, Pulaski was mortally wounded. He died two days later, Oct. 11, 1779, on board the frigate Wasp.

See Scott. No. 690

THADDEUS KOSCIUSZKO
TADEUZ ANDRZEJ BONAWENTURA KOSCIUSZKO
(1746-1817)

Thaddeus Kosciuszko had studied fortification and art in military academies in Poland and France and taught mathematics in his native Poland. His devotion to the cause of liberty led him to America in 1776 to offer his military and engineering skills to the Patriots. A Corps of Engineers was established and "Thad Kosci," as the Americans called him, was made Colonel of Engineers. The fortifications he prepared on Bemis Heights helped stop Burgoyne at Saratoga and contributed greatly to the first major American victory of the war. The next two years were spent designing and building his masterpiece —the fortress at West Point. As chief engineer in the 1780-82 southern campaign he built many forts, bridges and camps, including those used in the siege of Charleston and the Battle of Yorktown.

After the Revolution, Congress thanked him by giving him the rank of Brigadier-General and a large annual pension. He was also given a large piece of land, and the privilege of becoming a United States citizen. He returned home, however, to fight for Poland's independence and territorial rights against Russian partition. Kosciuszko's deep devotion to freedom and independence and his gallant struggle against overwhelming odds have made him one of the world's great heroes.

See Scott No. 734

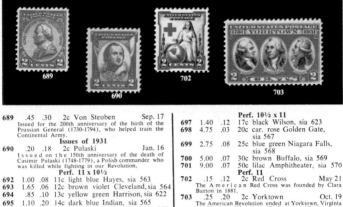

689   690   702   703

689	.45	.30	2c Von Steuben	Sep. 17

Issued for the 200th anniversary of the birth of the Prussian General (1730-1794), who helped train the Continental Army.

Issues of 1931

690	.20	.18	2c Pulaski	Jan. 16

Issued on the 150th anniversary of the death of Casimir Pulaski (1748-1779), a Polish commander who was killed while fighting in our Revolution.

Perf. 11 x 10½

692	1.00	.08	11c light blue Hayes, sia 563
693	1.65	.06	12c brown violet Cleveland, sia 564
694	.85	.10	13c yellow green Harrison, sia 622
695	1.10	.20	14c dark blue Indian, sia 565
696	3.50	.04	15c gray Statue of Liberty, sia 566

Perf. 10½ x 11

697	1.40	.12	17c black Wilson, sia 623
698	4.75	.03	20c car. rose Golden Gate, sia 567
699	2.75	.08	25c blue green Niagara Falls, sia 568
700	5.00	.07	30c brown Buffalo, sia 569
701	9.00	.07	50c lilac Amphitheater, sia 570

Perf. 11

702	.15	.12	2c Red Cross	May 21

The American Red Cross was founded by Clara Barton in 1881.

703	.25	.20	2c Yorktown	Oct. 19

The American Revolution ended at Yorktown, Virginia in 1781 when Washington, DeGrasse and Rochambeau defeated Cornwallis.

THE BATTLE OF YORKTOWN

When General Cornwallis surrendered his entire British force to the Americans at Yorktown, Virginia on October 19, 1781, a military band played "The World Turned Upside Down" and Lafayette solemnly remarked, "The play is over; the fifth act has come to an end."

For all intents and purposes the great French patriot and friend of the Americans was right; Yorktown was the last decisive battle of the Revolutionary War. That it ended on a note of triumph for the United States was, in large part, due to the aid given the Continental Army by Lafayette's fellow Frenchmen, De Grasse and Rochambeau.

The Yorktown campaign began when a French fleet of thirty-six ships under De Grasse converged on Yorktown where Cornwallis and 8,000 British troops were encamped. De Grasse successfully blockaded the Chesapeake Bay and cut off British supplies, reinforcements, communications, and escape. On land, Washington and Rochambeau encircled Yorktown with a combined force of 16,000 men, and by September Cornwallis was surrounded by the Allies. The siege itself began on September 28 and continued until October 17 when Cornwallis sent out a white flag of truce.

See Scott Stamp No. 703

France Scott No. 622

Issues of 1932, Perf. 11 x 10½					

Washington Bicentennial Issue, Jan. 1
Various Portraits

704	.06	.05	½c	Portrait by Charles W. Peale
705	.08	.04	1c	Bust by Jean Antoine Houdon
706	.18	.06	1½c	Portrait by Charles W. Peale
707	.07	.03	2c	Portrait by Gilbert Stuart
708	.30	.06	3c	Portrait by Charles W. Peale
709	.25	.06	4c	Portrait by Charles P. Polk
710	1.20	.08	5c	Portrait by Charles W. Peale
711	2.65	.06	6c	Portrait by John Trumbull
712	.40	.12	7c	Portrait by John Trumbull
713	2.65	.70	8c	Portrait by Charles B.J.F. Saint Memin
714	2.00	.25	9c	Portrait by W. Williams
715	7.00	.10	10c	Portrait by Gilbert Stuart

Issued for the 200th anniversary of the birth of George Washington.

Perf. 11

716	.18	.15	2c Olympic Games	Jan. 25

The Olympic Winter Games of 1932 were held at Lake Placid in New York.

Perf. 11 x 10½

717	.15	.08	2c Arbor Day	Apr. 22

In Nebraska trees are planted every year on Arbor Day. Nebraskan Julius Sterling Morton created Arbor Day.

10th Olympic Games Issue, June 15

718	.30	.06	3c Runner at Starting Mark	
719	.45	.20	5c Myron's Discobolus	

In 1932 the Olympic Summer Games were held in Los Angeles, California.

720	.15	.03	3c Washington	Jun. 16
720b	17.50	5.00	Booklet pane of 6	

Coil Stamps
Perf. 10 Vertically

721	.50	.08	3c Washington	Jun. 24

FREDERICK WILLIAM
AUGUSTUS HENRY FERDINAND,
BARON vonSTEUBEN (1730-1794)

The inexperienced Americans who faced the veteran British in the Revolutionary War were at a severe disadvantage until Baron von Steuben came to their aid. Often called "The Drillmaster of the Continental Army," he arrived at Valley Forge in February 1778 as Washington's Inspector General. The condition of the men was shocking to the meticulous Prussian officer. They had no uniforms, many of them had no shoes, much of their equipment lay rusting in the snow and discipline was non-existent.

Shouting orders in German, von Steuben drilled the ragged troops into an army that could maneuver smoothly and in unison. In May an officer at Valley Forge wrote, "As they became more skillful, their soldierly pride increased and a new morale, never more to be extinguished, soon prevailed in the ranks of the Continental Army."

See Scott No. 689

Even before the Revolutionary War began, the French were in sympathy with the colonists' struggle for independence. Their military supplies and volunteers had been arriving secretly since the fall of 1775 and immediately after the English defeat at Saratoga the French Government recognized American independence and declared war on England. French ships, men, supplies and gold were officially sent to America. Without that help, the struggle might have gone on for years longer. Two of the French officers who helped shorten the Revolution were Comte de Rochambeau and Admiral de Grasse.

JEAN BAPTISTE DONATIEN de VIMEUR, COMTE de ROCHAMBEAU, was a member of a fine old military family, but because of ill health he had been sent to Jesuit rather than military school. By the time he was sixteen his health had improved and he left the Jesuits to become a soldier. Rochambeau had a noteworthy career in the wars of Louis XV and after the Seven Years' War (French and Indian War) received the Order of St. Louis for faithful and gallant service. In 1780 Louis XVI promoted him to Lieutenant-General and put him in command of the French troops, munitions and supplies bound for America. Rochambeau's army united with Washington's army north of New York City in July 1781 and in August they began their rapid march to Virginia to join de Grasse and Lafayette at Yorktown.

FRANCOIS JOSEPH de GRASSE was a son of a French family that traced their lineage back to the 10th Century and boasted many royal intermarriages. Although his father was a captain in the army, de Grasse preferred the sea. He was a captain in the French navy when war was declared between France and England. In 1781 he was Admiral of a fleet bringing heavy reinforcements to America. He arrived at Chesapeake in August and was promptly attacked by the British fleet under Admirals Graves and Hood. De Grasse's victory in that important battle secured the allied water routes to Yorktown.
See Scott No. 703

Perf. 10 Horizontally

722   .35   .15   3c Washington   Oct. 12

Perf. 10 Vertically

723   2.25   .15   6c Garfield   Aug. 18

Perf. 11

724   .20   .10   3c William Penn   Oct. 24
English Quaker William Penn (1644-1718) founded Pennsylvania; laid out Philadelphia in 1682.

725   .25   .12   3c Daniel Webster   Oct. 24
Issued for the 150 anniversary of the birth of the Massachusetts orator and statesman (1782-1852), who was twice Secretary of State, a Congressman, and Senator.

Issues of 1933

726   .25   .10   3c Georgia 200th Anniv. Feb. 12
Englishman James Oglethorpe (1696-1785) established Georgia as a refuge for imprisoned debtors in 1733.

Perf. 10½ x 11

727   .14   .08   3c Peace of 1783   Apr. 19
In 1783, peace between the United States and the British was proclaimed.

Century of Progress Issue, May 25

728   .10   .06   1c Restoration of Ft. Dearborn
729   .12   .04   3c Fed. Building at Chicago 1933
The Century of Progress Exposition held in Chicago, Ill. in 1933, marked the "Windy City's" 100th anniversary.

**American Philatelic Society Issue
Souvenir Sheets, Aug. 25
Without Gum, Imperf.**

730   30.00   17.50   1c deep yellow green sheet
         of 25, sia 728
730a   .65   .35   Single stamp
731   20.00   15.00   3c dp. vio. sheet of 25, sia 729
731a   .50   .30   Single stamp

Issued in sheets of 25 with marginal inscriptions commemorating the 1933 convention of the American Philatelic Society, held in Chicago.

Perf. 10½x11

732   .14   .03   3c National Recovery Act
         Aug. 15
Issued to publicize the National Recovery Act, F.D.R.s program of aid for the depression-stricken country.

Perf. 11

733   .70   .60   3c Byrd's Antarctic Expedition,
         Oct. 9
Issued in connection with Rear Admiral Richard E. Byrd's second South Pole expedition.

734   .60   .20   5c Tadeusz Kosciuszko Oct. 13
Polish patriot Tadeusz Kosciuszko (1746-1817) fought in our Revolution and was awarded American citizenship in 1783.

THE SMITHSONIAN INSTITUTION

An Englishman who never saw the United States contributed greatly to its research activities and to the preservation of its heritage. That man was scientist John Smithson (1765-1829) who willed $500,000 to the United States for the "increase and diffusion of knowledge among men."

Established by an Act of Congress in 1846, the Smithsonian Institution now consists of several galleries, museums, and laboratories, with exhibitions ranging over every area of science and Americana.

The Smithsonian also is the home of the national stamp collection. Many of the stamps displayed at the institution on Scott Album pages have a fascinating tale to tell about the history of the United States; other stamps in the collection are rare treasures in themselves.
See Scott Stamp No. 943

Issues of 1934
National Stamp Exhibition Issue
Souvenir Sheet, Feb. 10
Without Gum, Imperf.

735	11.50	8.50	3c dk. blue sheet of 6, sia 733
735a	1.50	1.25	Single stamp

Issued in sheets of six with marginal inscription commemorating the National Stamp Exhibition of 1934, held in New York City.

Perf. 11

736	.20	.15	3c Maryland 300th Anniversary Mar. 23

Lord Baltimore founded Maryland in 1634.

Mothers of America Issue, May 2
Perf. 11x10-1/2

737	.12	.06	3c Whistler's Mother

Perf. 11

738	.20	.18	3c Whistler's Mother

Issued in honor of Mothers Day. Stamp shows adaption of the well-known painting of Whistler's Mother.

739	.20	.12	3c Wisconsin 300th Anniversary Jul. 7

French explorer Jean Nicolet arrived at Green Bay, in present-day Wisconsin in 1634.

National Parks Issue

740	.06	.06	1c El Capitan, Yosemite, Calif.

NATIONAL PARKS AND MONUMENTS

The land was ours before we were the land's. Robert Frost

Long after the government of the United States acquired the land in which we live, Americans were struggling to adapt to the land and tame its wilderness, to cross its deserts and build cities in the midst of mountains.

The story of this struggle is today kept alive in the nation's parks and monuments, which preserve the country's most historic sites and scenic wonders.

The policy of setting land aside for the public dates from 1872 when the Yellowstone Act forbade the destruction of that wilderness. In 1906 President

741	.10	.06	2c Grand Canyon, Arizona
742	.15	.06	3c Mt. Rainier and Mirror Lake, Washington
743	.40	.30	4c Mesa Verde, Colorado
744	.50	.30	5c Old Faithful, Yellowstone, Wyoming
745	.85	.50	6c Crater Lake, Oregon
746	.40	.35	7c Great Head, Acadia Park, Maine
747	1.20	.90	8c Great White Throne, Zion Park, Utah
748	1.00	.40	9c Mt. Rockwell and Two Medicine Lake, Glacier National Park, Montana
749	2.20	.50	10c Great Smoky Mountains, North Carolina

This series was issued in honor of National Parks Year.

American Philatelic Society Issue
Souvenir Sheet
Imperf.

750	24.00	13.50	3c deep violet sheet of six, sia 742 Aug. 28
750a	2.35	1.75	Single stamp

Issued in sheets of six with marginal inscription commemorating the 1934 convention of the American Philatelic Society held in Atlantic City, N. J.

Theodore Roosevelt designated the first national monument, Devils Tower in Wyoming, under the provisions of the Act for the Preservation of American Antiquities.

When the National Park Service was created in 1916, twelve parks and many monuments existed, ranging from caves, natural bridges, and forests to ancient mountains and Indian cliff dwellings.

Today thirty-five national parks and scores of monuments are found from coast to coast. Administered by the National Park Service of the Interior Department, they are America's gift to the American people.

See Scott Stamp Nos. 740-749, 1084, 1314, 1448-1454, C84

772

773

774 777

751	9.50	6.00	1c green sheet of 6, sia 740
			Oct. 10
751a	1.00	.80	single stamp

Issued in inscribed sheets of six to commemorate the 1934 convention of the Trans-Mississippi Philatelic Society, held in Omaha, Nebraska.

Special Printing (Nos. 752 to 771 inclusive)
Issued March 15, 1935
Without Gum

In 1940, the Post Office Department offered to and did gum full sheets of Nos. 754 to 771 sent in by owners.

Issues of 1935, Perf. 10½ x 11

752	.14	.08	3c violet, Peace of 1783, sia 727 Mar. 15
			Issued in sheets of 400

Perf. 11

753	.50	.50	3c dk. blue Byrd's Antarctic Expedition, sia 733

Imperf.

754	.30	.30	3c dp. vio. Whistler's Mother, sia 737
755	.30	.30	3c dp. vio. Wisconsin 300th Anniv., sia 739
756	.15	.15	1c green Yosemite, sia 740
757	.20	.20	2c red Grand Canyon, sia 741
758	.40	.40	3c dp. vio. Mt. Rainier, sia 742
759	.60	.50	4c brown Mesa Verde, sia 743
760	.65	.50	5c blue Yellowstone, sia 744
761	.95	.70	6c dk. blue Crater Lake, sia 745
762	.75	.60	7c black Acadia, sia 746
763	.90	.70	8c sage green Zion, sia 747
764	.90	.75	9c red orange Glacier Nat'l., sia 748
765	1.75	1.50	10c gray black Smoky Mts., sia 749

Nos. 753-765 were issued in sheets of 200.
Note: Postive identification of Nos. 752, 753, and 766-771 is by blocks or pairs showing wide gutters between stamps.

RICHARD E. BYRD (1888-1957)

One of the great modern explorers was American naval officer Richard E. Byrd. In 1926 he made the first flight over the North Pole; three years later he was the first to fly over the South Pole.

Byrd, whose South Pole flight earned him the rank of rear admiral, traveled to Antarctica several times. In 1928 he helped set up Little America, an exploration base manned by forty-two men on Ross Shelf Ice, south of the Bay of Whales. Five years later he returned to Little America and explored the more remote areas of Antarctica, this time moving some 123 miles closer to the Pole.

Byrd headed scientific expeditions to the South Pole in 1946 and 1947, and was involved in the International Geophysical Year. The author of five books about his explorations, he died in 1957.

See Scott Stamp No. 733

British Antarctic Territory Scott No. 23

766	27.50	16.00	1c yellow green, sia 728
			Pane of 25 from sheet of 225 (9 panes)
766a	.50	.35	Single stamp
767	18.50	13.50	3c violet, sia 729
			Pane of 25 from sheet of 225 (9 panes)
767a	.45	.30	Single stamp
768	11.00	8.00	3c dark blue, sia 733
			Pane of 6 from sheet of 150 (25 panes)
768a	1.20	1.00	Single stamp
769	8.25	6.00	1c green, sia 740
			Pane of 6 from sheet of 120 (20 panes)
769a	.60	.60	Single stamp
770	17.50	13.00	3c deep violet, sia 742
			Pane of 6 from sheet of 120 (20 panes)
770a	1.50	1.50	Single stamp
771	1.75	1.75	15c dark blue Seal of U.S., sia CE2, issued in sheets of 200

Perf. 11 x 10½

772	.10	.06	3c Connecticut 300th Anniv. Apr. 26

Connecticut was settled in 1635. The Founders hid their charter in the Charter Oak (shown).

773	.10	.06	3c California–Pacific Exposition May 29

The 1935 Exposition was held in San Diego.

Perf. 11

774	.10	.06	3c Boulder Dam Sep. 30

Boulder Dam, now Hoover Dam, was dedicated on September 30, 1935.

Perf. 11 x 10½

775	.10	.06	3c Mich. 100th Anniv. Nov. 1

Michigan became a state in 1835.

Issues of 1936

776	.10	.06	3c Texas 100th Anniv. Mar. 2

Texas became a Republic in 1836.

Perf. 10½ x 11

777	.12	.06	3c Rhode Island 300th Anniv. May 4

Rhode Island was founded by dissenters from the Massachusetts Bay Colony led by Roger Williams, in 1636.

775 776 782 784 783

ROGER WILLIAMS (1603-1683)

"Cowammaunsh—I love you." First word of vocabulary in "Key to the Indian Language" by Roger Williams.

Reverend Roger Williams ranks with William Penn and Lord Baltimore as a leader in the struggle for toleration of all religions in the colonies. A Cambridge graduate, he came to Boston in 1631 to teach. A few years later he became minister of the church in Salem. There he alarmed the Puritan leaders of Massachusetts by preaching separation of church and state. He preached complete freedom of religion and a government based on the will of the people. The self-appointed leaders of "The Godly Commonwealth of Massachusetts" had required all colonists to take an oath of loyalty to their regime and to attend church regularly. Only members of a Puritan congregation were allowed to vote. They could not tolerate "new and dangerous opinions against the authority of magistrates."

In 1635, Williams was tried and banished as a trouble-maker. The following spring he founded the Colony of Rhode Island and Providence Plantations on land purchased from his Narraganset Indian friends. The colony was a model of democracy for the whole world, fostering ideals that have become the principles of the United States. Followers came from England and Massachusetts to settle in the first society dedicated to the proposition that all men are created free and equal. There were no taxes levied to support the church, no religious qualifications for voting, and all men were allowed to speak freely and worship as they pleased.

Williams went to England in 1643 to secure a charter from Parliament and again in 1651 to have the charter confirmed to protect Rhode Island from being forcibly annexed by its Puritan neighbors. On his return in 1654, he was elected first president of the colony and served three terms.

See Scott Number 777

785

786

787

788

789

THE UNITED STATES ARMY

To be prepared for war is one of the most effectual means of preserving peace. George Washington

The United States Army began before there was a United States. In 1775, the Continental Congress created a Continental Army to win freedom from the British.

Led by the brilliant Washington, Nathanael Greene, and other generals, the Continental Army survived freezing winters and a lack of food and clothing to win the Revolutionary War. Men like Andrew Jackson ("Old Hickory") in the War of 1812 and fiery Winfield Scott in the Mexican War helped perpetuate military excellence.

In 1802 Congress authorized the creation of a military academy at West Point, New York, to train army officers. Distinguished West Point graduates include the opposing heroes of the Civil War: Generals Sherman, Grant, and Sheridan of the North; Lee and "Stonewall" Jackson of the South.

Led by heroes such as Generals Pershing, Patton, Eisenhower, and MacArthur, the twentieth century army has led the United States to victory in two World Wars.

See Scott Stamp Nos. 785-789, 934

Grenada Scott No. 377

790

791

792

793

794

THE UNITED STATES NAVY

I have not yet begun to fight!
John Paul Jones

The story of the navy is a log of famous battles, ships, and men. In the Revolutionary War, John Paul Jones and John Barry fathered the United States Navy. In the 1801-05 war against the Barbary pirates, Stephen Decatur distinguished himself in a daring raid on Tripoli harbor. In the War of 1812, Thomas MacDonough defeated the British on Lake Champlain.

During the Civil War David D. Porter and his adopted brother David Farragut, the first U. S. Admirals, successfully blockaded the South for the Union.

The Spanish-American War of 1898 was a further demonstration of the navy's might. Admirals Dewey, Schley, and Sampson distinguished themselves in conflicts from Santiago, Cuba to the Philippines.

Ships of the modern navy are stationed around the world. Twentieth century naval heroes include Admirals Mayo, Halsey, King, and Nimitz.

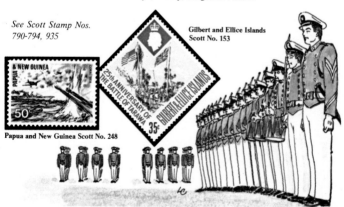

See Scott Stamp Nos. 790-794, 935

Gilbert and Ellice Islands
Scott No. 153

Papua and New Guinea Scott No. 248

795   796   798

799   800   801

802

THE FRAMING OF THE CONSTITUTION

We the People of the United States, in order to form a more perfect Union… The Constitution

On May 14, 1787, fifty-five delegates from all the states (except Rhode Island) met in historic Philadelphia to revise the inadequate Articles of Confederation. George Washington was elected president of the convention. Other delegates were the patriots Benjamin Franklin, James Madison, and Alexander Hamilton. Deliberating in secrecy, these distinguished men drew on their experience in self-government and on their knowledge of the British common law to form a strong, yet flexible framework of government. Their four month effort produced the Constitution of the United States, "the most wonderful work ever struck off at a given time by the brain and purpose of man" (William Gladstone).

This remarkable document, which became the law of the land in March of 1789, is the solid bedrock upon which the American democratic system is built. Its first three Articles establish and enumerate the divisions of the Federal government — the legislative, executive, and judicial branches. Under its unique system of "checks and balances" a unified nation has grown, liberty flourished, and the dream of its framers become reality.

See Scott Stamp Nos. 798, 835

NORTHWEST ORDINANCE OF 1787

"I doubt whether one single law of any lawgiver, ancient or modern, has provided effects of more distant, marked, and lasting character than the Ordinance of 1787."   *Daniel Webster*

The most important conflict facing the Continental Congress at the end of the American Revolution concerned our western lands. During the Colonial period Massachusetts, Connecticut, New York, Virginia, the Carolinas and Georgia had acquired claims on territory that stretched as far west as the Mississippi River. States with fixed borders, fearful of being dominated by larger neighbors, demanded that Congress should control the West. Maryland argued, "It had been secured by the blood and treasure of all" and ought to become "common stock, to be parcelled out by Congress into free, convenient, and independent Governments." Within a few years after Congress promised the land would be used for common benefit, all states claiming portions of the Northwest Territory ceded their claims to the new nation.

In 1786 a group of Army officers headed by General Rufus Putnam, an engineer from Massachusetts, formed the Ohio Company of Associates. The company intended to purchase a large tract of land in the territory and re-sell it in small tracts suitable for homesites. Congress, not authorized to hold or govern territory was quite willing to sell. Manasseh Cutler, a Massachusetts clergyman well-known for his business ability, was sent to represent the company in the negotiations. Cutler insisted a form of government for the new land had to be provided by Congress before the purchase could be completed.

With his help, the Continental Congress worked out the Ordinance of 1787 providing temporary government of the territory by officials appointed by Congress. When the adult male population in any one part of the territory reached 5,000, authority would reside in an elected legislature. When there were 60,000 inhabitants in one of these territories, that section could adopt a constitution, elect it own officers and enter the Confederation on equal terms with the original states. It guaranteed the settlers freedom of speech, press and religious worship, introduced a free system of education and prohibited slavery. In 1800 Indiana Territory was formed, followed soon thereafter by the State of Ohio. By mid-century Michigan, Illinois and Wisconsin had been admitted to Statehood.

The democratic principles of the Ordinance of 1787 set a precedent for the organization of all other United States territories that have been admitted into the Union. The "full equality" provision explains how it was possible for our country to grow from thirteen to fifty states in less than two hundred years.

See Scott No. 795

Issues of 1937

795   .12   .06   3c Northwest Ordinance
150th Anniversary   Jul. 13
The Northwest Territory was created in 1787. It included the present states of Ohio, Indiana, Illinois, Michigan, Wisconsin, and part of Minnesota.

Perf. 11

796   .35   .20   5c Virginia Dare   Aug. 18
Marks the 350th anniversary of the birth of the first child born in America of English parents, at Roanoke Island.

Society of Philatelic Americans
Imperf. Souvenir Sheet

797   .55   .35   10c blue green, sia 749   Aug. 26
Issued in sheets of one stamp with marginal inscription commemorating the 43rd Annual Convention of the Society of Philatelic Americans held in Asheville, North Carolina.

Perf. 11 x 10½

798   .15   .07   3c Constitution 150th Anniv.
Sep. 17
Issued on the 150th anniversary of the signing of the Constitution, Sep. 17, 1787.

Territorial Issues
Perf. 10½ x 11

799   .15   .07   3c Alaska   Oct. 18

Perf. 11 x 10½

800   .15   .07   3c Hawaii   Nov. 12
801   .15   .07   3c Puerto Rico   Nov. 25
802   .15   .07   3c Virgin Islands   Dec. 15
These stamps show a statue of King Kamehameha I (Hawaii), Mt. McKinley (Alaska), Fortaleza Castle (Puerto Rico), and Charlotte Amalie (Virgin Islands).

Presidential Issue, 1938–54

803	.03	.03	½c Benjamin Franklin
804	.04	.03	1c George Washington
804b	1.25	.30	Booklet pane of six
805	.05	.03	1½c Martha Washington
806	.06	.03	2c John Adams
806b	2.75	.85	Booklet pane of six
807	.08	.03	3c Thomas Jefferson
807a	6.00	1.50	Booklet pane of six
808	.15	.04	4c James Madison
809	.15	.06	4½c White House
810	.18	.03	5c James Monroe
811	.20	.03	6c John Q. Adams
812	.25	.05	7c Andrew Jackson
813	.25	.04	8c Martin Van Buren
814	.30	.04	9c William H. Harrison
815	.25	.03	10c John Tyler
816	.35	.08	11c James K. Polk
817	.45	.06	12c Zachary Taylor
818	.55	.08	13c Millard Filmore
819	.55	.10	14c Franklin Pierce
820	.45	.03	15c James Buchanan
821	.65	.25	16c Abraham Lincoln
822	.65	.12	17c Andrew Johnson
823	.70	.08	18c Ulysses S. Grant
824	.80	.30	19c Rutherford B. Hayes
825	.60	.03	20c James A. Garfield
826	.85	.10	21c Chester A. Arthur
827	.85	.35	22c Grover Cleveland
828	.95	.25	24c Benjamin Harrison
829	.70	.03	25c William McKinley
830	2.35	.05	30c Theodore Roosevelt
831	5.00	.06	50c William Howard Taft
			Perf. 11
832	5.50	.10	$1 Woodrow Wilson
832b	40.00	11.00	Wmkd. USIR sia 832
833	12.50	2.00	$2 Warren G. Harding
834	62.50	1.75	$5 Calvin Coolidge

JOHN ADAMS (1735-1826), SECOND PRESIDENT OF THE U. S.

One of the most scholarly and brilliant presidents, John Adams was also one of the most candid. Adams' frankness made him a poor diplomat but served him well in other spheres.

During the stormy era of the Revolution he was a staunch, outspoken patriot who took part in both Continental Congresses, argued for the Declaration of Independence, and was responsible for Washington's appointment as commander-in-chief of the Continental Army. A Federalist and the first president to occupy the White House, Adams served as Chief Executive from 1797 until 1801. Like Jefferson he died on the fiftieth anniversary of the adoption of the Declaration of Independence, July 4, 1826.

See Scott Stamp No. 806

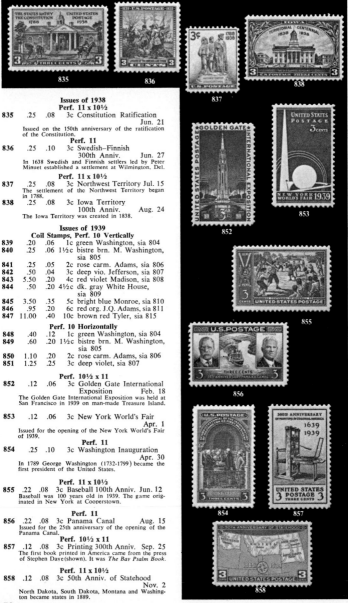

Issues of 1938
Perf. 11 x 10½

835   .25   .08   3c Constitution Ratification   Jun. 21

Issued on the 150th anniversary of the ratification of the Constitution.

Perf. 11

836   .25   .10   3c Swedish–Finnish 300th Anniv.   Jun. 27

In 1638 Swedish and Finnish settlers led by Peter Minuet established a settlement at Wilmington, Del.

Perf. 11 x 10½

837   .25   .08   3c Northwest Territory Jul. 15

The settlement of the Northwest Territory began in 1788.

838   .25   .08   3c Iowa Territory 100th Anniv.   Aug. 24

The Iowa Territory was created in 1838.

Issues of 1939
Coil Stamps, Perf. 10 Vertically

839   .20   .06   1c green Washington, sia 804
840   .25   .06   1½c bistre brn. M. Washington, sia 805
841   .25   .05   2c rose carm. Adams, sia 806
842   .50   .04   3c deep vio. Jefferson, sia 807
843   5.50   .20   4c red violet Madison, sia 808
844   .50   .20   4½c dk. gray White House, sia 809
845   3.50   .35   5c bright blue Monroe, sia 810
846   .95   .20   6c red org. J.Q. Adams, sia 811
847   11.00   .40   10c brown red Tyler, sia 815

Perf. 10 Horizontally

848   .40   .12   1c green Washington, sia 804
849   .60   .20   1½c bistre brn. M. Washington, sia 805
850   1.10   .20   2c rose carm. Adams, sia 806
851   1.25   .25   3c deep violet, sia 807

Perf. 10½ x 11

852   .12   .06   3c Golden Gate International Exposition   Feb. 1

The Golden Gate International Exposition was held at San Francisco in 1939 on man-made Treasure Island.

853   .12   .06   3c New York World's Fair   Apr. 1

Issued for the opening of the New York World's Fair of 1939.

Perf. 11

854   .25   .10   3c Washington Inauguration   Apr. 30

In 1789 George Washington (1732-1799) became the first president of the United States.

Perf. 11 x 10½

855   .22   .08   3c Baseball 100th Anniv. Jun. 12

Baseball was 100 years old in 1939. The game originated in New York at Cooperstown.

Perf. 11

856   .22   .08   3c Panama Canal   Aug. 15

Issued for the 25th anniversary of the opening of the Panama Canal.

Perf. 10½ x 11

857   .12   .08   3c Printing 300th Anniv. Sep. 25

The first book printed in America came from the press of Stephen Daye (shown). It was *The Bay Psalm Book.*

Perf. 11 x 10½

858   .12   .08   3c 50th Anniv. of Statehood   Nov. 2

North Dakota, South Dakota, Montana and Washington became states in 1889.

Famous Americans Issue, 1940, Perf. 10½ x 11

Authors

859	.06	.06	1c Washington Irving
860	.10	.08	2c James Fenimore Cooper
861	.12	.06	3c Ralph Waldo Emerson
862	.22	.22	5c Louisa May Alcott
863	2.00	1.10	10c Samuel L. Clemens
			(Mark Twain)

Poets

864	.12	.08	1c Henry W. Longfellow
865	.10	.08	2c John Greenleaf Whittier
866	.18	.06	3c James Russell Lowell
867	.22	.20	5c Walt Whitman
868	3.00	1.30	10c James Whitcomb Riley

It was *"The Sketchbook of Geoffrey Crayon, Gent,"* that reversed the criticism of American literary ability. The tremendous success of this collection of short stories published in 1819 made Washington Irving an outstanding author at home and abroad.

Irving, youngest of eleven children of an austere Presbyterian father and a genial Anglican mother, was spoiled and indulged by his older brothers and sisters, partly because he was the "baby," partly because he was a frail, sensitive youth. He studied law, but preferred writing and in 1809 published *"A History of New York From the Beginning of the World to the End of the Dutch Dynasty"* under the pseudonym Diedrick Knickerbocker. This satire of the Dutch in New Amsterdam was hailed as "the first great book of comic literature written by an American."

He passed his bar examainations "by the grace of God," practiced law briefly in his brother John's office, and in 1815 went to England to look after the family's business interests in Liverpool. The business did not do well, but the literary friendships Irving formed in London were profitable. The Sketch Book was a direct result of encouragement given him by Sir Walter Scott.

Later, as translator at the American Embassy in Madrid, he became deeply absorbed in Spanish history. It was during this period he wrote several biographies of Columbus, also *Conquest of Granada* and *The Alhambra,* the latter a Spanish counterpart of the Sketch book. He returned home in 1832 and soon thereafter departed on a journey to the Far West, which inspired several more works.

Except for four years as Minister to Spain (1842-1846), Irving spent the remainder of his life at "Sunnyside," his home on the Hudson, writing books about his travels and a five-volume biography of his namesake, George Washington. Though his works fill many volumes, he is best remembered for two stories from The Sketch Book— "The Legend of Sleepy Hollow," and "Rip Van Winkle."

WASHINGTON IRVING
(1783-1859)

"In all the four corners of the globe, who reads an American book?"
Sidney Smith,
English Humorist.

See Scott Nos. 859, 1548

BOOKER TALIAFERRO WASHINGTON (1856-1915)

"Up From Slavery"

Take a blind mule, a broken-down shanty, and an abandoned church. Add 30 students and a principal with a vision and you have Tuskegee Institute the day it opened . . . the Fourth of July, 1881.

Booker T. Washington, son of a negro slave and a white father, was born a slave in the Virginia hills. After emancipation, determined to have an education, he worked as a janitor at the Hampton (Virginia) Normal and Agricultural Institute to pay his tuition. When only twenty-five he was appointed principal of the new Negro school at Tuskegee, Alabama.

Undaunted when he found the school practically non-existent, Washington tramped the hot countryside to advertise the Institute and to recruit young men and women from the farms for training in agriculture and the trades. Helped by well-wishers of both races, he purchased a nearby farm. The students designed and constructed new buildings, made their own clothing, and raised food on their own farm as part of his program of learning by doing.

The school grew, as did Washington's prestige. Rising from the social level of the slave cabin to acceptance at the White House as an inter-racial statesman, he lectured, wrote books, and worked closely with presidents and industrialists. He established several organizations to promote the education, advancement, and welfare of the Black people. He received an honorary degree of Master of Art from Harvard University (1896) and of Doctor of Laws from Dartmouth College (1901).

In an age just beginning to learn that the color of a man's skin has nothing to do with his potential contribution to society, Dr. Booker T. Washington emerged as the most influential spokesman for the American Negro. "More and more," he taught, "we must learn to think not in terms of race or color or language or religion or political boundries, but in terms of humanity."

See Scott Nos. 873, 1074

JAMES FENIMORE COOPER (1789-1851)

Cooperstown, New York, a frontier settlement founded by Judge William Cooper in 1786, was the childhood home of his famous son, James Fenimore Cooper. The family mansion was on Otsego Lake and the boy spent many happy hours along its shores with trappers and woodsmen, fascinated by their tales of Indian warfare and the American Revolution.

A brilliant student, he entered Yale at the age of thirteen. The school prankster, he was expelled in his third year for exploding a charge of gunpowder in the lock of a teacher's door. He spent the next five years at sea, the last three as a United States Midshipman. In 1811 he married, resigned from the Navy, and settled down to the life of a country gentleman on the Cooperstown estate.

He wrote *Precaution* in 1820 on a dare from his wife, but it was a dismal failure. The following year he wrote a novel about the American Revolution, basing it on stories he had heard as a boy. *The Spy* was an international success and Cooper, at age thirty-two, became one of America's best known novelists. His most popular works are stories of the frontier and of the sea. Most successful are the Leatherstocking Tales. The land and sea adventures of their chief character, whose name was usually Natty Bumppo, still live in *The Deerslayer, The Pathfinder, The Pioneer, The Prairie,* and *The Last of the Mohicans.*

In addition to being the home of Baseball's Hall of Fame, Cooperstown is also headquarters of the New York State Historical Society which operates Fenimore House as a museum in the village.

See Scott No. 860

869 870 871 872 873

			Educators					Scientists
869	.09	.08	1c Horace Mann	874	.06	.06	1c John James Audubon
870	.10	.06	2c Mark Hopkins	875	.08	.06	2c Dr. Crawford W. Long
871	.30	.06	3c Charles W. Eliot	876	.10	.06	3c Luther Burbank
872	.35	.22	5c Frances E. Willard	877	.20	.18	5c Dr. Walter Reed
873	1.35	.85	10c Booker T. Washington	878	1.20	.80	10c Jane Addams

WALT WHITMAN (1819-92)

I hear America singing, the varied carols I hear. Leaves of Grass

Walt Whitman, a native of Long Island and one of nine children, is the great poetic voice of the democratic ideal, as he proclaimed himself in his longest poem, "Song of Myself." His classic *Leaves of Grass* (1855) is his poetic celebration of America.

During the Civil War Whitman served as a war correspondent and unofficial nurse. This turbulent experience produced *Drum-Taps* (1865), followed by *Sequel to Drum-Taps* (1866), which contains Whitman's elegies of Lincoln—"O Captain! My Captain!" and "When Lilacs Last in the Dooryard Bloom'd." His prose works are *Democratic Vistas* and *Specimen Days and Collect.*

See Scott Stamp No. 867

Czechoslovakia
Scott No. 726

1187

FREDERIC REMINGTON (1861-1909)

Rarely has the action, mystery, and beauty of the Old West been portrayed as realistically as in the art of Frederic Remington.

Born in Canton, New York, Remington moved to the West while still a youth to seek a remedy for his poor health. The rugged life of the frontier intrigued the young artist and became the subject-matter for his sculpture, paintings, and his writings.

From honest colorful depictions of pioneers to bronze statues such as "Wounded Bunkie" and the "Bronco Buster", Remington created in his art a living record of the winning of the West.

See Scott Stamp Nos. 888 and 1187

874 875 876 877 878

Composers			
879	.06	.06	1c Stephen Collins Foster
880	.08	.06	2c John Philip Sousa
881	.15	.06	3c Victor Herbert
882	.25	.20	5c Edward MacDowell
883	3.00	1.00	10c Ethelbert Nevin
Artists			
884	.06	.06	1c Gilbert Charles Stuart
885	.08	.06	2c James A. McNeill Whistler

886	.10	.06	3c Augustus Saint–Gaudens
887	.25	.22	5c Daniel Chester French
888	1.40	1.10	10c Frederic Remington
Inventors			
889	.12	.08	1c Eli Whitney
890	.08	.06	2c Samuel F. B. Morse
891	.20	.06	3c Cyrus Hall McCormick
892	1.00	.30	5c Elias Howe
893	5.75	1.25	10c Alexander Graham Bell

STEPHEN COLLINS FOSTER (1826-64)

All up and down the whole creation, sadly I roam
Still longing for the old plantation, and for the old folks at home.

Stephen Foster began his career as a professional bookkeeper and amateur songwriter. He had no formal musical training; genius was his schooling. Known to have written about two hundred ballads, such as "Swanee River" and "My Old Kentucky Home", Foster translated his environment into memorable lyrical expression. A Negro minstrel group called Christy's Minstrels caught his eye, and he began writing what he termed "Ethiopian" songs for their shows.

With the onslaught of the Gold Rush, his ever-popular "Oh Susanna" became the theme song of the Forty-Niners and carried Foster's reputation across the nation.

See Scott Stamp No. 879

Issues of 1940
Perf. 11x10-1/2

894	.50	.20	3c Pony Express	Apr. 3

The famed Pony Express began to carry mail across the continent in 1860.

Perf. 10-1/2x11

895	.45	.15	3c Pan American Union	Apr. 14

The Pan American Union was established in 1890. The stamp shows the "Three Graces" from Botticelli's "Spring".

Perf. 11x10-1/2

896	.20	.08	3c Idaho Statehood 50th Anniv.	

Idaho became a state in 1890. Jul. 3

Perf. 10-1/2x11

897	.20	.08	3c Wyoming Statehood 50th Anniv.	Jul. 10

Wyoming became a state in 1890.

898	.20	.08	3c Coronado Expedition	Sep. 7

In 1540, Coronado, the discoverer of Grand Canyon, led a Spanish expedition through the Southwest. The explorer hoped to find the golden "Cities of Cibola".

ALEXANDER GRAHAM BELL (1847-1922)

"Mr. Watson, come here; I want you," the first telephone transmission, ushered in a new era in communication. But for Alexander Graham Bell, the inventor of the telephone, it meant the end of a long struggle to perfect the revolutionary instrument.

Bell's lifelong interest in sound stimulated his invention of the telephone. A native of Scotland, he came to the United States by way of Canada. After settling in Boston he set up a training school for teachers of the deaf, and in 1873 he joined the faculty of Boston University as professor of vocal physiology.

By 1875 Bell and his assistant, Thomas Watson, had developed a machine that would become the modern telephone. This machine used electricity to transmit vocal sounds. On February 4, 1876 Bell applied for a patent on his revolutionary apparatus and on March 10, 1876 he spoke the first complete sentence over the telephone.

See Scott Stamp No. 893

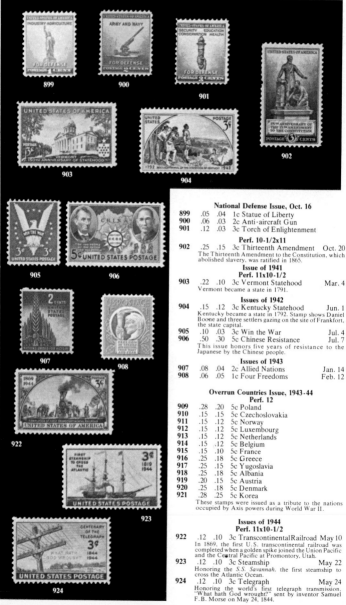

National Defense Issue, Oct. 16

899	.05	.04	1c Statue of Liberty	
900	.06	.03	2c Anti-aircraft Gun	
901	.12	.03	3c Torch of Enlightenment	

Perf. 10-1/2x11

902 .25 .15 3c Thirteenth Amendment Oct. 20
The Thirteenth Amendment to the Constitution, which abolished slavery, was ratified in 1865.

Issue of 1941
Perf. 11x10-1/2

903 .22 .10 3c Vermont Statehood Mar. 4
Vermont became a state in 1791.

Issues of 1942

904 .15 .12 3c Kentucky Statehood Jun. 1
Kentucky became a state in 1792. Stamp shows Daniel Boone and three settlers gazing on the site of Frankfort, the state capital.

905 .10 .03 3c Win the War Jul. 4
906 .50 .30 5c Chinese Resistance Jul. 7
This issue honors five years of resistance to the Japanese by the Chinese people.

Issues of 1943

907 .08 .04 2c Allied Nations Jan. 14
908 .06 .05 1c Four Freedoms Feb. 12

Overrun Countries Issue, 1943-44
Perf. 12

909	.28	.20	5c Poland
910	.15	.15	5c Czechoslovakia
911	.15	.12	5c Norway
912	.15	.12	5c Luxembourg
913	.15	.12	5c Netherlands
914	.15	.12	5c Belgium
915	.15	.10	5c France
916	.25	.18	5c Greece
917	.25	.15	5c Yugoslavia
918	.25	.18	5c Albania
919	.20	.15	5c Austria
920	.25	.18	5c Denmark
921	.28	.25	5c Korea

These stamps were issued as a tribute to the nations occupied by Axis powers during World War II.

Issues of 1944
Perf. 11x10-1/2

922 .12 .10 3c Transcontinental Railroad May 10
In 1869, the first U.S. transcontinental railroad was completed when a golden spike joined the Union Pacific and the Central Pacific at Promontory, Utah.

923 .12 .10 3c Steamship May 22
Honoring the S.S. *Savannah*, the first steamship to cross the Atlantic Ocean.

924 .12 .10 3c Telegraph May 24
Honoring the world's first telegraph transmission, "What hath God wrought?" sent by inventor Samuel F.B. Morse on May 24, 1844.

909 910 911

912 913 914

SAMUEL F. B. MORSE (1791-1872)

Samuel F. B. Morse, the inventor of the telegraph, began his career not as a scientist, but as an artist. In 1829, the young Yale graduate began a three year art tour of Europe. His return voyage proved to be the turning point in his career. While at sea his idea for a telegraph began to germinate.

For three years Morse worked on the idea, and on Sept. 21, 1837, he exhibited the successful instrument. He petitioned Congress for funds to build a practical working telegraph, but the lawmakers were not interested. More discouraging, neither England, nor Russia, nor France bought his patent. Finally in 1843, after a six year delay, Congress granted funds, and in 1844 Morse's telegraph linked Baltimore and Washington. On May 24th of that year, he tapped out his famous first message, "What hath God wrought?"

See Scott Stamp Nos. 890, 924

915 916 917 918 919 920 921

925   .12   .10   3c Philippines   Sep. 27
A tribute to the U.S.-Philippine resistance to the Japanese at Corregidor, Jan.-May 1942.

926   .12   .10   3c Motion Picture 50th Anniv.

                                     Oct. 31
In 1892, Edison's "Kinetoscope," the first motion picture, had its first public showing.

Issues of 1945

927   .10   .08   3c Florida Statehood   Mar. 3
Florida became a U.S. territory in 1822; a state in 1845.

928   .10   .08   5c United Nations Conference

                                      Apr. 25
The United Nations Conference of April 25, 1945 was a 46 nation effort to establish the U.N. and to draft a charter for it.

ROMANCE OF THE RAILROADS

On February 28, 1827, the Baltimore and Ohio was the first railroad company in America to be chartered as a common carrier of freight and passengers. Almost immediately, several other lines came into being. By the end of the Civil War more than 30,000 miles of railroad had been built east of the Missouri River. In the period of industrial expansion after the war the country needed an efficient way to move people, goods and mail throughout all the states to bind the nation into one economic unit.

The pioneers who had settled in the far west in the 1830's to the 1860's felt very far away from their former homes and friends. They were able to get general news in their daily newspapers by means of the recently-invented telegraph, but letters from their families back East took three or four months to reach them. Even after roads were built, the stage coaches carrying mail took more than a month for the trip. Products of the West had to be moved by way of the Gulf Ports to New Orleans, the commercial center of the Mississippi Valley. Great was the joy of those western families when the announcement was made that a railroad was to be built straight across the country—from sea to sea!

The building of the track is part of the thrilling saga of the West. The railroad had to be mapped out through wild, unknown country beyond the Missouri. Two lines of track were begun at the same time, one going east from Sacramento, the other west from Omaha. Thousands of men worked laying the track. For three years they fought blizzards, avalanches and each other while an enthusiastic nation waited to see whether the eastern or western construction crews would lay the most track.

Finally, on May 10, 1869 the "impossible" task was completed. The Central Pacific had built 689 miles of track from the west, the Union Pacific 1,086. The meeting took place at Promontory Point near Ogden, Utah. All rivalry was forgotten as special trains came from east and west with, as author-poet Bret Harte put it, "Two engines on a single track, half a world behind each back."

Telegraph wires were kept open throughout the nation to report each step of the historic event. Governor Stanford of California raised a silver sledgehammer to drive the final gold spike, a telegraph wire attached to it to transmit the actual blows across the country. (He missed the spike, but the telegraph operator, prepared for the emergency, simulated the blow with his key.) At that moment a large ball slid down the pole above the Capitol dome in Washington, fire bells clanged in San Francisco, cannons thundered and factory whistles pierced the air in cities from coast to coast. An Infantry band played "America" as the two trains edged cautiously over the new rail to touch cow-catchers and their engineers were given drinks from foamy bottles of champagne. The evening ended with a giant torchlight parade, a banquet and a very festive ball.

See Scott Nos. 114, 295, 922, 947, 993, 1006, Q5

930	**931**	**932**	**933**	
934		**935**		**936**

Perf. 10-1/2x11

929 .10 .05 3c Iwo Jima (Marines) Jul. 11
A tribute to U.S. Marines who fought in World War II.

Issues of 1945-46
Perf. 11x10-1/2
Franklin D. Roosevelt Issue

930 .05 .05 1c F.D.R. and home at Hyde Park
931 .08 .08 2c Roosevelt and "Little White House," Ga.

932 .10 .06 3c Roosevelt and White House
933 .12 .08 5c F.D.R., Globe and Four Freedoms
In memory of Franklin Delano Roosevelt (1882-1945), 32nd president of the United States (1933-1945).

934 .10 .05 3c U.S. Army in Paris Sep. 28
A tribute to U.S. soldiers who fought in World War II.
935 .10 .05 3c U.S. Navy Oct. 27
A tribute to U.S. sailors who served in World War II.
936 .10 .05 3c U.S. Coast Guard Nov. 10
A tribute to the members of the Coast Guard who served in World War II.

THE STORY OF STEAM

Aeolipile, a primitive steam driven device, was described by Greek mathematician Herod around the 1st century, A.D. Through the centuries many minds worked to improve this simple apparatus and in 1698 Thomas Savery was able to patent the first practical steam engine. Other men, including Thomas Newcomen, worked to improve on Savery's patent in the hopes of making an engine capable of pumping water out of coal mines in low-lying areas of England. The Newcomen engine served the purpose for many years, but it was a huge piece of equipment that used tremendous quantities of kindling.

In 1764 a broken Newcomen engine was given to Scottish engineer James Watt for repairs. After putting the machine in order, he made a scientific study of the properties of steam. His research led to the development of a smaller, more powerful engine which he patented in 1769. In addition to being an efficient pump, Watt's engine was also capable of driving other types of machinery through the use of a piston rod.

Even before the steam engine had been improved, experimental steamboats had been attempted, including one as early as 1690 by the noted French physicist Denis Papin. These early efforts were doomed to failure because of the problems of size and weight. Steam, at best, was considered only as a source of stationary power. Watt's smaller engine changed that attitude and inspired new and more successful attempts at steam navigation.

James Rumsey of Maryland designed a boat propelled by steam pressure and in 1787 the Rumsey Society received a grant to navigate the waters of New York, Maryland and Virginia. Their boats achieved a speed of four miles an hour. In 1790 John Fitch's steam boats carried passengers between Philadelphia and Burlington at the remarkable speed of eight miles an hour.

William Symington ran a steam propelled paddle-wheel vessel on a pond in Scotland to demonstrate its utility for towing purposes. Robert Fulton witnessed the success of this type of craft and returned home to build the "Clermont." (See Robert Fulton) The "Clermont" was a commercial success and in a few years paddle-wheel steam boats were providing speedy, low-cost transportation on the Mississippi, the Great Lakes and along the Atlantic coast.

Before long, ship owners began to think about crossing the Atlantic by steam instead of sailing vessels. The "Savannah," a full-rigged sailing ship, was fitted with engines and side paddle wheels. On May 22, 1819 she steamed out of Savannah, Georgia and continued to use engines for over 85 hours of the twenty-nine day voyage to Liverpool. Although regular steamship passage was still more than twenty years in the future, the "Savannah" was the first steam fitted ocean-going vessel to cross the Atlantic.

See Scott No. 923.

937 938
939
941
942
943
944
940
945
946

GEORGE S. PATTON (1885-1945)

General George S. Patton, Jr., World War II commander of the Third Army, was one of the most colorful American soldiers of all time. Nicknamed "Old Blood and Guts", Patton was a controversial figure due to his demanding discipline in battle.

The most brilliant phase of his career began at Normandy on D-Day, June 6, 1944. Spearheading the final thrusts of the American forces, he routed the Germans at St. Lô. Moving on toward Germany, Patton's army was the savior of the Allied forces at the Battle of the Bulge. On March 22, 1945 the general and his troops crossed the Rhine into the German heartland, and Allied victory was assured.

See Scott Stamp No. 1026

Belgium Scott No. B610

Belgium
Scott No. B608

937 .10 .04 3c Alfred E. Smith Nov. 26
Alfred E. Smith (1873-1944) was governor of N. Y. (1919-20, 1923-28). He was the Democratic Presidential candidate in 1928.

938 .10 .05 3c Texas Statehood Dec. 29
Texas became a state in 1845. It had been independent for nine years.

Issues of 1946

939 .10 .05 3c Merchant Marines Feb. 26
A tribute to Merchant Mariners who served in World War II.

940 .10 .04 3c Veterans of World War II May 9
Issued to honor the Veterans of World War II.

941 .10 .05 3c Tennessee Statehood Jun. 1
Tennessee became a state in 1796. Stamp shows two state heroes, Andrew Jackson and John Sevier, first governor of Tennessee.

942 .10 .05 3c Iowa Statehood Aug. 3
Iowa became a state in 1846.

943 .10 .05 3c Smithsonian Institution Aug. 10
The Smithsonian Institution in Washington, D. C. was funded by the will of English scientist John Smithson. Established in 1846, it houses the national stamp collection and has exhibitions in all areas of science.

944 .10 .05 3c Kearny Expedition Oct. 16
General Stephen Watts Kearny (1794-1848) captured Los Angeles and Santa Fe in 1846, thereby bringing to an end our war with Mexico.

Issues of 1947
Perf. 10-1/2x11

945 .10 .05 3c Thomas A. Edison Feb. 11
Issued for the 100th anniversary of the birth of Thomas A. Edison (1847-1931), inventor of the phonograph and sound movies.

Perf. 11x10-1/2

946 .10 .05 3c Joseph Pulitzer Apr. 10
Issued for the 100th anniversary of the birth of journalist Joseph Pulitzer (1847-1911). The first Pulitzer Prize was awarded in 1917.

Monaco
Scott No. 355

France No. B400

Tunisia
Scott No. B132

Germany
Scott No. B201

Mexico
Scott No. 826

FRANKLIN DELANO ROOSEVELT
(1882-1945)

Franklin D. Roosevelt, the 32nd president of the United States, guided Americans through the worst economic depression and the worst war in the country's history.

In 1932 when he was first elected to the office he would hold for twelve years, the country was caught in a critical economic crisis. During the historic first "Hundred Days" of his administration, he pushed thirteen emergency measures into law and the country was on its way to recovery. Early legislation included passage of the Social Security Act.

Roosevelt, the World War II leader, knew the horrors of war and dreamed of peace. In 1944, when he was elected president for the fourth and final time, he began to plan for the establishment of a United Nations. By 1945 his dream appeared to be coming true. World War II was coming to an end and delegates from countries all around the globe were about to meet in San Francisco to draw up the United Nations Charter. On April 12, however, shortly before this gathering took place, Roosevelt died of a cerebral hemorrhage while writing at his desk.

Throughout his life Roosevelt was an avid stamp collector. He once had this to say about his hobby: *"The best thing about stamp collecting is that the enthusiasm which it arouses in youth increases as the years pass. It dispels boredom, enlarges the vision, broadens our knowledge, and in innumerable ways enriches our life. I also commend stamp collecting because I really believe it makes one a better citizen."*

See Scott Stamp Nos. 930-933

Monaco Scott No. C16

Monaco Scott No. 202

Philippines Scott No. 544

Germany
Scott No. 9NB6

France Scott No. 1078

Hungary Scott No. 1261a

Indonesia Scott No. 642

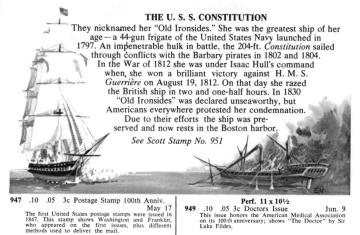

THE U. S. S. CONSTITUTION

They nicknamed her "Old Ironsides." She was the greatest ship of her age — a 44-gun frigate of the United States Navy launched in 1797. An impenetrable hulk in battle, the 204-ft. *Constitution* sailed through conflicts with the Barbary pirates in 1802 and 1804. In the War of 1812 she was under Isaac Hull's command when she won a brilliant victory against H. M. S. *Guerrière* on August 19, 1812. On that day she razed the British ship in two and one-half hours. In 1830 "Old Ironsides" was declared unseaworthy, but Americans everywhere protested her condemnation. Due to their efforts the ship was preserved and now rests in the Boston harbor.

See Scott Stamp No. 951

947 .10 .05 3c Postage Stamp 100th Anniv. May 17
The first United States postage stamps were issued in 1847. This stamp shows Washington and Franklin, who appeared on the first issues, plus different methods used to deliver the mail.

Imperf.

948 .75 .40 Souvenir sheet of two May 19
948a .25 .15 5c blue, single stamp, sia 1
948b .35 .20 10c brn. org., single stamp, sia 2
Issued in sheets of two with marginal inscription commemorating the 100th anniversary of U.S. postage stamps and the Centenary International Philatelic Exhition, held in New York in 1947.

Perf. 11 x 10½

949 .10 .05 3c Doctors Issue Jun. 9
This issue honors the American Medical Association on its 100th anniversary; shows "The Doctor" by Sir Luke Fildes.

950 .10 .05 3c Utah Issue Jul. 24
The settlement of Utah began in 1847. The stamp shows Mormon pioneers entering the state.

951 .10 .05 3c U.S. Frigate Constitution Oct. 21
Issued for the 150th anniversary of the launching of the U. S. Frigate *Constitution* ("Old Ironsides").

947   949   950

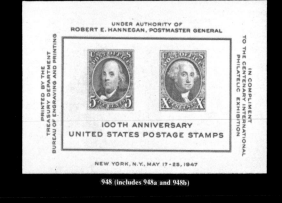

948 (includes 948a and 948b)

951

952

954

955

956

953

957

958

	Perf. 10-1/2x11			
952	.10	.05	3c Everglades Nat'l. Park	Dec. 5

The Everglades National Park in Florida was dedicated on Dec. 6, 1947.

Issues of 1948

953	.10	.05	3c Dr. George Washington Carver	Jan. 5

George Washington Carver (1864-1943), noted agricultural chemist, died five years before the stamp was issued.

Perf. 11x10-1/2

954	.10	.05	3c Calif. Gold 100th Anniv.	Jan. 24

In 1848, gold was found in Sutter's Mill in California.

955	.10	.05	3c Mississippi Territory	Apr. 7

The Mississippi Territory was established in 1798. It comprised the present states of Mississippi and Alabama.

956	.10	.05	3c Four Chaplains	May 28

George L. Fox, Clark V. Poling, John P. Washington and Alexander D. Goode sacrificed their lives in the sinking of the *S. S. Dorchester*, Feb. 3, 1943, when they gave their life preservers to their fellow passengers.

957	.10	.05	3c Wis. Statehood	May 29

Wisconsin became a state in 1848.

958	.15	.10	5c Swedish Pioneer	Jun. 4

In the nineteenth century, 1-1/2 million Swedish Pioneers helped to settle thirteen states in the Midwest.

THE FOUR CHAPLAINS

The date was February 3, 1943. The S.S. Dorchester, an old freighter-turned-troopship, was pushing her way through freezing waters, carrying American soldiers to their bleak outpost in Greenland. Suddenly, with a thunderous roar from the engine room, jets of steam and oil erupted, killing at least one hundred men in less than a minute. The vessel had been hit broadside by a German torpedo!

Frightened men raced to the decks in wild confusion. The ship's officers and medical men were assisted in their heroic attempt to save lives by four Army Lieutenants—Clark V. Poling and George L. Fox, Protestant ministers, John P. Washington, a Catholic priest, and Alexander D. Goode, a Jewish rabbi. The four chaplains, while encouraging and praying with the men, handed out life jackets and assisted them into the lifeboats.
With the lifeboats filled and the jackets all gone, each chaplain removed his own precious jacket and gave it to another man—knowingly sacrificing his own life.

As the crippled S.S. Dorchester was sinking beneath the icy waves, men in the lifeboats and in the water could see the four chaplains on the deck, linked arm in arm, their voices raised in prayer.
See Scott No. 956

959 · 961 · 962 · 960 · 965 · 963 · 964

959 .10 .05 3c Progress of Women Jul. 19
Issued for the first Women's Rights Convention, held in 1848 at Seneca Falls, New York. The stamp shows three important leaders of the movement, Lucretia Mott, Carrie Catt, and Elizabeth Stanton.

Perf. 10-1/2x11
960 .10 .06 3c William Allen White Jul. 31
Issued to honor William Allen White (1868-1944), American editor and author.

Perf. 11x10-1/2
961 .10 .05 3c U.S.-Canada Friendship Aug. 2
Issue notes a century of friendship between the United States and Canada.

962 .10 .05 3c Francis Scott Key Aug. 9
Lawyer Francis Scott Key (1779-1843) composed the "Star Spangled Banner".

963 .10 .06 3c Salute to Youth Aug. 11
Honoring the Youth of America, the nation's "Leaders of Tomorrow."

964 .12 .10 3c Oregon Territory Aug. 14
The Oregon Territory was established in 1848. The stamp shows pioneers Jason Lee and John McLoughlin.

Perf. 10-1/2x11
965 .15 .08 3c Harlan Fiske Stone Aug. 25
Issued to honor U.S. Chief Justice Harlan Fiske Stone (1872-1942).

966 .25 .10 3c Palomar Mt. Obs. Aug. 30
Issued for the dedication of Palomar Mountain Observatory, California, home of the 200-inch Hale reflecting telescope, largest in the world.

THE NATIONAL ANTHEM
And the rocket's red glare, the bombs bursting in air...

The stirring battle scene immortalized by Francis Scott Key in the national anthem took place in the War of 1812. In 1814 Key, a young lawyer, went aboard a British ship to plead for the release of a friend held captive there. By a quirk of fate he himself was imprisoned while the ship bombarded Fort McHenry, Maryland. All through the night of September 14 Key watched and prayed that the Americans could withstand the British onslaught. When the morning mist had cleared and he saw the U. S. flag above the fort, Key jotted down the prayer of thanks that became the "Star-Spangled Banner." In 1931 the song became the national anthem.

See Scott Stamp Nos. 962, 1142, 1346

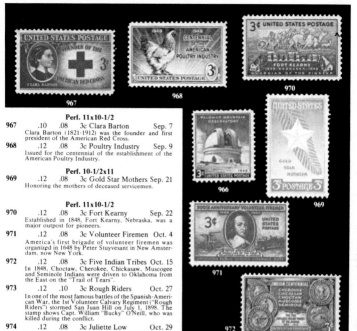

Perf. 11x10-1/2

967   .10   .08   3c Clara Barton   Sep. 7
Clara Barton (1821-1912) was the founder and first president of the American Red Cross.

968   .12   .08   3c Poultry Industry   Sep. 9
Issued for the centennial of the establishment of the American Poultry Industry.

Perf. 10-1/2x11

969   .12   .08   3c Gold Star Mothers   Sep. 21
Honoring the mothers of deceased servicemen.

Perf. 11x10-1/2

970   .12   .08   3c Fort Kearny   Sep. 22
Established in 1848, Fort Kearny, Nebraska, was a major outpost for pioneers.

971   .12   .08   3c Volunteer Firemen   Oct. 4
America's first brigade of volunteer firemen was organized in 1648 by Peter Stuyvesant in New Amsterdam, now New York.

972   .12   .08   3c Five Indian Tribes   Oct. 15
In 1848, Choctaw, Cherokee, Chickasaw, Muscogee and Seminole Indians were driven to Oklahoma from the East on the "Trail of Tears".

973   .12   .10   3c Rough Riders   Oct. 27
In one of the most famous battles of the Spanish-American War, the 1st Volunteer Calvary Regiment ("Rough Riders") stormed San Juan Hill on July 1, 1898. The stamp shows Capt. William "Bucky" O'Neill, who was killed during the conflict.

974   .12   .08   3c Juliette Low   Oct. 29
Issued to honor the founder of the Girl Scouts of America.

CLARA BARTON (1821-1912)

At the outbreak of the Civil War, Clarissa Harlowe Barton was a clerk in the U.S. Patent Office in Washington. When she started hearing stories of terrible suffering on the battlefields due to lack of medical assistance, she quit her job and became an army nurse. Although only five feet tall, she had strength and resolution and risked her own life repeatedly to give first aid to men on the battlefields.

In 1869 she attended the International Red Cross Conference in Switzerland. The following year when the Franco-Prussian War erupted Miss Barton went to the aid of the wounded with the Red Cross in Germany. Impressed by the work they were doing, she returned home determined to establish a United States branch of the organization. Her initiative and perseverance were successful; in 1882 Clara Barton became the first president of the American Red Cross. (It was largely through her efforts revisions were made in the charter providing Red Cross relief not only in war, but in other catastrophes.)

See Scott Nos. 702, 967, 1016

WILL ROGERS
(1879-1935)

"Just live your life so you wouldn't be afraid to sell your talking parrot to the town gossip."

William Penn Adair Rogers learned to rope on his father's ranch almost as soon as he learned to walk. "Talking politics" came naturally. His father was an influential man in community and Cherokee Indian affairs and the Rogers' home in Oologah, Indian Territory, was the scene of many political gatherings. Will always said he was born on election day because women weren't allowed to vote and his mother wanted to do something while the men were away, so she stayed home and had a baby. "I decided to get even with the Government. That's why I've always had it in for politicians."

Traveling with wild west shows and rodeos as a rope-throwing cowboy suited his restless spirit. He came to New York with a circus and, although there wasn't much work for a cowboy in a large eastern city, he decided to stay. In 1915 he appeared in Ziegfeld's "Midnight Frolic" twirling his lariat, chewing a wad of gum and carrying on a humorous political monologue. In what he called his "Oklahoma grammar," he'd comment on topics like taxes, inflation and the political scene. Congressmen and government officials were the favorite targets of his sharp wit, but Will's basic kindness took the sting out of the lampooning.

Will's homespun philosophy developed into a syndicated newspaper column and a series of books. Through stage, radio and motion pictures his salty remarks about contemporary people and events reached deep into the hearts and tickled the funnybones of what Will called "the big Honest Majority." He was their watchdog and their spokesman. In practically no time, Will Rogers became an American institution.

In spite of his claim that "All I know is just what I read in the papers," his wit was based on wisdom, a combination that led him to yet another distinguished career. As President Calvin Coolidge's "Ambassador of Good Will" to Europe and Mexico, his brilliant observations expressed in a friendly drawl led to a much greater understanding between countries.

An early booster of airplane travel, Will died in August, 1935, along with his good friend, pioneer aviator Wiley Post, when their light plane crashed near Point Barrow, Alaska. At the time of his death the man who had "never met a man I didn't like," was the top motion picture box office attraction, newspaper columnist, after dinner speaker and lecturer in the United States. More important, he had no doubt never met a man who didn't like him.

See Scott No. 975

973

974

975

976

977

978

979

980

981

982

983   984   985

986   987   988

Perf. 10-1/2x11

975   .12   .08   3c Will Rogers   Nov. 4
Issued in honor of Will Rogers (1879-1935), humorist, philosopher, author, and actor.

976   .25   .08   3c Fort Bliss 100th Anniv. Nov. 5
Fort Bliss, Texas, now a major missile center, was established in 1848.

Perf. 11x10-1/2

977   .12   .08   3c Moina Michael   Nov. 9
Moina Michael created the Memorial poppy. Countless numbers of these artificial flowers have been sold to aid disabled veterans.

978   .12   .08   3c Gettysburg Address Nov. 19
Lincoln's famous speech was given in 1863 as a dedication for the military cemetery at Gettysburg, Pennsylvania.

Perf. 10-1/2x11

979   .12   .08   3c American Turners   Nov. 20
Issued for the centennial of the American Turners Society, which promotes athletics.

980   .12   .08   3c Joel Chandler Harris   Dec. 9
Joel Chandler Harris (1848-1908) created the "Uncle Remus" stories.

Issues of 1949
Perf. 11x10-1/2

981   .10   .05   3c Minnesota Territory Mar. 3
The Minnesota Territory was established in 1849.

982   .10   .05   3c Washington & Lee University
     Apr. 12
Virginia's Washington and Lee University was established in 1749.

983   .10   .05   3c Puerto Rico Election
     Apr. 27
In 1949 Luis Muños-Marin became Puerto Rico's first elected governor.

984   .10   .05   3c Annapolis 300th Anniv.
     May 23
Established in 1694, Annapolis, the capital of Maryland, was named for Queen Anne of England.

985   .10   .05   3c Grand Army of the
     Republic   Aug. 29
The final encampment of the Grand Army of the Republic (Civil War Union Veterans) took place in 1949.

Perf. 10-1/2x11

986   .10   .05   3c Edgar Allen Poe   Oct. 7
Issued on the 100th anniversary of the death of Edgar Allen Poe (1809-1849), poet and short story author.

Issues of 1950
Perf. 11x10-1/2

987   .10   .05   3c American Bankers
     Association   Jan. 3
Issued for the 75th anniversary of the American Bankers Association.

Perf. 10-1/2x11

988   .10   .05   3c Samuel Gompers   Jan. 27
The American labor leader (1850-1924) served as president of the A.F.L. (American-Federation of Labor).

GIRL SCOUTS OF THE U.S.A.

On my honor, I will try:
To serve God,
My country and mankind,
And to live the Girl Scout Law.
Girl Scout Promise

The Girl Scouts of America is part of a larger organization called the World Association of Girl Guides and Girl Scouts.

Juliette Gordon Low founded the Girl Scouts in 1912. The group, patterned after the British Guides headed by Lady Baden-Powell, was first called the U. S. Girl Guides, but this name was soon changed.

Including girls from seven to seventeen, today's Scouts have fun while they learn the high ideals of citizenship and morality. Working together for badges that teach valuable skills, Girl Scouts help others while advancing from Brownie and Jr. Scout to Cadette and Senior Scout.

See Scott Stamp Nos. 974, 1199

Montserrat
Scott No. 252

National Capital 150th Anniv. Issue Perf. 10-1/2x11, 11x10-1/2			
989	.10	.05	3c Statue of Freedom
990	.10	.05	3c Executive Mansion
991	.10	.05	3c Supreme Court Building
992	.10	.05	3c U. S. Capitol Building

Washington, D.C., the nation's capital, was 150 years old in 1950. It was built on a site chosen by Washington.

Perf. 11x10-1/2			
993	.10	.05	3c Railroad Engineers Apr. 29

Issued to honor the railroad engineers of America. Stamp shows Casey Jones, who ran the crack "Cannonball Express."

994	.10	.05	3c Kansas City, Mo.	Jun. 3

Incorporated in 1850, Kansas City is a leading midwest city known for commerce, industry, and transportation.

THE NATION'S CAPITAL

For the young United States, 1800 meant more than the start of a brand-new century; it also meant the inauguration of a brand-new capital. In that year the Federal Government moved from Philadelphia to Washington, D. C.; from older, finished buildings into partially completed structures made of rough stone and boards.

The new capital city, named for the first President and built on a site chosen by him, was designed by Pierre L'Enfant. Being a far-sighted planner, L'Enfant laid out a design which allowed for growth over the years.

Not so organized, however, were the men who built the Capitol building. They began construction without any detailed architectural plans. When the Capitol, with the White House, was burned by the British in 1814 it had seen only three administrations.

The Capitol we see today was primarily designed by Charles Bullfinch and practically completed in 1863. The White House, or Executive Mansion, was designed by James Hoban.

A far cry from the boardwalks and mud roads of 1800, Washington is now a lovely city filled with parks and avenues. Its people are constantly in touch with the past as they work for the future.

See Scott Stamp Nos. 989-992, C64

BOY SCOUTS OF AMERICA

*A scout is trustworthy, loyal, help-
ful, friendly...The Scout law.*

Sir Robert Baden-Powell, a great
lover of outdoor living, is known to
countless American boys as the founder of the Boy Scouts. It was he who
originated the Scout motto "Be Prepared" and the custom of doing a daily
good deed. American William Boyce
introduced scouting to America (1910)
after being inspired by a British Boy
Scout who refused pay for helping him.

The Boy Scouts of America, six-
million strong, are organized by age
into Cub Scouts (8-10), Boy Scouts
(11-13), and Explorer Scouts (14 and
older). The Scout, from Tenderfoot
to Eagle, is advanced in rank on basis
of merit, citizenship, and outstanding
adherence to the high Scout ideal.

See Scott Stamp Nos. 995, 1145

995	.10	.06	3c Boy Scouts	Jun. 30

Issued to honor the Boy Scouts of America, whose
Second National Jamboree was held in 1950 at Valley
Forge, Pennsylvania.

996	.10	.05	3c Indiana Territory	Jul. 4

The Indiana Territory was created in 1800. William
Henry Harrison, shown on stamp, was governor of the
territory before becoming president of the United
States.

997	.10	.05	3c California Statehood	Sep. 9

In 1850, California joined the Union.

Issues of 1951

998	.10		3c United Confederate Veterans	
			Final Reunion	May 30

The last reunion of the United Confederate Veterans
took place in 1951 at Norfolk, Virginia.

999	.10	.05	3c Nevada 100th Anniv.	Jul. 14

Nevada was settled in 1851. Stamp shows Carson Valley, named for frontiersman Kit Carson.

1000	.10	.05	3c Landing of Cadillac	Jul. 24

Detroit, the "Motor City," was founded by Cadillac in
1701.

1001	.10	.05	3c Colorado Statehood	Aug. 1

Colorado became a state in 1876.

1002	.10	.05	3c American Chem. Soc.	Sep. 4

One of the world's largest scientific societies the American Chemical Society was established in 1876.

MOUNT RUSHMORE

In the Black Hills of South Dakota, likenesses of four great Americans survey the countryside from the granite cliffs of Mount Rushmore. The sixty-feet high busts of Washington, Jefferson, Theodore Roosevelt, and Lincoln are the work of sculptor Gutzon Borglum (1867-1941).

Borglum died before the awesome effigies were finished, but his son, Lincoln, and a team of dedicated helpers completed his work. The colossal faces, designed to a scale of men 465 feet tall, were blasted from rock with dynamite, then drilled to perfection.

Mount Rushmore, located near Rapid City, South Dakota, rises more than a mile above sea level and juts over 500 feet above the narrow valley at its base. The monument, one of the country's most famous landmarks, attracts thousands of visitors each year.

See Scott Nos. 1011, C88

1003   .10   .05   3c Battle of Brooklyn   Dec. 10
In 1776 Washington saved his troops at Brooklyn in the Battle of Long Island.

Issues of 1952

1004   .10   .05   3c Betsy Ross   Jan. 2
Issued for the 200th anniversary of the birth of Betsy Ross. According to legend, she made the first official U. S. Flag in 1777.

1005   .10   .05   3c 4-H Club   Jan. 15
The 4-H Club movement works to improve the head, heart, hands and health of the nation's youth.

1006   .10   .05   3c B&O Railroad   Feb. 28
Chartered in 1827, the B&O used horse-drawn cars to carry its first passengers. Stamp also shows the line's first steam engine, the "Tom Thumb", and a modern diesel.

1007   .10   .05   3c American Auto. Assn.   Mar. 4
Issued to promote highway safety on the 50th anniversary of the American Automobile Association.

1008   .10   .03   3c NATO   Apr. 4
The North Atlantic Treaty Organization is a mutual defense pact for the Western European nations, Canada and the United States. It was created in 1949.

1003   1004   1005

1006   1008   1007

1009

1011

1010

1012

1013

1014

| 1009 | .10 | .05 | 3c Grand Coulee Dam May 15 |
| | | | |

Issued on the 50th anniversary of the U.S. Bureau of Reclamation. this stamp shows Grand Coulee Dam, one of the largest in the world.

| 1010 | .10 | .05 | 3c General Lafayette Jun. 13 |

Lafayette came to America in 1777 to help the fledgling Continental Army in its fight for independence from Great Britain.

Perf. 10-1/2x11

| 1011 | .10 | .05 | 3c Mt. Rushmore Mem. Aug. 11 |

Mount Rushmore. in South Dakota. is famous for its giant busts of Lincoln. Washington. Jefferson and Theodore Roosevelt.

Perf. 11x10-1/2

| 1012 | .10 | .05 | 3c Engineering Anniversary Sep.6 |

The two bridges illustrated on this stamp symbolize 100 years of civil engineering progress in America. One is an early covered wooden bridge; the other, the modern George Washington Bridge between New Jersey and New York.

| 1013 | .10 | .05 | 3c Service Women Sep. 11 |

Issued as a tribute to the women members of the Army, Navy, Air Force and Marines.

| 1014 | .10 | .05 | 3c Gutenberg Bible Sep. 30 |

Johann Gutenberg (c. 1397-1468) printed the first book from movable type in 1456. This was the Holy Bible.

MARQUIS DE LAFAYETTE (1757-1834)

In 1777 the Marquis de Lafayette, a French nobleman, equipped a ship at his own expense and sailed to the United States to help the Americans win the Revolutionary

War. A young and wealthy idealist in the cause of liberty, Lafayette volunteered his services to General Washington. One month before his 20th birthday Congress made him a major general in Washington's army.

Although Lafayette was an able soldier, his most valuable service to the Continental Army was political. In 1779 he returned to France and persuaded King Louis XVI to send a naval force under Rochambeau to the United States. Rochambeau's aid was crucial to the American victory at Yorktown.

Following Cornwallis' surrender in 1781, Lafayette returned to France, where he later became involved in the French Revolution. A moderate who wished to retain the monarchy, Lafayette was imprisoned from 1792-97. In 1824 he returned to the United States for a one year triumphal tour—a renewal of his friendship with a grateful American people.

See Scott Stamp Nos. 1010, 1097

1015   .10   .05   3c Newspaper Boys   Oct. 4
Issued "In recognition of the important service rendered their communities and their nation by America's newspaper boys."

1016   .10   .05   3c Red Cross   Nov. 21
The International Red Cross was created in 1864 by Geneva Convention at the urging of Jean Dunant, the first Nobel Peace Prize Winner.

Issues of 1953

1017   .10   .05   3c National Guard   Feb. 23
A tribute to the National Guard which serves the United States in peace and war.

1018   .10   .05   3c Ohio Statehood   Mar. 2
Ohio joined the Union as the seventeenth state in 1803.

1019   .10   .05   3c Washington Territory   Mar. 2
Organized on March 2, 1853 the Washington Territory was carved from the Pacific Northwest by courageous pioneers who went there to settle and build homes.

1020   .10   .05   3c Louisiana Purchase Apr. 30
Issued for the 150th anniversary of the Louisiana Purchase.

1021   .15   .10   5c Opening of Japan 100th Anniversary   Jul. 14
In 1853, Commodore Matthew Perry negotiated the first U.S.-Japanese trade agreement.

NEW YORK CITY

Give my regards to Broadway ...
George M. Cohan

Broadway, Wall Street, the Empire State Building, and Lincoln Center! All the sights and sounds of America's largest city typify the twentieth century. But even a giant has humble beginnings.

In 1626 Peter Minuet, an enterprising Dutchman, bought Manhattan Island for $24. The island, named New Amsterdam by the Dutch, became New York when it was granted to the English Duke of York in 1664.

The scene of Washington's inauguration and the nation's capital from 1785 to 1790, New York City is now a huge metropolis. Each of its five boroughs—Manhattan, Brooklyn, the Bronx, Queens, and Staten Island—is large enough to be a city in itself. Representing almost every culture in the world, its eight million residents look upon their home as the cultural and commercial capital of the country.

See Scott Stamp Nos. 614, 1027, C38, 1397

| 1022 | .10 | .05 | 3c American Bar Assn. Aug. 24 |
Issued for the American Bar Association's 75th anniversary, this stamp depicts four symbolic figures representing "Wisdom," "Justice," "Truth," and "Divine Inspiration."

| 1023 | .10 | .05 | 3c Sagamore Hill Sep. 14 |
Sagamore Hill, Theodore Roosevelt's home in Oyster Bay, New York was opened as a national shrine in 1953.

| 1024 | .10 | .05 | 3c Future Farmers Oct. 13 |
Issued on the 25th anniversary of the Future Farmers of America.

| 1025 | .10 | .05 | 3c Trucking Industry Oct. 27 |
The American Trucking Association was created in 1903.

| 1026 | .10 | .05 | 3c General Patton Nov. 11 |
General George S. Patton, Jr. (1885-1945) commanded the Third Army in the Second World War.

| 1027 | .10 | .05 | 3c New York City 300th Anniversary Nov. 20 |
Settled by the Dutch in the 17th century, New York City is the nation's largest city.

| 1028 | .10 | .05 | 3c Gadsden Purchase Dec. 30 |
The 1853 Gadsden Purchase adjusted the boundary between Mexico and the United States.

Issues of 1954

| 1029 | .10 | .05 | 3c Columbia University 200th Anniversary Jan. 4 |
Columbia University was founded in 1754 as Kings College. Stamp depicts the school's Low Memorial Library.

THE FFA AND 4-H CLUBS

Two of the largest rural youth service organizations in the United States are the Future Farmers of America (FFA) and the 4-H Clubs, which offer fun and learning to the leaders of tomorrow.

FFA members gain experience in public speaking, in judging farm products, and in buying and selling cooperatively. The FFA motto is "Learning to do, Doing to learn, Earning to live, Living to serve."

4-H Clubs train boys and girls in agriculture or in homemaking. At present about half the members live on farms; the rest are non-farm rural and urban residents. The four H's stand for "Head, Heart, Hand, and Health."

See Scott Stamp Nos. 1005, 1024

1023

1024

1025

1026

1027

1028

1029

Liberty Issue, 1954–68
Perf. 11 x 10½, 10½ x 11

1030	.03	.03	½c Benjamin Franklin
1031	.04	.03	1c George Washington
1031A	.05	.05	1¼c Palace of the Governors, Santa Fe
1032	.05	.04	1½c Mount Vernon
1033	.05	.03	2c Thomas Jefferson
1034	.06	.05	2½c Bunker Hill Monument and Massachusetts flag
1035	.08	.03	3c Statue of Liberty
1035a	1.75	.50	Booklet pane of six
1036	.10	.03	4c Abraham Lincoln
1036a	2.00	.50	Booklet pane of six
1037	.12	.08	4½c The Hermitage
1038	.12	.03	5c James Monroe
1039	.15	.03	6c Theodore Roosevelt
1040	.16	.03	7c Woodrow Wilson

Perf. 11

1041	.25	.06	8c Statue of Liberty
1042	.20	.03	8c Statue of Liberty redrawn

Perf. 11 x 10½, 10½ x 11

1042A	.20	.03	8c John J. Pershing
1043	.20	.04	9c The Alamo
1044	.22	.03	10c Independence Hall

Perf. 11

1044A	.30	.06	11c Statue of Liberty

Perf. 11 x 10½, 10½ x 11

1045	.24	.05	12c Benjamin Harrison
1046	.35	.03	15c John Jay

1047	.50	.03	20c Monticello
1048	.55	.03	25c Paul Revere
1049	.65	.08	30c Robert E. Lee
1050	1.10	.10	40c John Marshall
1051	1.40	.04	50c Susan B. Anthony
1052	4.50	.06	$1 Patrick Henry

Perf. 11

1053	25.00	2.00	$5 Alexander Hamilton

Coil Stamps
Perf. 10 Vertically

1054	.05	.03	1c dark green Washington, sia 1031

Perf. 10 Horizontally

1054A	.45	.06	1¼c turquoise, Palace of the Governors, Santa Fe, sia 1031A

Perf. 10 Vertically

1055	.06	.03	2c carmine Jefferson, sia 1033
1056	.45	.07	2½c gray blue, Bunker Hill Monument and Massa– chusetts flag, sia 1034
1057	.12	.03	3c deep violet Statue of Liberty, sia 1035
1058	.15	.04	4c red vio. Lincoln, sia 1036

Perf. 10 Horizontally

1059	2.50	.10	4½c blue green Hermitage, sia 1037

Perf. 10 Vertically

1059A	.60	.20	25c grn. P. Revere, sia 1048

THE STATUE OF LIBERTY

Give me your tired, your poor,
Your huddled masses yearning to breathe free,
The wretched refuse of your teeming shore,
Send these, the homeless, tempest-tossed, to me;
I lift my lamp beside the golden door... Emma Lazarus

So reads the inscription on the base of the Statue of Liberty; the proud woman who stands at the entrance to the New York harbor.

The Statue of Liberty was presented to the people of the United States by the people of France on July 4, 1884. Since then she has welcomed millions of visitors and immigrants to the United States. In the early part of this century especially, she served as a beacon for the countless Europeans who came to the United States to seek a better life and, in turn, helped make the United States a better country.

The creation of Frederic Auguste Bartholdi, the Statue of Liberty is the largest statue ever made. She stands 151 feet high and weighs 450,000 pounds. Her right arm holds a great torch and her left arm grasps a tablet bearing the date of the adoption of the Declaration of Independence.

See Scott Stamp Nos.
1041, 1042, 1044A

France
Scott No. B44

Issues of 1954, Perf. 11x10-1/2				
1060	.10	.05	3c Nebraska Territory	May 7

The Nebraska Territory was created in 1854 under terms of the Kansas-Nebraska Act, which gave settlers free choice in the slavery issue.

1061 .10 .05 3c Kansas Territory May 31

The Kansas Territory was established in 1854.

Perf. 10-1/2x11

1062 .10 .05 3c George Eastman Jul. 12

Inventor and philanthropist, George Eastman was born in 1854.

Perf. 11x10-1/2

1063 .10 .05 3c Lewis and Clark Expedition Jul. 28

The 1804-06 Lewis and Clark Expedition charted much of the Louisiana Territory, purchased by the U.S. in 1803.

Issues of 1955, Perf. 10-1/2x11

1064 .10 .05 3c Pennsylvania Academy of Fine Arts Jan. 15

The Pennsylvania Academy of Fine Arts was founded in 1805 by artist Charles Wilson Peale, whose self-portrait is depicted on the stamp.

Perf. 11x10-1/2

1065 .10 .05 3c Land Grant Colleges Feb. 12

The first two U.S. land grant colleges, Michigan State University and Pennsylvania State University, were established in 1855.

1066 .20 .12 8c Rotary International Feb. 23

Issued to honor the 50th anniversary of Rotary International.

1067 .10 .05 3c Armed Forces Res. May 21

A tribute to the Armed Forces Reserve.

Perf. 10-1/2x11

1068 .10 .05 3c New Hampshire Jun. 21

Immortalized by Hawthorne as "The Great Stone Face," the "Old Man of the Mountains," shown on stamp, is New Hampshire's best-known scenic wonder.

GEORGE EASTMAN (1854-1932)

George Eastman was an American industrialist and philanthropist who made photography possible as an everyday hobby. While a basic camera had taken pictures as early as 1826, it was Eastman who improved the dryplate process and invented flexible film which could be wound in a camera. It was also Eastman who brought forth the famous Kodak in 1888. This simple box camera sold for $25 and revolutionized photography.

A business pioneer throughout his life, Eastman invested in large-scale advertising, industrial research, and other projects. Throughout the years he donated over $100 million to leading colleges and universities, including the Massachusetts Institute of Technology, the University of Rochester, and the Eastman School of Music.

See Scott Stamp No. 1062

1069

1072

1068

1073

Perf. 11x10-1/2
1069 .10 .05 3c Soo Locks Jun. 28
The Soo Locks of the Sault Ste. Marie Canal link Lake Huron and Lake Superior. They were opened in 1855.
1070 .10 .05 3c Atoms for Peace Jul. 28
Issued to promote Eisenhower's Atoms for Peace policy, this stamp quotes a speech he made to the U.N. on the peaceful uses of atomic energy.
1071 .10 .05 3c Fort Ticonderoga Sep. 18
Fort Ticonderoga was the scene of many battles in the Revolution and the French and Indian War. In one of the most famous of these, Ethan Allen, shown on stamp, stormed the Fort and won it from the British in 1775.

Perf. 10-1/2x11
1072 .10 .05 3c Andrew W. Mellon Dec. 20
Born in 1855, Andrew Mellon was a noted financier, industrialist and philanthropist.

Issues of 1956
1073 .10 .05 3c Benjamin Franklin Jan. 17
Issued on the 250th anniversary of the birth of Benjamin Franklin.

Perf. 11x10-1/2
1074 .10 .05 3c Booker T. Washington Apr. 5
Black educator Booker T. Washington was born in 1856. Stamp shows cabin similar to his birthplace.

Fifth International Philatelic Exhibition
Souvenir Sheet, Imperf.
1075 3.50 2.50 Sheet of two Apr. 28
1075a 1.25 .80 3c deep violet, sia 1035
1075b 1.65 1.10 8c dk. vio. bl. & car., sia 1041
Issued in sheets of two with marginal inscription commemorating the Fifth International Philatelic Exhibition held in New York City.

Perf. 11x10-1/2
1076 .10 .05 3c New York Coliseum and Columbus Monument Apr. 30
Stamp honors the opening of the New York Coliseum and the Fifth International Philatelic Exhibition held there in 1956.

1070

1071

1074

1076

1075

1077   1078   1079

1080   1082

1081

1083

Wildlife Conservation Issue

1077	.10	.05	3c Wild Turkey	May 5
1078	.10	.05	3c Pronghorn Antelope	Jun. 22
1079	.10	.05	3c King Salmon	Nov. 9

The Wildlife Conservation Series calls attention to the need to save our wildlife from extinction. King Salmon, pronghorn antelope and the wild turkey have been helped by conservationists.

Perf. 10-1/2x11

1080	.10	.05	3c Pure Food and Drug Laws	Jun. 27

Chemist Harvey W. Wiley, shown on stamp, helped enact the first Pure Food and Drug Act in 1906.

Perf. 11x10-1/2

1081	.10	.05	3c Wheatland	Aug. 5

Wheatland was the home of President James Buchanan (1791-1868). It is located in Lancaster, Pa.

Perf. 10-1/2x11

1082	.10	.05	3c Labor Day	Sep. 3

Labor Day has been a U.S. legal holiday since 1894.

Perf. 11x10-1/2

1083	.10	.05	3c Nassau Hall	Sep. 22

Constructed in 1756, Nassau Hall is Princeton University's most famous building.

Perf. 10-1/2x11

1084	.10	.05	3c Devils Tower	Sep. 24

In 1906 Devils Tower in Wyoming became the first U.S. national monument.

Perf. 11x10-1/2

1085	.10	.05	3c Children's Issue	Dec. 15

Designed by a high school student, this stamp promotes friendship as the key to peace throughout the world.

Issues of 1957

1086	.10	.05	3c Alexander Hamilton	Jan. 11

Issued for the 200th anniversary of the birth of Alexander Hamilton.

Perf. 10-1/2x11

1087	.10	.05	3c Polio Issue	Jan. 15

A tribute to the March of Dimes and the National Foundation for Infantile Paralysis.

WILDLIFE CONSERVATION

To waste, to destroy, our natural resources, to skin and exhaust the land…will result in undermining (it) in the days of our children… Theodore Roosevelt

Today forty-four species of U. S. wildlife, victims of man's thoughtlessness, are in danger of extinction. Once the private cause of a few dedicated conservationists, the preservation of our wildlife has become the public will. Stringent measures are being taken to protect world wildlife. Laws now protect the fur seal whose numbers were decimated in the 19th century. In 1969 President Nixon signed the Endangered Species Conservation Act, which prohibits the import into the U. S. of skins (or trophies) of any world wildlife threatened with extinction. Integral to the conservation of wildlife is the preservation of its sanctuaries. During the 1960's sixty-four new additions were made to the national parks and forests.

See Scott Stamp Nos. 1077-1079, 1098, 1306, 1362, 1427-1430, 1464-1467

1085

1086

1084

1087

Perf. 11x10-1/2

1088 .10 .05 3c Coast and Geodetic Survey Feb. 11
The Coast and Geodetic Survey, established in 1807, charts coasts and navigation routes; records tides.

1089 .10 .05 3c Architects Feb. 23
The American Institute of Architects was created in 1857.

Perf. 10-1/2x11

1090 .10 .05 3c Steel Industry May 22
The U.S. is one of the world's leading steel producers. The industry was 100 years old in 1957.

Perf. 11x10-1/2

1091 .10 .05 3c Int'l. Naval Review Jun. 10
The International Naval Review was held in 1957 in connection with the 250th anniversary of Jamestown, Virginia.

1092 .10 .05 3c Oklahoma Statehood Jun. 14
From 1828 to 1846, Oklahoma was an Indian Reservation. In 1907 it became a state.

1093 .10 .05 3c School Teachers Jul. 1
A tribute to the school teachers of America.

Perf. 11

1094 .12 .08 4c Flag Issue Jul. 4
This stamp which depicts the 48-star flag was the first U.S. issue printed by Giori Press. The press can print three colors simultaneously.

Perf. 10-1/2x11

1095 .10 .05 3c Shipbuilding Aug. 15
The *"Virginia of Sagadahock,"* the first U.S. international trading vessel, was constructed in 1607.

Perf. 11

1096 .20 .15 8c Champion of Liberty Aug. 31
Ramon Magsaysay, honored here, was president of the Philippines from 1953 to 1957.

Perf. 10-1/2x11

1097 .10 .05 3c Lafayette Sep. 6
Issued for the 200th anniversary of the birth of the Marquis de Lafayette.

1090

1088

1089

1091

1092

1093

1094

1095

1096

1097

ABRAHAM LINCOLN (1809-65)

*With malice toward none; with charity for all...let us strive to finish the work we are in; to bind up the nation's wounds...*Second Inaugural Address

On the eve of the Civil War Abraham Lincoln became the sixteenth president of the United States. On a bleak March day the new President took his oath "to preserve, protect and defend" the Union. Six weeks later the guns of Fort Sumter challenged the existence of that Union.

Despite dissension in the Cabinet and Congress, Lincoln's wise and just leadership carried the nation through the war. He claimed special powers which he felt were necessary in this unique crisis. "The moment came," he said, "when I felt that slavery must die that the nation might live." So, not waiting for congressional action, Lincoln freed all slaves by the Emancipation Proclamation on January 1, 1863.

Lincoln's attitude toward the defeated South typified his great humanity. At the war's end he urged charity and reconciliation between the North and South. The assassin's bullet fired by John Wilkes Booth on April 14, 1865, however, was to change the course of Reconstruction.

See Scott Stamp Nos. 367-369, 906, 978, 1113-1116, C59

Perf. 11

1098 .10 .05 3c Wildlife Conservation Nov. 22
The almost extinct whooping crane points up urgent need for wildlife conservation.

Perf. 10-1/2x11

1099 .10 .05 3c Religious Freedom Dec. 27
The Flushing Remonstrance of 1657 helped create religious freedom in America.

Issues of 1958

1100 .10 .05 3c Gardening-Horticulture Mar. 15
Horticulture issue honors birth in 1858 of botanist Liberty Hyde Bailey.

Perf. 11x10-1/2

1104 .10 .05 3c Brussels Fair Apr. 17
Issued for the opening of the Brussels World's Fair, this stamp shows the United States Pavilion at the Fair.

1105 .10 .05 3c James Monroe Apr. 28
Issued for the 200th anniversary of the birth of James Monroe (1758-1831), fifth president of the United States.

1106 .10 .05 3c Minnesota Statehood May 11
Minnesota became a state in 1858.

Perf. 11

1107 .15 .05 3c Geophysical Year May 31
The International Geophysical Year of 1957-58 was a team effort by world scientists for research and discovery. The stamp shows part of Michelangelo's famous fresco, "The Creation of Adam."

Perf. 10-1/2x11

1108 .10 .05 3c Gunston Hall Jun. 12
Gunston Hall was the Virginia home of George Mason (1725-92), author of Virginia's constitution.

Perf. 11x10-1/2

1109 .10 .05 3c Mackinac Bridge Jun. 25
Dedicated in 1958, the Mackinac Bridge connects the two peninsulas of Michigan.

1110 .10 .05 4c Champion of Liberty Jul. 24

Perf. 11

1111 .20 .15 8c Champion of Liberty
Simon Bolivar (1783-1830) liberated much of South America from Spanish domination.

Perf. 11x10-1/2

1112 .10 .05 4c Atlantic Cable 100th Anniversary Aug. 15
The first Atlantic cable, between London and New York was finished in 1858.

Lincoln 150th Anniv. Issue, 1958-59
Perf. 10-1/2x11, 11x10-1/2

1113 .05 .05 1c Portrait by George Healy

1114 .10 .06 3c Sculptured Head by Gutzon Borglum

1115 .10 .05 4c Lincoln and Stephen Douglas Debating

1116 .10 .05 4c Statue in Lincoln Memorial by Daniel Chester French
Issued for the 150th anniversary of the birth of Abraham Lincoln.

Issues of 1958
Perf. 10-1/2x11

1117 .10 .05 4c Champion of Liberty Sep. 19

Perf. 11

1118 .20 .12 8c Champion of Liberty
Lajos Kossuth (1802-1892), patriot of Hungary, was a leading figure in that nation's revolution.

Perf. 10-1/2x11

1119 .10 .05 4c Freedom of Press Sep. 22
The world's first journalism school was established in 1908 at the University of Missouri.

Perf. 11x10-1/2

1120 .10 .05 4c Overland Mail Oct. 10
The first overland mail coach arrived in San Francisco, California in 1858. It began its journey in Tipton, Missouri.

Perf. 10-1/2x11

1121 .10 .05 4c Noah Webster Oct. 16
Noah Webster (1758-1843) was a noted scholar and a lexicographer.

Perf. 11

1122 .10 .05 4c Forest Conservation Oct. 27
Issued on the 100th anniversary of the birth of Theodore Roosevelt, an ardent conservationist.

NORTH POLE EXPEDITIONS

The contrast between two North Pole expeditions vividly points up scientific progress in the 1900's.

In 1909, Robert Peary (1856-1920) reached the Pole by foot and dogsled; in 1958 the submarine *Nautilus* used atomic power to repeat his feat.

Peary, who made many journeys to the frozen North, arrived at the Pole on his fourth Arctic expedition. Returning to the States he wrote several books about his explorations and was made a rear admiral in 1911.

The 1958 voyage to the Pole by the first atomic submarine was fast and effortless compared to Peary's. On that historic trip, the *Nautilus* and her sister-ship the *Skate* cruised under the polar ice cap, the first submarines to do so.

See Scott Stamp No. 1128

THE ST. LAWRENCE SEAWAY

When French explorers discovered the St. Lawrence River in 1535, they hoped it might be a new route to China. Later pioneers realized its value as a shipping route from the Atlantic Ocean to the Great Lakes. As early as 1895 a Canadian-U. S. commission urged that a deep-sea channel be dredged in the St. Lawrence. The U. S. Congress delayed action for almost sixty years. Finally Canada announced it would proceed alone. Congress, faced with the Canadian challenge, approved the St. Lawrence Seaway Development Corporation in 1954.

The Seaway, 2,300 miles of canals and locks, stretches from the mouth of the St. Lawrence to the western tip of Lake Superior. During construction peaks, the power and navigation works, costing an estimated $1 billion, employed as many as 20,000 men. By July 1, 1958, Ontario and upper New York State received power from the hydroelectric plant at International Rapids. On June 26, 1959, Queen Elizabeth II and President Dwight D. Eisenhower dedicated the completed Seaway, a great river highway to the middle of a continent.

See Scott Stamp No. 1131

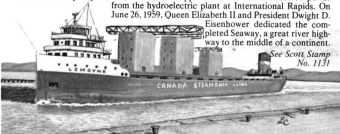

Perf. 11

1131 .10 .05 4c St. Lawrence Seaway Jun. 26
This stamp was issued jointly by both Canada and the United States for the opening of the St. Lawrence Seaway.

1132 .10 .05 4c 49-Star Flag Jul. 4
The 49-star flag of 1959 marked Alaska's entry to the Union.

1133 .10 .05 4c Soil Conservation Aug. 26
Contour plowing, shown on stamp, is an effective means of conserving soil.

Perf. 10-1/2x11

1134 .10 .05 4c Petroleum Industry Aug. 27
Oil was found at Titusville, Pennsylvania in 1859 when Col. Drake hit "black gold" at 69-1/2 feet.

Perf. 11x10-1/2

1135 .10 .05 4c Dental Health Sep. 14
The American Dental Association was established in 1859.

Perf. 10-1/2x11

1136 .10 .05 4c Champion of Liberty Sep. 29

Perf. 11

1137 .20 .12 8c Champion of Liberty
Ernst Reuter, honored here, was mayor of Berlin during the blockade of 1948-1949.

Perf. 10-1/2x11

1138 .10 .05 4c Dr. Ephraim McDowell Dec. 3
Dr. Ephraim McDowell (1771-1830) performed the first operation in ovarian surgery.

Issues of 1960-61, Perf. 11
American Credo Issue

1139	.15	.05	4c Quotation from Washington's Farewell Address
1140	.15	.05	4c B. Franklin Quotation
1141	.15	.05	4c T. Jefferson Quotation
1142	.15	.05	4c Francis Scott Key Quotation
1143	.15	.05	4c Lincoln Quotation
1144	.15	.05	4c Patrick Henry Quotation

Issued to perpetuate and emphasize American ideals.

1145	.10	.05	4c Boy Scout Jubilee	Feb. 8

Issued for the 50th anniversary of the founding of the Boy Scouts of America.

Perf. 10-1/2x11

1146	.10	.05	4c Olympic Winter Games	Feb. 18

The Olympic Winter Games of 1960 were held in Squaw Valley, California.

1147	.10	.05	4c Champion of Liberty	Mar. 7

Perf. 11

1148	.20	.12	4c Champion of Liberty	

Thomas Masaryk (1850-1937) was the founder and first president of the Czechoslovakian Republic.

Perf. 11x10-1/2

1149	.10	.05	4c World Refugee Year	Apr. 7

World Refugee Year lasted from July 1, 1959 until June 30, 1960.

Perf. 11

1150	.10	.05	4c Water Conservation	Apr. 18

Water Conservation Issue depicts the ecological water cycle: rain runoff to watershed to reservoir to city use.

Perf. 10-1/2x11

1151	.10	.05	4c Seato	May 31

The South-East Asia Treaty Organization is a mutual defense pact for some Asian nations and the U.S.

Perf. 11x10-1/2

1152	.10	.05	4c American Woman	Jun. 2

A tribute to the women of America.

Perf. 11

1153	.10	.05	4c 50-Star Flag	Jul. 4

When Hawaii joined the Union (in 1959) the fiftieth star was added to the flag.

Perf. 11x10-1/2

1154	.10	.05	4c Pony Express 100th Anniv.	Jul. 19

The Pony Express was founded in 1860.

Perf. 10-1/2x11

1155	.10	.05	4c Employ the Handicapped	Aug. 28

"Employ the Handicapped" was the theme of the Eighth World Congress of the International Society for the welfare of crippled persons.

1156	.10	.05	4c World Forestry Congress	Aug. 29

The Fifth World Forestry Congress was held in Seattle, Washington in 1960.

Perf. 11

1157	.10	.05	4c Mexican Independence	Sep. 16

Issued for the 150th anniversary of Mexican independence.

1158	.10	.05	4c U.S.-Japan Treaty	Sep. 28

The U.S. Japan Treaty of Amity and Commerce was ratified in 1860.

THE PONY EXPRESS
The mail must go through.

In 1861 a Pony Express rider crossed the country in record-breaking time: seven days and seventeen hours. The urgent news he carried was the text of President Abraham Lincoln's first inaugural address. The usual schedule for the mail trip from St. Joseph, Missouri to Placerville, California was eight days, about 24 days faster than the journey of a mail coach traveling by the southern route.

The Pony Express began on the eve of the Civil War as a means of rapid communication between California and the East — a necessity during this time of crisis. Operated by the Overland Mail Company, this legendary mail service had operated for a mere eighteen months when it was replaced by a telegraph line. Even so, it has enjoyed an enduring fame due to the heroism and stamina of the anonymous Pony Express rider. Passing through the hostile Indian country of the Great Plains, this lone horseman braved the snow of the Rockies and the heat of the desert to accomplish his duty: the delivery of the United States Mail.

See Scott Stamp Nos. 894, 1120, 1154

San Marino Scott No. 271 shows the first U.S. postage stamps.

Perf. 10-1/2x11

| 1159 | .10 | .05 | 4c Champion of Liberty | Oct. 8 |

Perf. 11

| 1160 | .20 | .12 | 8c Champion of Liberty |

Issued to honor I.J. Paderewski (1860-1941), Polish pianist and statesman.

Perf. 10-1/2x11

| 1161 | .10 | .05 | 4c Sen. Taft Memorial | Oct. 10 |

Robert A. Taft (1889-1953) was a U.S. Senator from 1939-1953.

Perf. 11x10-1/2

| 1162 | .10 | .05 | 4c Wheels of Freedom | Oct. 15 |

Issued in connection with the National Automobile Show, held in Detroit in 1960.

| 1163 | .10 | .05 | 4c Boys' Clubs of America | Oct. 18 |

The Boys' Clubs of America movement was organized in 1860.

| 1164 | .10 | .05 | 4c Automated P.O. | Oct. 20 |

The first U.S. automated post office opened on October 20, 1960, in Providence, Rhode Island.

Perf. 10-1/2x11

| 1165 | .10 | .05 | 4c Champion of Liberty | Oct. 26 |

Perf. 11

| 1166 | .20 | .12 | 8c Champion of Liberty |

Baron Gustaf Mannerheim (1867-1951) was president of Finland from 1944 to 1946.

| 1167 | .10 | .05 | 4c Camp Fire Girls | Nov. 1 |

The Camp Fire Girls was organized in 1910.

Perf. 10-1/2x11

| 1168 | .10 | .05 | 4c Champion of Liberty | Nov. 2 |

Giuseppe Garibaldi (1807-1882) was a leader in the fight to unify all Italy.

BOYS' CLUBS OF AMERICA

Building boys is better than mending men. The Boys' Clubs motto.

The Boys' Clubs of America is a national organization with a membership of 850,000 urban youth. For minimal dues it offers boys a recreational meeting place which is open after school hours and six days a week. Larger clubs have swimming pools, libraries, gymnasiums, workshops, and clubrooms. When possible Boys' Clubs sponsor summer camps and provide medical examinations to promote good health.

The first Boys' Club was organized in 1860 for the sons of Hartford, Connecticut millworkers. Boys' Clubs now exist throughout the nation. In cities or small towns they serve boys of all backgrounds and ages (from eight years up) and perpetuate high ideals through word, example, and fun.

See Scott Stamp No. 1163

1162

1163

1167

1164

1165

1166

1168

1169

CAMP FIRE GIRLS

Worship God, seek beauty, give service, pursue knowledge, be trustworthy, hold on to health, glorify work, be happy.

The Camp Fire Girl Law.

The Camp Fire Girls were established in 1910 by Luther and Charlotte Gulick of New York City, whose summer camp in Maine was one of the first girls' camps in the country. The group has always emphasized camping, learning by doing, and the giving of service. Since 1910 over four million girls have learned the value and joy of community service through their Camp Fire Girl experience.

The Girls are organized into three age brackets: the Blue Birds (7-10), Camp Fire Girls (10-15), and Horizon Club Girls (15-18). The fun and learning activities are based on the seven crafts: home, creative arts, outdoors, frontiers, business, sports and games, and citizenship. As she progresses from Trail Seeker to Torch Bearer, this wide range of activity helps the Campfire Girl to develop into a good homemaker and citizen, the Camp Fire ideal.

See Scott Stamp No. 1167

Perf. 11

1169   .20   .12   8c Champion of Liberty

Perf. 10-1/2x11

1170   .10   .05   4c Sen. George Memorial   Nov. 5
Walter F. George (1878-1957) was Ambassador to NATO and a U.S. Senator.

1171   .10   .05   4c Andrew Carnegie   Nov. 25
Steel magnate Andrew Carnegie (1835-1919) gave $350 million to various educational institutions.

1172   .10   .05   4c John Foster Dulles Memorial
                                                             Dec. 6
John Foster Dulles (1888-1959) served as Secretary of State under Eisenhower.

Perf. 11x10-1/2

1173   .45   .12   4c Echo I — Communications
                                 for Peace   Dec. 15
The world's first communications satellite, Echo I, was placed in orbit on August 12, 1960.

Issues of 1961
Perf. 10-1/2x11

1174   .10   .05   4c Champion of Liberty   Jan. 26

Perf. 11

1175   .20   .12   8c Champion of Liberty
Pacifist Mahatma Gandhi (1869-1948) led India to freedom from the British in 1947.

1176   .10   .05   4c Range Conservation   Feb. 2
Issue dramatizes the development of range conservation from the age of the pioneers to the age of modern science.

Perf. 10-1/2x11

1177   .10   .05   4c Horace Greeley   Feb. 3
Journalist Horace Greeley (1811-1872) was editor and publisher of the *N. Y. Tribune*.

1178   1179   1180   1181   1182   1186

Civil War 100th Anniv. Issue, 1961-1965
Perf. 11x10-1/2

1178	.18	.05	4c Fort Sumter Centenary, 1961
1179	.15	.05	4c Shiloh Centenary, 1962

Perf. 11

1180	.15	.05	5c Gettysburg Centenary, 1963
1181	.15	.05	5c Wilderness Centenary, 1964
1182	.18	.05	5c Appomattox Centenary, 1965

Issued for the Civil War Centennial.

Issues of 1961

1183	.10	.05	4c Kansas Statehood	May. 10

Kansas became a state in 1861.

Perf. 11x10-1/2

1184	.10	.05	4c Sen. George W. Norris	Jul. 11

U.S. Senator George Norris (1861-1944) helped father the Tennessee Valley Authority in 1933.

THE CIVIL WAR

A house divided against itself cannot stand. Abraham Lincoln

The Civil War (1861-65) was the most costly struggle in the nation's history. Arising out of years of controversy over slavery and states' rights, it tested the right of the South to withdraw from the Union to preserve a way of life.

The cotton culture of the South, made possible by the invention of the cotton gin, was sustained by slavery. As the United States grew and expanded, the question soon arose whether new states entering the Union would be "slave" or "free". Compromise after compromise failed to solve the problem and tempers flared. Wrangling over the status of fugitive slaves, the activities of Northern abolitionists and the repeal of the Missouri Compromise (a "half-slave", "half-free" solution) added fuel to the fire. Southerners began to talk about secession, while a man from Illinois, Abraham Lincoln, argued to preserve the Union.

When Lincoln was elected president in 1860, South Carolina left the Union, followed by Georgia, Alabama, Mississippi, Louisiana, Florida, and Texas. When the Confederates bombarded Charleston's federal Fort Sumter in 1861, Lincoln called for a militia of 75,000 troops to put down the rebellion. This appeal to arms decided the issue for Virginia, Arkansas, North Carolina, and Tennessee, who joined the Confederate States of America.

1185   .10   .05   4c Naval Aviation   Aug. 20
    Issued for the 50th anniversary of Naval aviation.

Perf. 10-1/2x11

1186   .10   .05   4c Workmen's Comp.   Sep. 4
    Issued for the 50th anniversary of the passage of the
    first successful Workmen's Compensation Law.

Perf. 11

1187   .15   .05   4c Frederic Remington   Oct. 4
    Artist Frederic Remington (1861-1909) captured the
    "Old West" in sculpture and on canvas. Stamp shows
    his work "The Smoke Signal."

Perf. 10-1/2x11

1188   .10   .05   4c Republic of China   Oct. 10
    Issued for the 50th anniversary of the Republic of
    China. Stamp shows Sun Yat-sen (1866-1925), first
    president of China.

1189   .10   .05   4c Naismith-Basketball   Nov. 6
    James Naismith invented basketball in 1891.

The armed struggle between North and South lasted over four long years, despite the North's superiority in numbers, wealth, industry, and sea power.

Early in the war Lincoln formed a three-fold plan for Union victory. He hoped to capture the Confederate capital at Richmond, take control of the Mississippi River, and blockade all Southern ports. Eventually this strategy was successful; initially it was thwarted by Robert E. Lee.

In 1862 the great Southern general started the campaign that led to Southern victories at Bull Run, Fredericksburg, and Chancellorsville. But when Lee moved north to Pennsylvania he was met by Meade at Gettysburg. The bloody battle fought there in July, 1863 ended in a Union victory and marked the turning point of the war on land.

The turning point of the naval phase of the war took place in March, 1862 when the first ironclad ships, the Northern *Monitor* and the Southern *Merrimac,* clashed at Hampton Roads. While neither ship emerged victorious, the battle was a defeat for the South because it failed to break the North's blockade of the Atlantic coast. This

blockade, which cut off valuable supplies and tools, slowly starved the South into submission.

The final phase of the war began in 1864. William Sherman's march to the sea crushed the South's ability and will to fight. General Grant's Wilderness campaign started his relentless thrust to Richmond. Lee's army, decimated by Grant, retreated from Petersburg to Richmond. On April 9, 1865, in Virginia's Appomattox Courthouse, Lee accepted Grant's surrender terms.

See Scott Stamp Nos. 1178-1182

1191

1192

1193

1195

1190

Perf. 11

1190 .10 .05 4c Nursing Dec. 28
A tribute to the nursing profession.

Issues of 1962

1191 .10 .05 4c New Mexico Statehood Jan. 6
This 50th anniversary issue depicts Shiprock, sacred mountain of the Navajos, in New Mexico.

1192 .20 .05 4c Arizona Statehood Feb. 14
In 1912 Arizona joined the Union. Stamp depicts the Arizona desert.

1193 .30 .12 4c Project Mercury Feb. 20
Issued for the first orbital flight of a U.S. astronaut. Flight made by Colonel John Glenn Feb. 20, 1962.

1194 .10 .05 4c Malaria Eradication Mar. 30
Many nations of the world, including the United States, joined the U.N.'s World Health Organization in its fight against malaria.

Perf. 10-1/2x11

1195 .10 .05 4c Charles Evans Hughes Apr. 11
Chief Justice Charles Evans Hughes (1862-1948) also governed the state of New York.

Perf. 11

1196 .10 .05 4c Seattle World's Fair Apr. 25
The "Century 21" International Exposition was held at Seattle in 1962.

1197 .10 .05 4c Louisiana Statehood Apr. 30
In 1812, Louisiana joined the Union.

Perf. 11x10-1/2

1198 .10 .05 4c Homestead Act May 20
The Homestead Act, signed into law by Lincoln in 1862, played a major role in settling the West.

1199 .10 .05 4c Girl Scout Jubilee Jul. 24
Issued for the 50th anniversary of the founding of the Girl Scouts of America.

1200 .10 .05 4c Sen. Brien McMahon Jul. 28
Senator Brien McMahon of Connecticut authored the McMahon Act for the peaceful uses of atomic energy.

1201 .10 .05 4c Apprenticeship Aug. 31
Enacted under the New Deal, the National Apprenticeship Act trained people in industry.

Perf. 11

1202 .10 .05 4c Sam Rayburn Sep. 16
Sam Rayburn of Texas (1882-1961) was Speaker of the House of Representatives for 17 years.

1203 .12 .05 4c Dag Hammarskjöld Oct. 23
Swedish diplomat Dag Hammarskjöld was Secretary General of the United Nations from 1953 until his death in 1961.

1204 .18 .08 4c Hammarskjöld Special Printing; black, brown and yellow (yellow inverted)

1205 .08 .03 4c Christmas Issue Nov. 1

1206 .10 .05 4c Higher Education Nov. 14
Issued as a tribute to U.S. colleges and universities.

1207 .10 .05 4c Winslow Homer Dec. 15
Artist Winslow Homer (1836-1910) was best-known for seascapes such as "Breezing Up," shown on stamp.

Flag Issue of 1963-66

1208 .12 .03 5c Flag over White House

Regular Issue of 1962-66
Perf. 11x10-1/2

1209 .03 .03 1c Andrew Jackson

1194

1196

1197

1198

1199

1200

BASKETBALL — JAMES NAISMITH (1861-1939)

Students at the YMCA training school at Springfield, Mass. in 1891 were no different from boys at any other school; they loved outdoor competitive games, but invented all kinds of excuses to avoid winter gym classes. Athletic Coach Naismith tried adapting football and soccer to an indoor arena—the results were several unplanned lessons in practical first aid. Naismith decided if the players were not allowed to run with the ball, there would be no need to tackle and the roughness could be eliminated. Almost anyone could catch and pass a large light ball, and if the goal were over the players' heads, the ball could be kept in sight. When his class came in the next day and saw peachbaskets nailed up at either end of the gym they snorted, "Huh, another new game!" But this one was a success from the time the first mid-court shot went through a basket. Word spread quickly—other students came to watch and before long everyone in Springfield was either playing or watching.

Athletic directors at other schools heard about the new game and wrote to Naismith for copies of the rules. Geneva College (Penn.), the University of Iowa and the University of Chicago were the first to introduce it to their students in 1892. The first intercollegiate game was played on January 18, 1896 between Iowa and Chicago, with Chicago winning 15-12. The first professional team originated in Trenton, N. J. and in 1898 the National Basketball League was formed.

Because of its eye-appealing excitement, the first major sport "Made in the U.S.A." has become the country's biggest spectator sport. There can be no accurate account of participants, for wherever there are youngsters and a place to nail a hoop, indoors or out, some form of basketball is sure to be played.

See Scott No. 1189

ELEANOR ROOSEVELT (1884-1962)

Anna Eleanor Roosevelt, humanitarian and diplomat, was the wife of Franklin D. Roosevelt. As First Lady she defied tradition by writing a syndicated column, "My Day", and by touring prisons, coal mines, and military bases all over the world. As a delegate to the United Nations, she headed its Commission on Human Rights (1945-51). Her work for world peace and human rights earned her the title "First Lady of the World".

See Scott Stamp No. 1236

Jamaica Scott No. 239.

1232

1233

1234

1236

1237

1235

1213	.10	.03	5c George Washington
1213a	2.00	.75	Booklet pane of 5 + label

Coil Stamps, Perf. 10 Vertically

1225	.05	.03	1c green Jackson, sia 1209
1229	.18	.03	5c dark blue gray Washington, sia 1213

Issues of 1963, Perf. 11

1230	.12	.05	5c Carolina Charter	Apr. 6

The granting of the Carolina Charter by King Charles II gave eight Englishmen vast lands for settlement in 1663.

1231	.12	.05	5c Food for Peace — Freedom from Hunger	Jun. 4

Issue publicizes joint U.S.-U.N. campaign to end starvation.

1232	.12	.05	5c W. Virginia Statehood	Jun. 20

In 1863, West Virginia joined the union.

1233	.12	.05	5c Emancipation Proclamation	Aug. 16

President Lincoln's Emancipation Proclamation of January, 1863, freed all slaves in the ten Southern states.

1234	.12	.05	5c Alliance for Progress	Aug. 17

Issued for the second anniversary of the Alliance for Progress.

Perf. 10-1/2x11

1235	.12	.05	5c Cordell Hull	Oct. 5

Cordell Hull (1871-1955) was Secretary of State from 1933-1944.

Perf. 11x10-1/2

1236	.12	.05	5c Eleanor Roosevelt	Oct. 11

Mrs. Franklin D. Roosevelt (1884-1962) was the 32nd First Lady (1933-1945). She also served as U.S. delegate to the U.N.

Perf. 11

1237	.12	.05	5c Science	Oct. 14

The National Academy of Science was founded in 1863.

1238	.12	.05	5c City Mail Delivery	Oct. 26

Issued for the 100th anniversary of free city mail delivery.

1239	.12	.05	5c Red Cross 100th Anniv.	Oct. 29

Issued for the 100th anniversary of the International Red Cross.

1240	.10	.03	5c Christmas Issue	Nov. 1
1241	.15	.05	5c John James Audubon	Dec. 7

Audubon (1785?-1851) was a famous painter, ornithologist and conservationist. Stamp shows "Columbia Jays" from his book *The Birds of America.*

Issues of 1964, Perf. 10-1/2x11

1242	.12	.05	5c Sam Houston	Jan. 10

Sam Houston (1793-1863) was president of the Republic of Texas and later a U.S. Senator from the state of Texas.

1239

1240

1238

Haiti Scott No. C313

Togo Scott No. 601

Ghana Scott No. 191

Liberia Scott No. 397

Montserrat Scott No. 207

Dominican Republic Scott No. 475

Burundi Scott No. C92

THE BLACK AMERICAN

Whether the first Black man came to the United States in 1526 as a Spanish slave or in 1619 on a Dutch Man-of-War has yet to be determined. What is clear is that the Black American has risen from the bonds of slavery to contribute to the growth of the United States in many spheres.

In all fields — from science to sports — he has left his mark. The scientist George Washington Carver revolutionized agriculture in the South, adding the peanut, sweet potato, and soybean to its one-crop cotton economy. Dr. Daniel Hale Williams performed one of the first two open-heart operations in 1893. Dr. Charles Richard Drew pioneered in the development of blood banks. In 1959 Lorraine Hansberry won the New York Drama Critics Circle award for "Raisin in the Sun", an ever-popular American drama . In the 1936 Olympics Jesse Owens won four gold medals. Twice, in less than forty years, the Nobel Peace Prize has been awarded to Black Americans — Dr. Ralph Bunche and Dr. Martin Luther King, Jr.

Paralleling the Black American's contribution in peace has been his service in war: about 5,000 served in the Continental Army, some 200,000 in the Union Army, 367,000 in World War I, and more than a million in World War II.

See Scott Stamp Nos. 873, 953, 1074, 1233, 1290, 1372, 1486

1241

1242

1243

1244

1245

Jordan Scott No. 506

Ajman Scott No. 24

El Salvador Scott No. 749

Dubai Scott No. C26

Nigeria Scott No. 160

Ajman Scott No. 22

JOHN F. KENNEDY (1917-1963)

Those who make peaceful revolution impossible will make violent revolution inevitable.

John F. Kennedy

John F. Kennedy, who became the 35th president of the United States in 1961 at the age of 43, was the youngest man to be elected chief executive. During his brief term in office his quick wit, magnetic personality, and style injected new and hopeful vigor into politics.

He put young men, most in their 30's and 40's, in the chief posts of his administration, which he called the "New Frontier." He established the Peace Corps, which was enthusiastically received. He proposed comprehensive legislation in the field of civil rights, a continuation of the movement of the Eisenhower era.

Internationally his short administration was beset by crises, including the Bay of Pigs invasion of Cuba, the erection of the Berlin Wall, and the Cuban missile crises, when the United States and the Soviet Union stood on the brink of war.

Late in 1962 the United States learned that the Soviet Union had fortified Cuba with offensive missiles. In response the young president imposed a naval quarantine on all shipments of arms from the U.S.S.R. to Cuba. Two weeks of negotiations followed, after which Premier Khrushchev agreed to dismantle the bases.

The Kennedy era came to a tragic end on November 22, 1963, when the president was assassinated by Lee Harvey Oswald in Dallas, Texas.

See Scott Stamp Nos. 1246, 1287, 1447

San Marino Scott No. 608

Rwanda Scott No. 134

Ivory Coast Scott No. C29

Malta Scott No. 354

Venezuela Scott No. 884

Gabon Scott No. C27

1246   1247   1248   1249   1250   1252   1251   1253

Perf. 11

1243   .15   .05   5c Charles M. Russell   Mar. 19
This stamp honors frontier artist Charles M. Russell (1864-1926). It depicts his painting, "Jerked Down."

1244   .20   .05   5c New York
      World's Fair   Apr. 22
Issued for the opening of the New York World's Fair of 1964-65.

Perf. 11

1245   .12   .05   5c John Muir   Apr. 29
Conservationist John Muir (1838-1914) worked to save California's redwood trees.

Perf. 11x10-1/2

1246   .12   .05   5c Kennedy Memorial   May. 29
A memorial to John F. Kennedy, president of the United States from 1961 until his death in 1963.

Perf. 10-1/2x11

1247   .12   .05   5c New Jersey 300th Anniv. Jun. 15
In 1664, the English colonized New Jersey.

Perf. 11

1248   .12   .05   5c Nevada Statehood   Jul. 22
Nevada became a state in 1864.

1249   .12   .05   5c Register and Vote   Aug. 1
Issued for the 1964 presidential elections.

Perf. 10-1/2x11

1250   .12   .05   5c Shakespeare   Aug. 14
English dramatist William Shakespeare was born in 1564, 400 years before this stamp was issued.

1251   .12   .05   5c Doctors Mayo   Sep. 11
A tribute to the Mayo brothers, surgeons who established the Mayo Foundation. The heads on the stamp are from a sculpture by James E. Fraser.

Perf. 11

1252   .12   .05   5c American Music   Oct. 15
Issued for the 50th anniversary of the founding of the American Society of Composers, Authors and Publishers (ASCAP).

1253   .12   .05   5c Homemakers   Oct. 26
Designed in the style of an early sampler, this stamp honors U.S. homemakers.

THE MAYO BROTHERS

William James Mayo (1861-1939) and Charles Horace Mayo (1865-1939) were Minnesota surgeons whose dedication to their work resulted in new hope for millions. With their father, William Worrall Mayo, they founded the Mayo Clinic in Rochester, Minnesota, in 1889.

The number of successful operations performed at the new clinic made it a mecca for the sick. The two brothers quickly gained an international reputation for their diagnostic ability and surgical technique.

In 1915 the Doctors Mayo contributed $2.8 million to establish the Mayo Foundation for Education and Research, which became a part of the University of Minnesota Graduate School. During World War I the two brothers served the army as chief consultants for all surgical services. One of the founders of the American College of Surgeons, William Mayo was president of numerous medical societies, including the American Medical Association (1905-06).

See Scott Stamp No. 1251

THE WAR OF 1812

A lasting peace with England was the positive result of the War of 1812, which began over the issue of freedom of the seas and ended with the emergence of a new national hero.

In 1806 England, then at war with France, began to blockade U.S. ships that carried war supplies to France. This blockade, coupled with the British practice of "conscripting" U.S. sailors from their ships, led Congress to declare war on June 18, 1812 at the urging of President James Madison.

The ensuing conflict proved a series of frustrating stalemates. Early U.S. naval triumphs, such as Commodore Oliver Perry's Lake Erie victory of 1812, were almost nullified by the burning of the Capitol by 4,000 British troops in 1814.

The Ghent Peace Treaty brought the war to an end in December, 1814, but before news of the Treaty reached America, the war's most famous battle took place. This was the Battle of New Orleans, a U. S. victory from which Andrew Jackson emerged a great hero.

See Scott Stamp No. 1261

Christmas Issue, Nov. 9

1254	.30	.03	5c Holly
1255	.30	.03	5c Mistletoe
1256	.30	.03	5c Poinsettia
1257	.30	.03	5c Sprig of Conifer
1257b	1.40	.25	Block of four

Perf. 10-1/2x11

1258 .12 .05 5c Verrazano-Narrows Bridge Nov. 21

The world's longest suspension bridge was opened on November 21, 1964. It connects Staten Island and Brooklyn, N.Y.

Perf. 11

1259 .12 .05 5c Fine Arts Dec. 2

Stamp depicts "Abstract Design" by Stuart Davis.

Perf. 10-1/2x11

1260 .12 .05 5c Amateur Radio Dec. 15

The American Radio Relay League for "ham operators" was established in 1914.

Issues of 1965, Perf. 11

1261 .12 .05 5c Battle of New Orleans Jan. 8

The Battle of New Orleans established 150 years of peace between the United States and Britain.

1262 .12 .05 5c Physical Fitness-Sokol Feb. 15

The Sokol Athletic Organization was founded in 1915. Issue also promotes physical fitness.

1263 .12 .05 5c Crusade Against Cancer Apr. 1

Issue publicized the fight against cancer; also stressed the importance of an early diagnosis.

Perf. 10-1/2x11

1264 .12 .05 5c Churchill Memorial May 13

In memory of the British statesman (1874-1965), Prime Minister and World War II leader.

Perf. 11

1265 .12 .05 5c Magna Carta Jun. 15

This famous document, signed by King John in 1215, is the basis of the common law of England and the U.S.

1266 .12 .05 5c Intl. Cooperation Year Jun. 26

Issued for International Cooperation Year and the 20th anniversary of the United Nations.

1267 .12 .05 5c Salvation Army Jul. 2

William Booth founded the Salvation Army in 1865.

Perf. 10-1/2x11

1268 .12 .05 5c Dante Alighieri Jul. 17

The Italian poet born in 1265, is best-known for the *Divine Comedy.*

1269 .12 .05 5c Herbert Hoover Aug. 10

The 31st president of the United States (1929-1933) was born in 1874. He died in 1964.

Perf. 11

1270 .12 .05 5c Robert Fulton Aug. 19

Fulton (1765-1815) invented the first commercial steamboat.

1271 .12 .05 5c Settlement of Florida Aug. 28

Established in 1565, St. Augustine, Florida was the first permanent European settlement in the U.S.

1272 .12 .05 5c Traffic Safety Sep. 3

Issued to help prevent traffic accidents and to publicize highway safety.

1273 .12 .05 5c John Singleton Copley Sep. 17

John Singleton Copley (1738-1815) was an important early U.S. painter. Detail on the stamp is from his oil "The Copley Family" and portrays his daughter.

1274 .35 .12 11c International Telecommunication Union Oct. 6

The International Telecommunication Union, now under the auspices of the United Nations, was established in 1865.

1275 .12 .05 5c Adlai E. Stevenson Oct. 23

Adlai E. Stevenson (1900-65) was governor of Illinois and U.S. Ambassador to the United Nations.

1276 .10 .03 5c Christmas Issue Nov. 2

This stamp was designed from an 1840 weathervane. It depicts an angel with a trumpet.

GEORGE CATLETT MARSHALL (1880-1959)

"First in war, First in peace" applied to General George Marshall just as much as it did to General George Washington. A career officer since 1901, he rose through the ranks and was named Chief of Staff of the Army at the outbreak of World War II. His diplomatic experience and achievements with the Allied Powers led President Truman to appoint him Secretary of State at the end of the war.

The world's post-war problems were enormous. Western Europe's agriculture, industry and transportation had been brought almost to a standstill by land fighting and bombing. Reconstruction was hampered by cold, hunger and unemployment. If nations were to ever again live in peace and hope, Europe's economy had to be stablized. Air travel having come of age during the war, America could no longer wrap itself in its oceans and retreat from international affairs. As a world power we were forced to accept global responsibilities.

On June 5, 1947 Secretary of State Marshall proposed what became known as the "Marshall Plan," to restore the prosperity of Western Europe.

"Our policy is not directed against any country or doctrine, but against hunger, poverty, desperation and chaos. It's purpose should be the revival of a working economy in the world so as to permit the emergence of political and social conditions in which free institutions can exist."

In April, 1948 Congress passed a bill appropriating 5.3 billion dollars for the European Recovery Program—official name of the Marshall Plan. Altogether between 1948 and 1951 the United States provided about 12 billion dollars in aid to help rebuild Europe's economy.

Marshall resigned as Secretary of State in 1949. Later that year he became president of the American Red Cross. The following year President Truman summoned him back to his Cabinet as Secretary of Defense. General George C. Marshall was awarded the 1953 Nobel Peace Prize in recognition of his contributions to the economic rehabilitation of Europe and his untiring efforts to promote world peace and understanding.

See Scott No. 1289

Germany Scott No. 821

Issues of 1965-73, Prominent Americans			
Perf. 11x10-1/2, 10-1/2x11			
1278	.03	.03	1c Thomas Jefferson
1278a	.75	.25	Booklet pane of eight
1278b	.60	.20	Booklet pane of 4
1279	.20	.05	1¼c Albert Gallatin
1280	.04	.03	2c Frank Lloyd Wright and Guggenheim Museum
1280a	1.00	.40	Booklet pane of 5+label
1281	.06	.03	3c Francis Parkman
1282	.08	.03	4c Abraham Lincoln
1283	.10	.03	5c George Washington
1283B	.15	.03	5c Washington redrawn
1284	.12	.03	6c Franklin D. Roosevelt
1284b	1.00	.50	Booklet pane of eight
1284c	1.00	.50	Booklet pane of 5 + label
1285	.16	.05	8c Albert Einstein
1286	.20	.03	10c Andrew Jackson
1286A	.24	.03	12c Henry Ford & 1909 Model T
1287	.26	.05	13c John F. Kennedy
1288	.30	.06	15c Oliver Wendell Holmes
1289	.40	.06	20c George Catlett Marshall
1290	.50	.03	25c Frederick Douglass
1291	.60	.08	30c John Dewey
1292	.80	.10	40c Thomas Paine
1293	1.00	.04	50c Lucy Stone
1294	2.00	.08	$1 Eugene O'Neill
1295	10.00	2.00	$5 John Bassett Moore
Coil Stamps, Issues of 1966-73			
Perf. 10 Horizontally			
1298	.50	.05	6c gray brown F.D.R., sia 1284
Perf. 10 Vertically			
1299	.03	.03	1c green Jefferson, sia 1278
1303	.08	.03	4c black Lincoln, sia 1282
1304	.12	.03	5c blue Washington, sia 1283
1305	.12	.05	6c Franklin D. Roosevelt
1305C	2.00	.20	$1 dull purple Eugene O'Neill, sia 1294

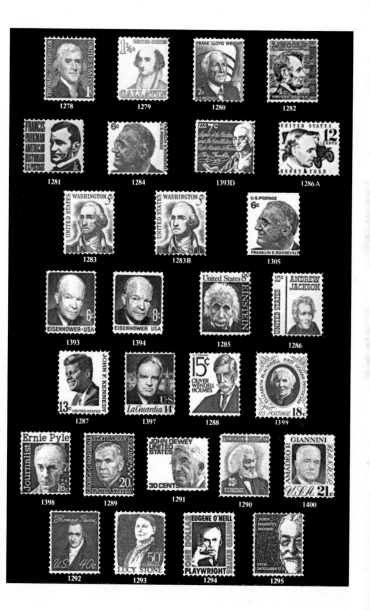

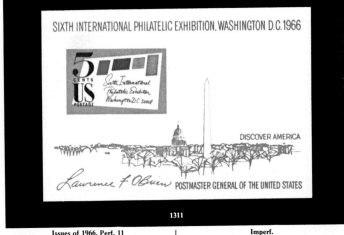

SIXTH INTERNATIONAL PHILATELIC EXHIBITION, WASHINGTON D.C. 1966

DISCOVER AMERICA

Lawrence F O'Brien POSTMASTER GENERAL OF THE UNITED STATES

1311

Issues of 1966, Perf. 11					
1306	.12	.05	5c Migratory Bird Treaty		Mar. 16

In 1916 Canada and the United States ratified this treaty to protect their migratory birds.

1307	.12	.05	5c Humane Treatment of Animals		Apr. 9

The American Society for the Prevention of Cruelty to Animals was established in 1866.

1308	.12	.05	5c Indiana Statehood		Apr. 16

In 1816, Indiana joined the Union.

1309	.12	.05	5c American Circus		May 2

This tribute to the circus also marked the 100th anniversary of the birth of John Ringling, circusmaster.

Sixth International Philatelic Exhibition Issues

1310	.12	.05	5c Stamped Cover		May 21

Imperf.					
1311	.18	.10	5c Souvenir Sheet		May 23

Issued in sheets of one stamp with marginal inscription commemorating the Sixth International Philatelic Exhibition (SIPEX), held in Washington, D.C. from May 21-30.

Perf. 11					
1312	.12	.05	5c Bill of Rights		Jul. 1

Issued for the 175th anniversary of the Bill of Rights.

Perf. 10-1/2x11					
1313	.12	.05	5c Polish Millennium		Jul. 30

The people of Poland adopted Christianity in 966 A.D.

Perf. 11					
1314	.12	.05	5c National Park Service		Aug. 25

Issued for the 50th anniversary of the National Park Service of the Department of the Interior.

ALBERT EINSTEIN (1879-1955)

Albert Einstein was one of the greatest, most creative thinkers of the 20th Century. In 1916 he published his general theory of relativity dealing with the relationships of time, motion and space. His famous equation $E=mc^2$ opened the way for the development of atomic energy. In 1921 his work in theoretical physics earned him a Nobel Prize.

Hitler's rapid rise to power took place while Einstein was a visiting professor at the California Institute of Technology. He foresaw the impending disasters that were to befall his native Germany under control of the Nazi regime. Because he was a Jew, he went to Belgium, resigned his positions in Berlin and returned to the United States.

In 1933 Einstein accepted a post at the Institute for Advanced Study in Princeton, New Jersey; and consequently, in 1940, became an American citizen.

Although his continued research led to the atomic bomb, Einstein held a high belief in humanity and social justice. By his statement, "God is subtle, but he is not malicious," it is obvious that his intent was not to create deaths, but peace.

See Scott Nos. 1070, 1285

1306

1307

1308

1309

1310

1312

1313

1314

THE BILL OF RIGHTS

Congress shall make no law...a-bridging the freedom of speech or of the press; or the right of the people peacefully to assemble...

Revolutions often breed dictatorships. Not so in the United States, where government by the people resulted from the Revolutionary War.

The founding fathers, anxious to preserve the freedoms fought for in the war, acted quickly to set up a democratic form of government at the war's conclusion. The Constitution, written in 1787, was the bulwark of this government.

When the Constitution was presented to the people for approval they demanded—and received—a bill of rights to preserve their civil liberties. Such a bill was not a new idea. Its roots lay deep in English history—in the Magna Carta, which established the right of trial by jury in 1215; and in the English Bill of Rights of 1689.

When the first ten amendments were added to the Constitution in 1791, liberty was truly made the Law of the Land.

See Scott Stamp No. 1312

1099

1119

908

1265

1315	.12	.05	5c Marine Corps Reserve Aug. 29		

The U.S. Marine Corps Reserve was established in 1916.

1316	.12	.05	5c General Federation of Women's Clubs Sep. 12

Issue notes "75 Years of Service for Freedom and Growth" by the General Federation of Women's Clubs.

1317	.12	.05	5c American Folklore Issue Sep. 24

Issued to honor Johnny Appleseed (John Chapman, 1774-1845), who roamed over 100,000 square miles planting apple trees.

1318	.12	.05	5c Beautification of America Oct. 5

This stamp helped encourage interest in the "Beautify America" campaign of President and Mrs. Lyndon Johnson. It carries the legend "Plant for a more beautiful America."

1319	.12	.05	5c Great River Road Oct. 21

The 5,600 mile Great River Road connects New Orleans with Kenora, Ontario. It follows the Mississippi River.

1320	.12	.05	5c Savings Bond-Servicemen Oct. 26

Issued for the 25th anniversary of U.S. Savings Bonds.

1321	.10	.03	5c Christmas Issue Nov. 1

This stamp shows a detail from the work "Madonna and Child with Angels" by the Flemisl. artist Hans Memling (c. 1430-1494).

1322	.15	.05	5c Mary Cassatt Nov. 17

Mary Cassatt (1845-1926) was an American impressionist painter. The stamp was designed from her work "The Boating Party."

Issues of 1967

1323	.12	.05	5c National Grange Apr. 17

The National Grange, a farmers' organization, was created in 1867.

MARY CASSATT (1844-1926)

"Woman's vocation in life is to bear children," painter Mary Cassatt once said. Never having any children of her own, but feeling them a very important part of life, Miss Cassatt created hundreds of children, as well as their mothers, on her canvases in the seventy years before she went blind.

Society daughter of a Pennsylvania banker, she attended the Pennsylvania Academy of Fine Arts. At a time when young ladies rarely left their home unescorted, she insisted upon continuing her studies in Europe. In spite of her father's strong objections, she went to the Continent to study and paint at the age of twenty-two.

Tall, prim, gaunt, she had not only wealth, but a discriminating mind, ambition and courage. She exhibited in the Paris Salon in 1872, the first of five successive years. Modern master Edgar Degas became her close friend and in 1877 invited her to show with the Impressionists. From them she learned how to better use space and form in painting and achieved a distinctively feminine touch in her work.

Though critically acclaimed in France, Mary Cassatt remained unrecognized as an artist in the United States during her lifetime. Today she is acknowledged as one of America's foremost painters.

See Scott No. 1322

1323

1324

1325

1326

1327

1328

1329

1330

1324	.12	.05	5c Canada 100th Anniv.	May 25

Issued for the 100th anniversary of Canada's Emergence as a nation.

1325	.12	.05	5c Erie Canal	Jul. 4

The construction of the Erie Canal began in 1817, 150 years before this stamp was issued.

1326	.12	.05	5c "Peace"—Lions	Jul. 5

"Search for Peace" was the theme of an essay contest sponsored by Lions International for its 50th anniversary.

1327	.12	.05	5c Henry David Thoreau	Jul. 12

A leading author of the nineteenth century, Thoreau is best-known for his book *Walden*.

1328	.12	.05	5c Nebraska Statehood	Jul. 29

Nebraska became a state in 1867.

1329	.12	.05	5c Voice of America	Aug. 1

Issued for the 25th anniversary of the Voice of America, the radio branch of the United States Information Agency.

1330	.12	.05	5c American Folklore Issue	

HENRY DAVID THOREAU (1817-62)

The mass of men lead lives of quiet desperation. Walden

On Independence Day, 1845, Henry David Thoreau began his two-year residence at Walden Pond, a few miles south of Concord, Massachusetts. Insisting that a man need not mortgage his life just to live, he built his house for $28 and lived off the land. In the same year, as a protest against slavery, he personally seceded from the Union, refused to pay the poll tax, and spent a night in the Concord jail. Although *Walden* is Thoreau's most famous work, his most influential has been *Civil Disobedience*. Objecting to the continuance of slavery, the treatment of Indians, and the Mexican War, he delineated his policy of passive resistance to unjust governments. His essay, inspiration to Mahatma Ghandi, has been the basis for many peaceful revolutions throughout the world.

See Scott Stamp No. 1327

FRONTIERS OF SPACE

Live television coverage of happenings in far-off lands...weather satellites that track down storms while orbiting in outer space...a race to Mars...

**U.S.S.R.
Scott No. 3224**

Ascension Scott No. 104

These are but a few of the miraculous achievements of the Space Age, which was launched in 1957 by Russia's Sputnik satellite. The United States, which followed Russia with Explorer 1 in 1958, has also landed the first men upon the moon; launched Early Bird, the first communications satellite; and orbited the weather satellites Nimbus and TIROS. Two United States unmanned expeditions, Viking and "Grand Tour" are planned for in the future. "Grand Tour" will go to Jupiter, Uranus, Neptune, Saturn, and Pluto. Viking will orbit Mars. In 1970, the Space Race, long the domain of the United States and the Soviet Union, was joined by the People's Republic of China, which launched a 380-pound earth satellite.

See Scott Stamp Nos. 1331-1332, 1371, C76

Space Accomplishments Issue, Sep. 29

1331	.75	.20	5c Space-Walking Astronaut
1331a	3.50	1.25	Pair
1332	.75	.20	5c Gemini 4 Capsule and Earth

Nos. 1331-1332, the first twin stamps in U.S. postal history, note U.S. accomplishments in outer space.

| 1333 | .12 | .05 | 5c Urban Planning | Oct. 2 |

"Plan for better cities" was the theme of this stamp, issued in conjunction with the International Conference of the American Institute of Planners, held in Washington, D.C. from Oct. 1-6.

| 1334 | .15 | .05 | 5c Finnish Independence | Oct. 6 |

Issued for the 50th anniversary of Finnish independence, this stamp reproduces Finland's coat of arms.

Perf. 12

| 1335 | .18 | .05 | 5c Thomas Eakins | Nov. 2 |

Painter Thomas Eakins (1844-1916), is honored on this stamp. Designed from an Eakins oil, "The Biglin Brothers Racing," it was the first U.S. stamp printed by the gravure method.

| 1336 | .12 | .04 | 5c Christmas Issue | Nov. 6 |

This stamp shows "Madonna and Child with Angels," by Hans Memling. The painting, which hangs in the National Gallery of Art, was also shown on the 1966 Christmas Issue.

| 1337 | .12 | .05 | 5c Mississippi Statehood | Dec. 11 |

In 1817, Mississippi joined the Union. Stamp depicts the Mississippi flower, the magnolia.

1338				
1339			1341	
1340	1342		1343	1344

	Issues of 1968-71				
1338	.12	.03	6c Flag and White House		
	Perf. 11x10-1/2				
1338D	.12	.03	6c dark blue, red & grn., sia 1338		
1338F	.16	.03	8c multicolored, sia 1338		
	Coil Stamps of 1969-71				
	Perf. 10 Vertically				
1338A	.12	.03	6c dk. blue, red & green, sia 1338		
1338G	.16	.03	8c multicolored, sia 1338		
	Issues of 1968, Perf. 11				
1339	.14	.05	6c Illinois Statehood		Feb. 12

Illinois became a state in 1818.

1340	.14	.05	6c Hemis Fair '68		Mar. 30

San Antonio, Texas was the site of the Hemis Fair '68 Exposition.

| 1341 | 2.25 | 1.25 | $1 Airlift · | | Apr. 4 |

Issued for airposting parcels to servicemen overseas.

| 1342 | .14 | .05 | 6c "Youth"—Elks | | May 1 |

National Youth Week of 1968 was sponsored by the Elks.

| 1343 | .14 | .05 | 6c Law and Order | | May 17 |

This stamp reaffirmed the role of the policeman as a friend and a protector of the citizen.

| 1344 | .14 | .05 | 6c Register and Vote | | Jun. 27 |

Issued to remind Americans to "Register and Vote" in the 1968 elections.

FOLK HEROES OF THE OLD FRONTIER

The names and exploits of Daniel Boone and Davy Crockett loom large in the legends of early frontier heroes—rugged, fearless men who, fiercely independent, thrived on a life of lonely danger.

Celebrated as the discoverer and founder of Kentucky, Daniel Boone (1734-1820), more than any other man, molded the frontier tradition. Legend says that he could trap a bear in record time, outrun any Indian, and better any shot. In 1775 he blazed the Wilderness Road into Kentucky and built Boonesboro, the town that bears his name. But when settlers poured into Kentucky, Boone grew restless. "If you can see smoke from your neighbor's chimney, it's time to move on," he said, and so he did, this time blazing a trail to Missouri.

Davy Crockett (1786-1836) acquired his legendary reputation both in Tennessee and at the Alamo. An expert marksman, a fine trapper, and a hunter, he brought the coonskin cap of the woodsman into Washington, D.C. when he became a Congressman in 1827 and again in 1832. Always a conspicuous and eccentric figure in the capital, he moved to Texas after his congressional defeat in 1835. There, he joined the fight for Texas independence, and with 186 other men died at the historic Battle of the Alamo.

See Scott Stamp Nos. 904, 1330, 1357

WALT DISNEY (1901-1966)

A brilliant fantasyland where Goofy, Donald Duck, Jiminy Cricket, Chip and Dale, Thumper the rabbit, Dumbo the elephant, the fairies Flora, Fauna, and Merriweather, and their cartoon relatives cavort is the magic legacy of Walt Disney, film producer and animation pioneer.

Over two dozen Academy Awards attest to the perennial popularity of Disney's films. Yet one of his best-loved characters, Mickey Mouse, did not capture the public imagination until Mickey's third picture, "Steamboat Willie" came around the bend and Walt let him talk. To the World War II effort, Disney contributed animated features for government training programs. Disneyland Park near Los Angeles, a children's fairyland since its birth in 1954, attracts thousands of young, middle-aged, and old "children" each year.

See Scott Stamp No. 1355

WALT DISNEY
UNITED STATES
6¢
1355

San Marino
Scott No. 744

U.S. POSTAGE 6¢
LIBERTY
FORT MOULTRIE FLAG 1776
1345

U.S. POSTAGE 6¢
U.S. FLAG (1795-1818) (FT. M'HENRY FLAG)
1346

U.S. POSTAGE 6¢
AN APPEAL TO HEAVEN
WASHINGTON'S CRUISERS FLAG 1775
1347

U.S. POSTAGE 6¢
76
BENNINGTON FLAG 1777
1348

U.S. POSTAGE 6¢
HOPE
RHODE ISLAND FLAG 1775
1349

U.S. POSTAGE 6¢
FIRST STARS AND STRIPES 1777
1350

U.S. POSTAGE 6¢
GRAND UNION FLAG 1776
1352

U.S. POSTAGE 6¢
BUNKER HILL FLAG 1775
1351

U.S. POSTAGE 6¢
PHILADELPHIA LIGHT HORSE FLAG 1775
1353

U.S. POSTAGE 6¢
DONT TREAD ON ME
FIRST NAVY JACK 1775
1354

128

1356

1357

1361

1358

1359

1360

THE VIKINGS AND LEIF ERIKSON

In the year 1,000 the Vikings — or sons of the rjords as they called themselves — were the undisputed rulers of the sea; master mariners who plundered coastal settlements from Sicily to Normandy and struck terror in the hearts of landsmen throughout Europe. In that year, according to Norse sagas, Leif the Lucky sailed from Norway to take Christianity to Greenland. But as fate would have it he failed to reach his destination. Blown off course by a storm he landed on an unknown shore filled with wild grapes which he named Vinland the Good.

Was Vinland a real place? Yes, say some modern scholars. Most of them believe it was located in North America, probably in Nova Scotia or in Newfoundland. Certain scholars think the Vikings tried to colonize the land but found the task too difficult. It remained for better-known explorers to seek Vinland out in a way that would alter history.

See Scott Stamp Nos. 621, 1359

1362

PLANT for more BEAUTIFUL CITIES — PLANT for more BEAUTIFUL PARKS — PLANT for more BEAUTIFUL HIGHWAYS — PLANT for more BEAUTIFUL STREETS

1368A

CHRISTMAS 6¢ — UNITED STATES — **1363**

Chief Joseph National Portrait Gallery — United States Postage 6¢ — **1364**

The American Legion — 50 years — Veterans as Citizens — U.S. POSTAGE 6 CENTS — **1369**

Grandma Moses — 6c U.S. POSTAGE — **1370**

In the beginning God... — APOLLO 8 — SIX CENTS · UNITED STATES — **1371**

CALIFORNIA — 1769 1969 — United States 6 cents — **1373**

W.C. HANDY father of the Blues — UNITED STATES — **1372**

JOHN WESLEY POWELL — 1869 EXPEDITION — 6¢ U.S. POSTAGE — **1374**

ALABAMA — 1819 1969 — UNITED STATES — **1375**

Pseudotsuga menziesii — 6¢ UNITED STATES — 37TH INTERNATIONAL — BOTANICAL — Cypripedium reginae — 6¢ UNITED STATES — Fouquieria splendens — 6¢ UNITED STATES — BOTANICAL — 6¢ UNITED STATES — Franklinia alatamaha — **1379A**

1362	.18	.05	6c Waterfowl Conservation Oct. 24

Issued to encourage waterfowl conservation and to honor Ducks Unlimited, an organization which has spent nearly $15 million on conservation.

1363	.18	.04	6c Christmas Issue Nov. 1

This stamp shows the Angel Gabriel, a detail from "The Annunciation" by Flemish painter Jan van Eyck (c. 1390-1441).

1364	.18	.05	6c American Indian Nov. 4

A tribute to the Indian, this stamp shows the great Chief Joseph (c. 1840-1904), leader of the Nez Percé tribe.

Issues of 1969
Beautification of America, Jan. 16

1365	.75	.06	6c Capitol, Azaleas and Tulips
1366	.75	.06	6c Washington Monument, Potomac River and Daffodils
1367	.75	.06	6c Poppies and Lupines along Highway
1368	.75	.06	6c Blooming Crabapples along Street
1368a	3.50	.40	Block of four

Nos. 1365-1368 were issued to promote the "Beautification of America" campaign.

JAZZ

Jazz, America's unique contribution to music, originated during the 19th century when the American Negro took the songs of his new home — folk songs, church hymns and other popular music — and transformed them into a distinctive Afro-American idiom — that is, into work songs, spirituals, and the blues.

In jazz, especially the brass-band variety, emphasis is on the improvisational abilities of the player, usually in "jam" sessions. Great artists in its history include Jelly-Roll Morton, Louis Armstrong, Duke Ellington, and Bix Beiderbecke.

Among the composers of blues, jazz steeped with emotion, W. C. Handy is probably the most famous. During his lifetime (1873-1958), he wrote "Memphis Blues", "St. Louis Blues", and about sixty other songs.

See Scott Stamp No. 1372

1369	.14	.05	6c American Legion	Mar. 15

The American Legion was founded in 1919 in Paris.

1370	.14	.05	6c American Folklore	May 1

Issued to honor Grandma Moses (1860-1961), American primitive painter.

1371	.30	.06	6c Apollo 8	May 5

The Apollo 8 mission of Dec. 21-27, 1968 put the first men into orbit around the moon.

1372	.14	.05	6c W. C. Handy	May 17

William Christopher Handy (1873-1958) was a jazz musician and composer ("The St. Louis Blues"). Stamp also notes the 150th anniversary of Memphis, Tennessee.

1373	.14	.05	6c California Settlement	Jul. 16

Issued for the 200th anniversary of the settlement of California by Father Junipero Serra and Gaspar de Portola.

1374	.14	.05	6c John Wesley Powell	Aug. 1

Geologist John Wesley Powell (1834-1902) explored the Green and Colorado Rivers.

1375	.14	.05	6c Alabama Statehood	Aug. 2

In 1819, Alabama joined the union. Stamp shows the yellowhammer and the camelia. Alabama's bird and flower.

Botanical Congress Issue

1376	1.00	.05	6c Douglas Fir (Northwest)
1377	1.00	.05	6c Lady's-slipper (Northeast)
1378	1.00	.05	6c Ocotillo (Southwest)
1379	1.00	.05	6c Franklinia (Southeast)
1379a	4.50	.30	Block of four

Issued in conjunction with the 11th International Botanical Congress, held in Seattle, Washington from Aug. 24-Sep. 2.

FOOTBALL

The first intercollegiate football game was played in 1869 at New Brunswick, New Jersey between Rutgers and Princeton Universities. Since then the game has gained steadily in popularity and prestige. Early players such as Jim Thorpe, "Red" Grange, and Clyde "Bulldog" Turner captured the popular imagination and before long the game became professional. In 1922 the National Football League (NFL) was organized and in 1959 the American Football League (AFL) was founded. In 1970 Alvin "Pete" Rozelle became the first comissioner of Pro Football, and the two leagues merged into the National Football League, which now has two conferences, the National and American. Each year the championship Super Bowl pits the top pro teams against one another in one of the country's most exciting sports events.

See Scott Stamp No. 1382

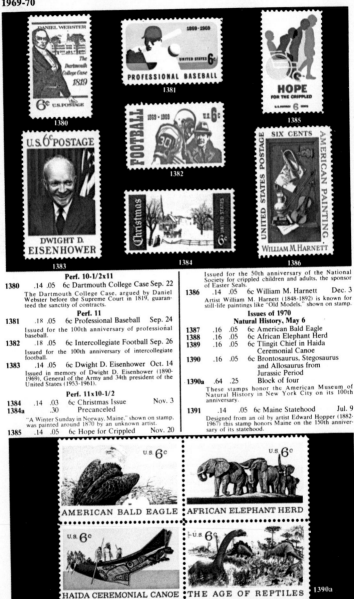

1380

1381

1385

1382

1383

1384

1386

Perf. 10-1/2x11

1380 .14 .05 6c Dartmouth College Case Sep. 22

The Dartmouth College Case, argued by Daniel Webster before the Supreme Court in 1819, guaranteed the sanctity of contracts.

Perf. 11

1381 .18 .05 6c Professional Baseball Sep. 24

Issued for the 100th anniversary of professional baseball.

1382 .18 .05 6c Intercollegiate Football Sep. 26

Issued for the 100th anniversary of intercollegiate football.

1383 .14 .05 6c Dwight D. Eisenhower Oct. 14

Issued in memory of Dwight D. Eisenhower (1890-1969), General of the Army and 34th president of the United States (1953-1961).

Perf. 11x10-1/2

1384 .14 .03 6c Christmas Issue Nov. 3
1384a .30 Precanceled

"A Winter Sunday in Norway, Maine," shown on stamp, was painted around 1870 by an unknown artist.

1385 .14 .05 6c Hope for Crippled Nov. 20

Issued for the 50th anniversary of the National Society for crippled children and adults, the sponsor of Easter Seals.

1386 .14 .05 6c William M. Harnett Dec. 3

Artist William M. Harnett (1848-1892) is known for still-life paintings like "Old Models," shown on stamp.

Issues of 1970
Natural History, May 6

1387 .16 .05 6c American Bald Eagle
1388 .16 .05 6c African Elephant Herd
1389 .16 .05 6c Tlingit Chief in Haida Ceremonial Canoe
1390 .16 .05 6c Brontosaurus, Stegosaurus and Allosaurus from Jurassic Period
1390a .64 .25 Block of four

These stamps honor the American Museum of Natural History in New York City on its 100th anniversary.

1391 .14 .05 6c Maine Statehood Jul. 9

Designed from an oil by artist Edward Hopper (1882-1967) this stamp honors Maine on the 150th anniversary of its statehood.

1390a

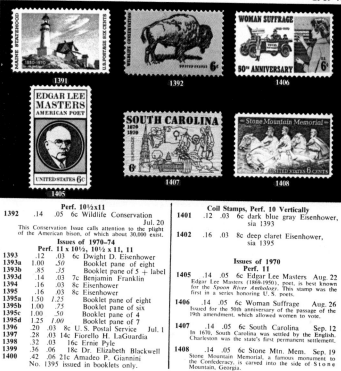

Perf. 10½x11

1392	.14	.05	6c Wildlife Conservation	Jul. 20

This Conservation Issue calls attention to the plight of the American bison, of which about 30,000 exist.

Issues of 1970-74

Perf. 11 x 10½, 10½ x 11, 11

1393	.12	.03	6c Dwight D. Eisenhower
1393a	1.00	.50	Booklet pane of eight
1393b	.85	.35	Booklet pane of 5 + label
1393d	.14	.03	7c Benjamin Franklin
1394	.16	.03	8c Eisenhower
1395	.16	.03	8c Eisenhower
1395a	1.50	1.25	Booklet pane of eight
1395b	1.00	.75	Booklet pane of six
1395c	1.00	.50	Booklet pane of 4
1395d	1.25	1.00	Booklet pane of 7
1396	.20	.03	8c U.S. Postal Service	Jul. 1
1397	.28	.03	14c Fiorello H. LaGuardia
1398	.32	.03	16c Ernie Pyle
1399	.36	.06	18c Dr. Elizabeth Blackwell
1400	.42	.06	21c Amadeo P. Giannini

No. 1395 issued in booklets only.

Coil Stamps, Perf. 10 Vertically

1401	.12	.03	6c dark blue gray Eisenhower, sia 1393
1402	.16	.03	8c deep claret Eisenhower, sia 1395

Issues of 1970

Perf. 11

1405	.14	.05	6c Edgar Lee Masters	Aug. 22

Edgar Lee Masters (1869-1950), poet, is best known for the *Spoon River Anthology*. This stamp was the first in a series honoring U. S. poets.

1406	.14	.05	6c Woman Suffrage	Aug. 26

Issued for the 50th anniversary of the passage of the 19th amendment. which allowed women to vote.

1407	.14	.05	6c South Carolina	Sep. 12

In 1670, South Carolina was settled by the English. Charleston was the state's first permanent settlement.

1408	.14	.05	6c Stone Mtn. Mem.	Sep. 19

Stone Mountain Memorial, a famous monument to the Confederacy, is carved into the side of S t o n e Mountain, Georgia.

Illustrations of stamps 1393, 1394, 1397-1400 on pg. 121.

BASEBALL

Tradition has it that Abner Doubleday created America's national pastime in 1839 at Cooperstown, New York. Since then, the cry "Play ball!" has started countless season and post-season clashes between members of the two professional leagues: the National (dating from 1876) and the American (dating from 1901).

In 1903 the Boston Red Sox defeated the Pittsburgh Pirates in the first World Series, now a yearly classic. In 1939, on baseball's 100th anniversary, the National Baseball Hall of Fame and Museum was built at Cooperstown. The first five "greats" honored on its roster were Ty Cobb, Babe Ruth, Walter Johnson, Honus Wagner, and Christy Mathewson.

It took 39 years for Babe Ruth's lifetime record of 714 home runs to be broken. On April 4, 1974 Hank Aaron of the Atlanta Braves tied this record. Four days later he established the new world record of 715 home run hits.

See Scott Stamp Nos. 855, 1381

THE MENACE OF POLLUTION
In recent years pollution has become a problem of nation-wide concern, for it threatens to destroy the resources on which life depends. Lakes and streams in parts of the United States are clogged with algae. City air is thick with smog. Chemicals have poisoned once-rich soil, and many forms of wildlife are on the verge of extinction. The situation is now so acute that nation-wide campaigns are being waged to save the country's cities, soil, air, and water. Ecology, a term once known only to scientists, has become a household word as children and adults fight to preserve the balance between man and his environment which sustains and nurtures life.

See Scott Stamp Nos. 1410-1413

1409	.14	.05	6c Fort Snelling Oct. 17

Established in 1820, Fort Snelling, Minnesota played a major role in the opening of the Northwest.

Perf. 11 x 10½
Anti–Pollution Issue, Oct. 28

1410	.35	.05	6c Save our Soil
1411	.35	.05	6c Save our Cities
1412	.35	.05	6c Save our Water

1413	.35	.05	6c Save our Air
1413a	1.60	.25	Block of four

Issued to call attention to the mounting problem of pollution.

Christmas Issue, Nov. 5
Perf. 10½ x 11

1414	.20	.03	6c Nativity, by Lorenzo Lotto
1414a		.25	Precancelled

1409

1413a

1418b

1414

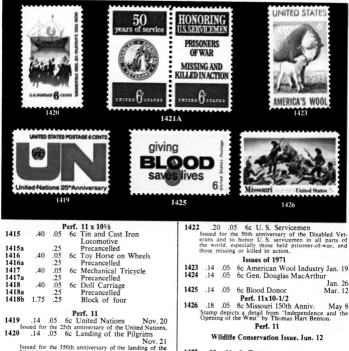

Perf. 11 x 10½			
1415	.40	.05	6c Tin and Cast Iron Locomotive
1415a		.25	Precancelled
1416	.40	.05	6c Toy Horse on Wheels
1416a		.25	Precancelled
1417	.40	.05	6c Mechanical Tricycle
1417a		.25	Precancelled
1418	.40	.05	6c Doll Carriage
1418a		.25	Precancelled
1418b	1.75	.25	Block of four

Perf. 11				
1419	.14	.05	6c United Nations	Nov. 20

Issued for the 25th anniversary of the United Nations.

1420	.14	.05	6c Landing of the Pilgrims	Nov. 21

Issued for the 350th anniversary of the landing of the Pilgrims.

Disabled Veterans and Servicemen Issue, Nov. 24

1421	.20	.05	6c Disabled American Veterans Emblem
1421a	.50	.12	Pair, sia 1421–1422

1422	.20	.05	6c U. S. Servicemen

Issued for the 50th anniversary of the Disabled Veterans and to honor U. S. servicemen in all parts of the world, especially those held prisoner-of-war, and those missing or killed in action.

Issues of 1971

1423	.14	.05	6c American Wool Industry	Jan. 19
1424	.14	.05	6c Gen. Douglas MacArthur	Jan. 26
1425	.14	.05	6c Blood Donor	Mar. 12
Perf. 11x10-1/2				
1426	.18	.05	8c Missouri 150th Anniv.	May 8

Stamp depicts a detail from "Independence and the Opening of the West" by Thomas Hart Benton.

Perf. 11

Wildlife Conservation Issue, Jun. 12

1427	.22	.06	8c Trout
1428	.22	.06	8c Alligator
1429	.22	.06	8c Polar Bear and Cubs
1430	.22	.06	8c California Condor
1430a	.88	.30	Block of four

1431   1432   1433

1431   .18   .05   8c Antarctic Treaty Issue   Jun. 23

Tenth anniversary of the Antarctic Treaty pledging peaceful uses of and scientific co-operation in Antarctica.

1432   .18   .05   8c American Revolution 200th Anniv.   Jul. 4

Special issue marks start of U.S. Revolution bicentennial celebration: shows official emblem of Bicentennial Commission.

1433   .18   .05   8c John Sloan Issue   Aug. 2

Issued to honor John Sloan (1871-1951), American painter. Stamp shows his work "The Wake of the Ferry".

Decade of Space Achievements Issue, Aug. 2

1434   .25   .05   8c Earth, Sun, Landing Craft on Moon
1434a   .60   .25   Pair, sia 1434-1435
1435   .25   .05   8c Lunar Rover and Astronauts

Stamps honor a decade of space achievements and the Apollo 15 mission of July 26-August 7.

UNITED STATES IN SPACE...   A DECADE OF ACHIEVEMENT

1434   1435

MEN ON THE MOON

That's one small step for a man, one giant leap for mankind. Neil A. Armstrong

On July 20, 1969 a concept of science fiction became fact when man took his first steps on the moon. Millions of people watched Apollo 11 astronauts Neil Armstrong and Edwin Aldrin Jr. descend to the landing site in the lunar module "Eagle". while Michael Collins continued to orbit the moon in the command module "Columbia". For 21 hours and 37 minutes the astronauts lived on the forbidding lunar surface. During their two-hour moon walk they collected about fifty pounds of moon rocks and soil samples for scientific analysis. Before leaving Armstrong and Aldrin planted a United States flag which, due to the absence of atmosphere, had to be flown on a metal support. An accompanying plaque, signed by President Nixon, states that the people of the United States achieved the moon landing for "peaceful purposes".

Since 1969 six more manned U.S. moon flights have been made. During the Apollo 15 mission of 1971 astronauts David Scott and James Irwin established the first U.S. post office on the moon.

See Scott Stamp Nos. 1434-1435, C76

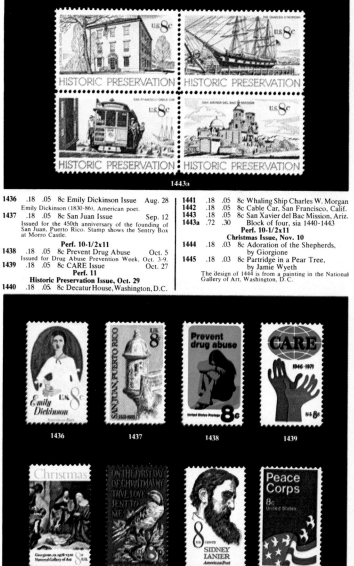

1443a

1436	.18	.05	8c Emily Dickinson Issue	Aug. 28

Emily Dickinson (1830-86), American poet.

1437	.18	.05	8c San Juan Issue	Sep. 12

Issued for the 450th anniversary of the founding of San Juan, Puerto Rico. Stamp shows the Sentry Box at Morro Castle.

Perf. 10-1/2x11

1438	.18	.05	8c Prevent Drug Abuse	Oct. 5

Issued for Drug Abuse Prevention Week, Oct. 3-9.

1439	.18	.05	8c CARE Issue	Oct. 27

Perf. 11

Historic Preservation Issue, Oct. 29

1440	.18	.05	8c Decatur House, Washington, D.C.
1441	.18	.05	8c Whaling Ship Charles W. Morgan
1442	.18	.05	8c Cable Car, San Francisco, Calif.
1443	.18	.05	8c San Xavier del Bac Mission, Ariz.
1443a	.72	.30	Block of four, sia 1440-1443

Perf. 10-1/2x11

Christmas Issue, Nov. 10

1444	.18	.03	8c Adoration of the Shepherds, by Giorgione
1445	.18	.03	8c Partridge in a Pear Tree, by Jamie Wyeth

The design of 1444 is from a painting in the National Gallery of Art, Washington, D.C.

1436   1437   1438   1439

1444   1445   1446   1447

1451a

1452

1453

1454

C84

Issues of 1972
Perf. 11

1446 .18 .05 8c Sidney Lanier Feb. 3
Sidney Lanier (1842-1881), poet, musician, lawyer, educator.

Perf. 10-1/2x11

1447 .18 .05 8c Peace Corps Feb. 11
The act creating the Peace Corps, a volunteer program operating in underdeveloped countries in all parts of the globe, was passed by Congress in 1961.

National Parks 100th Anniversary Issue
Perf. 11

1448	.06	.03	2c Hulk of Ship	Apr. 5
1449	.06	.03	2c Cape Hatteras Lighthouse	Apr. 5
1450	.06	.03	2c Laughing Gulls on Driftwood	Apr. 5
1451	.06	.03	2c Laughing Gulls and Dune	Apr. 5
1451a	.24	.16	Block of four, Cape Hatteras
1452	.12	.04	6c Wolf Trap Farm	Jun. 26
1453	.18	.05	8c Yellowstone	Mar. 1
1454	.35	.15	15c Mt. McKinley	Jul. 28

Yellowstone, created in 1872, was the first national park. Cape Hatteras National Seashore in North Carolina consists of 45 square miles of beach land. Wolf Trap Farm Park, 117 acres, is near Vienna, Virginia. Mt. McKinley National Park in Alaska, 3,020 square miles, was created in 1917.

Note: Beginning with this issue, the U.S.P.S. began to offer stamp collectors first day cancellations affixed to 8x10-1/2 souvenir pages. The pages are similar to the stamp announcements that have appeared on post office bulletin boards since Scott No. 1132.

1455 .16 .05 8c Family Planning Mar. 18
Issue focuses attention on family planning.

Perf. 11x10-1/2
American Revolution Bicentennial Issue, Jul. 4
Craftsmen in Colonial America

1456	.20	.05	8c Glassmaker
1457	.20	.05	8c Silversmith
1458	.20	.05	8c Wigmaker
1459	.20	.05	8c Hatter
1459a	.90	.20	Block of four

Issued in honor of colonial American craftsmen as part of the United States' bicentennial celebration.

Olympic Games Issue, Aug. 17

1460	.12	.04	6c Bicycling and Olympic Rings
1461	.16	.05	8c Bobsledding
1462	.30	.15	15c Running

Issued for the 11th Winter Olympic Games, held at Sapporo, Japan, from Feb. 3-13; and for the 20th Summer Olympic Games, held at Munich, Germany from Aug. 26-Sep. 11.

1463 .16 .05 8c P.T.A. 75th Anniv. Sep. 15
The Parent Teacher Association was founded by Mrs. Phoebe Hearst and Mrs. Alice Birney in 1897. Today, nearly ten million people belong to the organization.

Perf. 11
Wildlife Conservation Issue, Sep. 20

1464	.18	.05	8c Fur Seals
1465	.18	.05	8c Cardinal
1466	.18	.05	8c Brown Pelican
1467	.18	.05	8c Bighorn Sheep
1467a	.72	.20	Block of four

The 1972 wildlife conservation stamps depict birds and animals indigenous to different parts of the United States. The U.S.P.S. has pointed out that these are not necessarily endangered species but that all forms of wildlife should be of public concern.

Note: With this issue the U.S.P.S. introduced the "American Commemorative Series" S t a m p Panels. Each panel contains a block of four mint s t a m p s, mounted with text, and background illustrations.

Perf. 11x10-1/2

1468 .16 .05 8c Mail Order 100th Anniv. Sep. 27
The mail order business was originated in 1872 by Aaron Montgomery Ward of Chicago.

THE BOSTON TEA PARTY

During the years before the Revolutionary War the government of England levied heavy taxes on the thirteen colonies, but refused to sit their representatives in Parliament. The Stamp Act of 1765 and the Townshend tax on paper, tea, and other imports raised indignant cries of "taxation without representation" and inflamed the rebellious mood of the Americans.

One of the most bitterly resented taxes was the Tea Act imposed by Lord North in 1773. It not only taxed Americans for the privilege of drinking tea, but it also restricted the tea trade to the British East India Company and certain merchants whose loyalty to the Crown was above reproach.

American retaliation was immediate and swift. In Boston, where angry patriots vowed to stop the sale of tea, a "Tea Party" was held on the night of December 16, 1773. A group of citizens disguised as Mowhawk Indians went to the waterfront, boarded English ships, and dumped 342 chests of tea into the harbor.

When England learned about the Boston Tea Party it hesitated only three short months before responding with the so-called Intolerable Acts, which further aroused the colonies. Revolution was not far away. *See Scott Stamp Nos. 1480-1483*

Perf. 10-1/2x11

1469	.16	.05	8c Osteopathic Medicine	Oct. 9

Issued for the 75th anniversary of the American Osteopathic Association, founded by Dr. Andrew T. Still.

Perf. 11

1470	.16	.05	8c American Folklore Issue	
				Oct. 13

Created by Mark Twain, Tom Sawyer is one of the most famous characters in American literature.

Perf. 10-1/2x11
Christmas Issue, Nov. 9

1471	.16	.03	8c Angel from
			"Mary, Queen of Heaven"
1472	.16	.03	8c Santa Claus

The design of 1471 is from a painting by the Master of the St. Lucy Legend in the National Gallery of Art, Washington, D.C.

Perf. 11

1473	.16	.05	8c Pharmacy Issue	Nov. 11

Honoring American druggists, this stamp was issued in connection with the 120th anniversary of the American Pharmaceutical Association.

1474	.16	.05	8c Stamp Collecting Issue	Nov. 17

Issued to publicize stamp collecting and in honor of the 125th anniversary of U.S. postage stamps. The design reproduces the first U.S. stamp.

Issues of 1973
Perf. 11x10-1/2

1475	.16	.05	8c Love Issue	Jan. 26

This "special stamp for someone special" depicts "Love" by contemporary artist Robert Indiana.

Perf. 11
American Revolution Bicentennial
Communications in Colonial America

1476	.20	.05	8c Printer and Patriots	
			Examining Pamphlet	Feb. 16

1477	.20	.05	8c Posting a Broadside	Apr. 13
1478	.20	.05	8c Postrider	Jun. 22
1479	.20	.05	8c Drummer	Sep. 28

Boston Tea Party, Jul. 4

1480	.18	.05	8c British Merchantman	
1481	.18	.05	8c British Three-master	
1482	.18	.05	8c Boats and Ship's Hull	
1483	.18	.05	8c Boat and Dock	
1483a	.72	.20	Block of four, Boston Tea Party	

Nos. 1476-1479 depict the "Rise of the Spirit of Independence" and honor communications in colonial America. Nos. 1480-1483 recall the Boston Tea Party of 1773. These four stamps, printed in a block of four, combine to make a complete design.

American Arts Issue

1484	.16	.05	8c George Gershwin	Feb. 28

American composer George Gershwin (1899-1937) created *Porgy and Bess, Rhapsody in Blue* and *An American in Paris.*

1485	.16	.05	8c Robinson Jeffers	Aug. 13

American poet Robinson Jeffers (1887-1926) wrote *Tamar and Other Poems. The Double Axe* and several plays, including a modern adaptation of *Medea.*

1486	.16	.05	8c Henry Ossawa Tanner	Sep. 10

American artist Henry Ossawa Tanner (1859-1937) is remembered for oils, drawings and water colors based on themes from the Bible.

1487	.16	.05	8c Willa Cather	Sep. 20

The works of American novelist Willa Cather (1873-1947) deal with history and life in the Midwest. They include *O Pioneer!, My Antonia,* and *Death Comes to the Archbishop.*

1488	.16	.05	8c Nicolaus Copernicus	Apr. 23

Polish astronomer Nicolaus Copernicus (1473-1543) altered man's conception of the universe by declaring that the earth revolves around the sun.

GEORGE GERSHWIN
(1898-1937)

You call it a waste of time, this taste
For popular tunes, and yet
Goodbye to care when you whistle the air
Of the song that you can't forget.
  G. W. Carryl "The Organ Man"

The syncopated jazz form of the "American folk music of the Machine Age" was created by the son of Jewish-Russian immigrants. George Gershwin had some formal training in harmony, but got most of his musical training in "Tin Pan Alley" working as a 'song plugger' in a music publishing house. His first success, "Swanee" (1919) was immortalized by the great jazz singer Al Jolson. "Rhapsody in Blue," a classic example of symphonic jazz, was written in 1924 after he had already become famous as the composer of the scores of eleven Broadway musicals. His tone poem "An American in Paris" (1928) incorporates elements of jazz with realistic sound effect and popular dance tunes.

George and his brother Ira, a gifted lyricist, produced the music for shows such as "Strike Up the Band," "Lady Be Good," "Girl Crazy," "Shall We Dance?" "Funny Face," "George White's Scandals," and the uproarious political satire "Of Thee I Sing" which was awarded a Pulitzer Prize in 1931. His last, and probably finest, work was "Porgy and Bess," a folk opera about the Negro residents of Charleston's Catfish Row, was first staged in Boston on September 30, 1935. Especially known for the songs "I Got Plenty O' Nothin'," "It Ain't Necessarily So," and "Summertime," it has been presented on stages in cities all over the world, and in 1959 it was made into a motion picture. George Gershwin died in Hollywood in 1937 while working on the score of "The Goldwyn Follies."

See Scott No. 1484

1485

1484

1486

1487

POSTAL PEOPLE ISSUE

This innovative series, inspired by the 1973 observance of Postal Week, is designed to honor the nation's 700,000 postal workers. These men and women are responsible for moving almost half the world's mail, or about 90 billion pieces every year. For the first time in U.S. postal history, the gum (back) side of each stamp bears a printed text relating to the picture on the face.

THE UNITED STATES POSTAL SERVICE

Neither snow, nor rain, nor heat, nor gloom of night stays these couriers from the swift completion of their appointed rounds.

These words, adapted from the Greek historian Herodotus (484-425 B. C.) have long been the pledge of the U. S. government's 740,000 Post Office Department employees.

With the inauguration of a new postal service, however, the pledge was transferred to a brand-new corporation. On July 1, 1971 the old Post Office became the United States Postal Service, a quasi-independent public utility.

The position of postmaster general is no longer a presidential cabinet post. He and his deputy will be appointed by a nine-member Board of Governors, who will manage the postal service much as a board of directors manages a modern corporation. Under the Postal Reorganization Act it is hoped that the postal system will become a modern, efficient operation that can use new ideas, new methods, and new machines to handle the great load of mail that passes through the world's largest post office. No longer subject to political patronage, the directors of the Service plan to serve their 204 million customers on the basis of sound business practice.

See Scott Stamp Nos. 1396, 1489-1498

THE TRUMAN ERA

The responsibility of great states is to serve and not dominate the world. Harry S. Truman.

Harry S. Truman (1884-1972), the son of a poor Missouri farmer, rose to become the 33rd president of the United States. On April 12, 1945, when Franklin Roosevelt died, the presidency passed on to then Vice-President Truman. Shortly afterwards the new president made the difficult decision to drop the atomic bomb on Japan. This decision, the first of many made by Truman, hastened Japan's surrender and the end of World War II.

In 1947 General George C. Marshall, Truman's secretary of state, proposed the Marshall Plan of economic aid to war-devastated Europe. The Marshall Plan was an outgrowth of the "Truman Doctrine", a policy of economic and military aid to countries threatened by aggression. In 1949 the North Atlantic Treaty Organization (NATO) was approved.

During Truman's first full term in office, which began in 1949, postwar international problems continued to overshadow domestic affairs. In 1950 armed hostilities erupted in Korea and U.S. troops were sent to the Orient as part of the U. N. forces supporting the government of South Korea. On March 29, 1952, Truman, who was lauded by Winston Churchill for making "great and valiant decisions," announced that he would not seek another term.

See Scott Stamp Nos. 1008, 1127, 1289, 1426, 1499

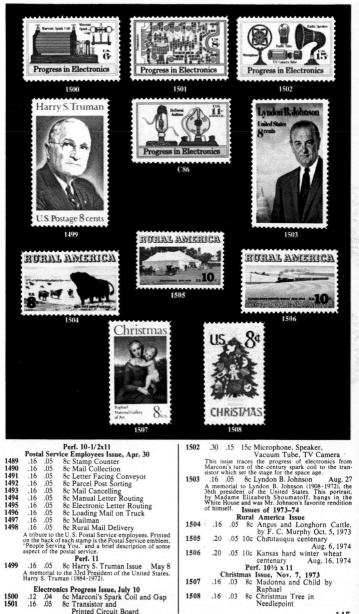

Perf. 10-1/2x11
Postal Service Employees Issue, Apr. 30

1489	.16	.05	8c Stamp Counter
1490	.16	.05	8c Mail Collection
1491	.16	.05	8c Letter Facing Conveyor
1492	.16	.05	8c Parcel Post Sorting
1493	.16	.05	8c Mail Cancelling
1494	.16	.05	8c Manual Letter Routing
1495	.16	.05	8c Electronic Letter Routing
1496	.16	.05	8c Loading Mail on Truck
1497	.16	.05	8c Mailman
1498	.16	.05	8c Rural Mail Delivery

A tribute to the U.S. Postal Service employees. Printed on the back of each stamp is the Postal Service emblem, "People Serving You," and a brief description of some aspect of the postal service.

Perf. 11

1499	.16	.05	8c Harry S. Truman Issue May 8

A memorial to the 33rd President of the United States, Harry S. Truman (1884-1972).

Electronics Progress Issue, July 10

1500	.12	.04	6c Marconi's Spark Coil and Gap
1501	.16	.05	8c Transistor and Printed Circuit Board
1502	.30	.15	15c Microphone, Speaker, Vacuum Tube, TV Camera

This issue traces the progress of electronics from Marconi's turn of the century spark coil to the transistor which set the stage for the space age.

1503	.16	.05	8c Lyndon B. Johnson Aug. 27

A memorial to Lyndon B. Johnson (1908-1972), the 36th president of the United States. This portrait, by Madame Elizabeth Shoumatoff, hangs in the White House and was Mr. Johnson's favorite rendition of himself. **Issues of 1973-74**

Rural America Issue

1504	.16	.05	8c Angus and Longhorn Cattle, by F. C. Murphy Oct. 5, 1973
1505	.20	.05	10c Chautauqua centenary Aug. 6, 1974
1506	.20	.05	10c Kansas hard winter wheat centenary Aug. 16, 1974

Perf. 10½ x 11
Christmas Issue, Nov. 7, 1973

1507	.16	.03	8c Madonna and Child by Raphael
1508	.16	.03	8c Christmas Tree in Needlepoint

SKYLAB STORY

What's it like to live on a space station? Nine astronauts found out—aboard Skylab, America's first space station. Orbiting 235 nautical miles in space, at 17,500 miles per hour, Skylab served as a home-workshop for three separate crews from May 1973 to February 1974. The first three man crew spent 28 days, and the second crew was aboard for 56 days. The third group of three returned to earth February 8, 1974, after a record-breaking 84 days in space. Today the space station still orbits the earth, silent and unmanned, awaiting the next family of astronauts.

During the nine months of the Skylab program, an incredible amount of scientific data was produced. Skylab proved beyond the shadow of a doubt that man can survive in space for months at a time without permanent ill effect and it gave us new insights into the natural resources of the earth. The program brought science a giant step closer to the secrets of the sun's energy transference, too. Skylab experiments also proved that welding, melting and purification of metals can be carried out far better in gravity-free space than they can on earth—which opens up the prospect of orbiting space factories in the future.

The astronauts of Skylab obtained some 182,800 astronomical photos. They also obtained 46,148 pictures and 54 miles of magnetically taped information of earth. Most of the data will take months, even years to process. We can only guess at the enormous significance that will eventually emerge from this mass of information.

No other major missions by American astronauts are planned now until the Apollo-Soyuz test project in July, 1975. In 1980 we shall see the beginning of the reusable space shuttle program. So the completion of the Skylab program marked the end of the first era of space flight. And it laid a firm foundation for man's far-flung future in space.

See Scott No. 1529

ROBERT FROST (1874-1963)

Robert Lee Frost wrote about New England, the land he knew and loved. His father, William Prescott Frost, Jr. was a head-master of a private school and later a newspaper reporter in San Francisco. It was in California that Robert Frost was born on March 26, 1874.

At the age of eleven, upon the death of his father, Frost moved to New England where, as as a young man, he worked as a farmer, editor and schoolmaster. In 1912, Frost sold his farm

and moved to England with his wife and children. "A Boy's Will" was accepted in 1913 by the first London publisher who read it. The next year, saw the publication of a new volume of poems, "North of Boston." Success and recognition were no longer denied to Robert Frost. Pultizer Prizes for poetry were awarded to him in 1924, 1931, 1937 and 1943. In 1960, the United States Congress voted Robert Frost a gold medal ". . . in recognition of his poetry . . ."

Inspired by landscapes and folkways, Robert Frost blended poetic forms with his own graceful style, always reaching for a deep involvement with nature. The poems of Robert Frost are both simple and profound . . . simple in so far as they reflect New England speech mannerisms and plain language, profound in that they capture the essence and quiet values of the New England way of life. It was for this reason that in January, 1961, Robert Frost was invited to recite his "The Gift Outright" at the inauguration of President John F. Kennedy.

See Scott No. 1526

Issues of 1974
Perf. 11 x 10½

1509	.20	.03	10c 50–Star and 13–Star Flags
1510	.20	.03	10c Jefferson Memorial and Signature
1510b	1.00		Booklet pane of 5
1510c	1.60		Booklet pane of 8
1510d	1.20		Booklet pane of 6
1511	.20	.03	10c Mail Transport; "Zip"

Coil Stamps, Perf. 10 Vertically

1518	.13	.07	6.3c Bells Oct. 1
1519	.20	.03	10c red & blue Flags, sia 1509
1520	.20	.03	10c blue Jefferson Memorial, sia 1510

Perf. 11

1525 .20 .05 10c V.F.W. Emblem   Mar. 11
75th anniversary of Veterans of Spanish-American and other Foreign Wars.

Perf. 10½ x 11

1526 .20 .05 10c Robert Frost   Mar. 26
Centenary of the birth of Robert Frost (1874-1963), American poet.

Perf. 11

1527 .20 .05 10c Cosmic Jumper and Smiling Sage, by Peter Max   Apr. 18
EXPO '74, Spokane, Wash. May 4-Nov. 4. Theme of the Exposition was "Preserve the Environment."

Perf. 11

1528 .20 .05 10c Horses Rounding Turn   May 4
Centenary of the Kentucky Derby, Churchill Downs.

Perf. 11

1529 .20 .05 10c Skylab II   May 14
First anniversary of the launching of Skylab I, and to honor all who participated in the Skylab projects.

Centenary of UPU Issue, June 6
Perf. 11

1530 .20 .05 10c Michelangelo, by Raphael

1531	.20	.05	10c "Five Feminine Virtues," by Hokusai
1532	.20	.05	10c Old Scraps, by John Fredrick Peto
1533	.20	.05	10c The Lovely Reader, by Jean Liotard
1534	.20	.05	10c Lady Writing Letter, by Gerard Terborch
1535	.20	.05	10c Inkwell and Quill, by Jean Chardin
1536	.20	.05	10c Mrs. John Douglas, by Thomas Gainsborough
1537	.20	.05	10c Don Antonio Noriega, by Francisco de Goya
1537a	1.60	.40	Block of eight, Nos. 1530–1537

Centenary of the Universal Postal Union. Nos. 1530-1537 printed in blocks of eight in panes of 32. The designs are details from famous paintings pertaining to letter writing. The quotation "Letters mingle souls" is from a letter by poet John Donne.

Mineral Heritage Issue, June 13
Perf. 11

1538	.20	.05	10c Petrified Wood
1539	.20	.05	10c Tourmaline
1540	.20	.05	10c Amethyst
1541	.20	.05	10c Rhodochrosite
1541a	.80	.20	Block of 4, Nos. 1538–1541

Nos. 1538–1541 printed in blocks of four in panes of 48.

Perf. 11

1542 .20 .05 10c Fort Harrod   June 15
Bicentenary of Fort Harrod, first settlement in Kentucky.

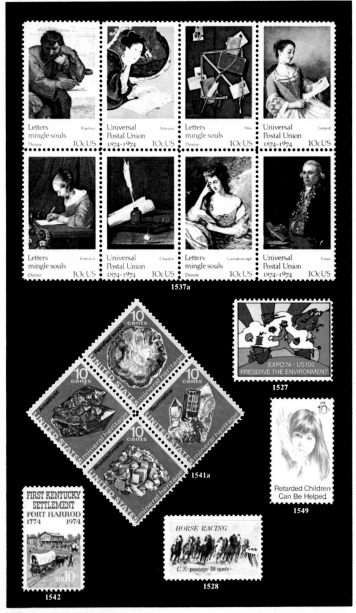

Letters mingle souls — Donne — Raphael — 10c US

Universal Postal Union 1874-1974 — Hokusai — 10c US

Letters mingle souls — Donne — Peto — 10c US

Universal Postal Union 1874-1974 — Liotard — 10c US

Letters mingle souls — Donne — Terborch — 10c US

Universal Postal Union 1874-1974 — Chardin — 10c US

Letters mingle souls — Donne — Gainsborough — 10c US

Universal Postal Union 1874-1974 — Goya — 10c US

1537a

10 cents — Petrified wood — UNITED STATES

10 cents — Amethyst — UNITED STATES — mineral heritage

10 cents — Tourmaline — UNITED STATES — mineral heritage

10 cents — Rhodochrosite — UNITED STATES — mineral heritage

1541a

EXPO'74 · US10c — PRESERVE THE ENVIRONMENT

1527

10c — Retarded Children Can Be Helped

1549

FIRST KENTUCKY SETTLEMENT FORT HARROD 1774 1974 — US 10c

1542

HORSE RACING — U.S. postage 10 cents

1528

148

THE UNIVERSAL POSTAL UNION

Possibly you've written letters to someone in another country. But chances are, you never stopped to think how many countries your letter may have to travel through before it reaches its destination...never stopped to wonder why a mailman in a foreign country will deliver your letter when the only stamps on it are United States stamps...not those of the country in which it is received. It's all part of international postal service, something we take for granted today. But if you'd mailed your letter just over a century ago, its path would have been difficult at best, and possibly never have been received.

It was under the administration of Montgomery Blair, the American Postmaster General in Lincoln's cabinet, that the idea of establishing an international agreement on postal rates and services originated. This resulted in the Paris Postal Congress of 1863. Delegates from the nations that had diplomatic relations with the U.S. gathered in Paris and drew up a list of recommendations for simplifying international postal service. The first step had been taken. The next one would be of even greater significance.

Heinrich von Stephan, brilliant young Minister of Posts of the German Empire, proposed a conference among European nations to discuss international postal service. Its purpose, to work out a world-wide postal agreement that would permit mail to cross borders as easily as it crossed cities. On September 15, 1874, delegates of 22 countries met in Berne, Switzerland.

At the time there were about 1,200 different postal rates for mail travelling between those 22 countries—each rate figured in local currency, and each based on different weight-and-measurement charts. In less than three conference weeks, that incredible tangle of rates was unraveled. On October 9, 1874, a treaty was signed that established uniform postal rates between nations, fixed international transit fees, and created out of 22 separate countries a single postal territory for the unhampered exchange of mail. At the same time, a permanent international postal organization was established with meetings to be held at regular intervals so that postal regulations could be kept up to date. It was called the General Postal Union at first. In 1878 the name was officially changed to the Universal Postal Union.

A permanent International Bureau was established at the 1874 Congress, too. It's located in Berne, Switzerland, supervised by the Swiss government, and financed by contributions from member countries. The Bureau serves as the Universal Postal Union's information center, its general accounting office, and as an intermediary for any changes in regulations that are proposed during the periods between full-scale meetings.

The Universal Postal Union's main regulation-making body, the Universal Postal Congress, meets every five years in a different member country. The 17th Congress, held in Lausanne, Switzerland from May to July, 1974, commemorated the 100th birthday of the Universal Postal Union. More than 150 member nations from all over the world were represented at this celebration. And they had something worth celebrating.

Despite political upheavals and global wars, the Universal Postal Union has, for more than a century, maintained international postal service.

See Scott Nos. 1530-37, C42-C44, C66

149

American Revolution Bicentennial
First Continental Congress, July 4
Perf. 11

1543	.20	.05	10c Carpenters' Hall
1544	.20	.05	10c "We ask but for Peace, Liberty and Safety"
1545	.20	.05	10c "Deriving their Just Powers.."
1546	.20	.05	10c Independence Hall
1546a	.80	.20	Block of four, Nos. 1543–1546

Nos. 1543–1546 printed in blocks of four in panes of 50.

Energy Conservation Issue
Perf. 11

1547	.20	.05	10c Molecules and drops of gasoline and oil Sept. 22

Protection and improvement of the environment while dealing with the fuel shortage. Issued during World Energy Conference, Detroit, Sept. 1974.

150

American Folklore Issue
Legend of Sleepy Hollow
Perf. 11

1548	.20	.05	10c The Headless Horseman Oct. 10

The Headless Horseman in pursuit of Ichabod Crane, from *Legend of Sleepy Hollow*, by Washington Irving.

Retarded Children Can Be Helped!
Perf. 11

1549	.20	.05	10c Little Girl Oct. 12

Annual Convention of the National Association of Retarded Children.

Christmas Issues, 1974, Oct. 23
Perf. 11

1550	.20	.03	10c Angel
1551	.20	.03	10c Sleigh Ride, by Currier and Ives

Imperf.
Self–adhesive

1552		.25	10c Weather Vane; precancelled

The weather vane shown on No. 1552 was designed by George Washington for Mount Vernon.

INDEX of U.S. Commemorative Issues

Stamps having related stories are indicated in **Bold Face** type.

151

Commemorative Stamps—Quantities Issued

The latest figures represented are based on reports of fiscal year July 1, 1973–June 30, 1974. All quantities listed are those stamps distributed to post offices.

Cat. No.	Quantity	Cat. No.	Quantity	Cat. No.	Quantity
230	449, 195, 550	646	9, 779, 896	740	84, 896, 350
231	1,464, 588, 750	647	5, 519, 897	741	74, 400, 200
232	11, 501, 250	648	1, 459, 897	742	95, 089, 000
233	19, 181, 550	649	51, 342, 273	743	19, 178, 650
234	35, 248, 250	650	10, 319, 700	744	30, 980, 100
235	4, 707, 550	651	16, 684, 674	745	16, 923, 350
236	10, 656, 550	654	31, 679, 200	746	15, 988, 250
237	16, 516, 950	655	210, 119, 474	747	15, 288, 700
238	1, 576, 950	656	133, 530, 000	748	17, 472, 600
239	617, 250	657	51, 451, 880	749	18, 874, 300
240	243, 750	658	13, 390, 000	750 (sheet of six)	511,391
241	55, 050	659	8, 240, 000	750a	3, 068, 346
242	45, 550	660	87, 410, 000	751 (sheet of six)	793, 551
243	27, 650	661	2, 540, 000	751a	4, 761, 306
244	26, 350	662	2, 290, 000	752	3, 274, 556
245	27, 350	663	2, 700, 000	753	2, 040, 760
285	70, 993, 400	664	1, 450, 000	754	2, 389, 288
286	159, 720, 800	665	1, 320, 000	755	2, 294, 948
287	4, 924, 500	666	1, 530, 000	756	3, 217, 636
288	7, 694, 180	667	1, 130, 000	757	2, 746, 640
289	2, 927, 200	668	2, 860, 000	758	2, 168, 088
290	4, 629, 760	669	8, 220, 000	759	1, 822, 684
291	530, 400	670	8, 990, 000	760	1, 724, 576
292	56, 900	671	73, 220, 000	761	1, 647, 696
293	56, 200	672	2, 110, 000	762	1, 682, 948
294	91, 401, 500	673	1, 600, 000	763	1, 638, 644
295	209, 759, 700	674	1, 860, 000	764	1, 625, 224
296	5, 737, 100	675	980, 000	765	1, 644, 900
297	7, 201, 300	676	850, 000	766 (pane of 25)	10,968
298	4, 921, 700	677	1, 480, 000	766a	2, 467, 800
299	5, 043, 700	678	530, 000	767 (pane of 25)	9, 546
323	79, 779, 200	679	1, 890, 000	767a	2, 147, 850
324	192, 732, 400	680	29, 338, 274	768 (pane of six)	10, 688
325	4, 542, 600	681	32, 680, 900	768a	1, 603, 200
326	6, 926, 700	682	74, 000, 774	769 (pane of six)	13, 998
327	4, 011, 200	683	25, 215, 574	769a	1, 679, 760
328	77, 728, 794	688	25, 609, 470	770 (pane of six)	10, 796
329	149, 497, 994	689	66, 487, 000	770a	1, 295, 520
330	7, 980, 594	690	96, 559, 400	771	1, 370, 560
367	148, 387, 191	702	99, 074, 600	772	70, 726, 800
368	1, 273, 900	703	25, 006, 400	773	100, 839, 600
369	637, 000	704	87, 969, 700	774	73, 610, 650
370	152, 887, 311	705	1, 265, 555, 100	775	75, 823, 900
371	525, 400	706	304, 926, 800	776	124, 324, 500
372	72, 634, 631	707	4, 222, 198, 300	777	67, 127, 650
373	216, 480	708	456, 198, 500	778 (sheet of four)	2, 809,039
397 410	334, 796, 926	709	151, 201, 300	778a	2, 809, 039
398 402	503, 713, 086	710	170, 565, 100	778b	2, 809, 039
399 403	29, 088, 726	711	111, 739, 400	778c	2, 809, 039
400 404	16, 968, 365	712	83, 257, 400	778d	2, 809, 039
537	99, 585, 200	713	96, 506, 100	782	72, 992, 650
548	137, 978, 207	714	75, 709, 200	783	74, 407, 450
549	196, 037, 327	715	147, 216, 000	784	269, 522, 200
550	11, 321, 607	716	51, 102, 800	785	105, 196, 150
610	1, 459, 487, 085	717	100, 869, 300	786	93, 848, 500
611	770, 000	718	168, 885, 300	787	87, 741, 150
612	99, 950, 300	719	52, 376, 100	788	35, 794, 150
614	51, 378, 023	724	49, 949, 000	789	36, 839, 250
615	77, 753, 423	725	49, 538, 500	790	104, 773, 450
616	5, 659, 023	726	61, 719, 200	791	92, 054, 550
617	15, 615, 000	727	73, 382, 400	792	93, 291, 650
618	26, 596, 600	728	348, 266, 800	793	34, 552, 950
619	5, 348, 800	729	480, 239, 300	794	36, 819, 050
620	9, 104, 983	730 (sheet of 25)	456, 704	795	84, 825, 250
621	1, 900, 983	730a	11, 417, 600	796	25, 040, 400
627	307, 731, 900	731 (sheet of 25)	441, 172	797	5, 277, 445
628	20, 280, 500	731a	11, 029, 300	798	99, 882, 300
629	40, 639, 485	732	1, 978, 707, 300	799	78, 454, 450
630 (sheet of 25)	107, 398	733	5, 735, 944	800	77, 004, 200
643	39, 974, 900	734	45, 137, 700	801	81, 292, 450
644	25, 628, 450	735 (sheet of six)	811,404	802	76, 474, 550
645	101, 330, 328	735a	4, 868, 424	835	73, 043, 650
		736	46, 258, 300	836	58, 564, 368
		737	193, 239, 100	837	65, 939, 500
		738	15, 432, 200	838	47, 064, 300
		739	64, 525, 400	852	114, 439, 600

Cat. No.	Quantity	Cat. No.	Quantity	Cat. No.	Quantity
853	101, 699, 550	941	132, 274, 500	1025	123, 709, 600
854	72, 764, 550	942	132, 430, 000	1026	114, 789, 600
855	81, 269, 600	943	139, 209, 500	1027	115, 759, 600
856	67, 813, 350	944	114, 684, 450	1028	116, 134, 600
857	71, 394, 750	945	156, 540, 510	1029	118, 540, 000
858	66, 835, 000	946	120, 452, 600	1060	115, 810, 000
859	56, 348, 320	947	127, 104, 300	1061	113, 603, 700
860	53, 177, 110	948	10, 299, 600	1062	128, 002, 000
861	53, 260, 270	949	132, 902, 000	1063	116, 078, 150
862	22, 104, 950	950	131, 968, 000	1064	116, 139, 800
863	13, 201, 270	951	131, 488, 000	1065	120, 484, 800
864	51, 603, 580	952	122, 362, 000	1066	53, 854, 750
865	52, 100, 510	953	121, 548, 000	1067	176, 075, 000
866	51, 666, 580	954	131, 109, 500	1068	125, 944, 400
867	22, 207, 780	955	122, 650, 500	1069	122, 284, 600
868	11, 835, 530	956	121, 953, 500	1070	133, 638, 850
869	52, 471, 160	957	115, 250, 000	1071	118, 664, 600
870	52, 366, 440	958	64, 198, 500	1072	112, 434, 000
871	51, 636, 270	959	117, 642, 500	1073	129, 384, 550
872	20, 729, 030	960	77, 649, 600	1074	121, 184, 600
873	14, 125, 580	961	113, 474, 500	1075	2, 900, 731
874	59, 409, 000	962	120, 868, 500	1076	119, 784, 200
875	57, 888, 600	963	77, 800, 500	1077	123, 159, 400
876	58, 273, 180	964	52, 214, 000	1078	123, 138, 800
877	23, 779, 000	965	53, 958, 100	1079	109, 275, 000
878	15, 112, 580	966	61, 112, 010	1080	112, 932, 200
879	57, 322, 790	967	57, 823, 000	1081	125, 475, 000
880	58, 281, 580	968	52, 975, 000	1082	117, 855, 000
881	56, 398, 790	969	77, 149, 000	1083	122, 100, 000
882	21, 147, 000	970	58, 332, 000	1084	118, 180, 000
883	13, 328, 000	971	56, 228, 000	1085	100, 975, 000
884	54, 389, 510	972	57, 832, 000	1086	115, 299, 450
885	53, 636, 580	973	53, 875, 000	1087	186, 949, 627
886	55, 313, 230	974	63, 834, 000	1088	115, 235, 000
887	21, 720, 580	975	67, 162, 200	1089	106, 647, 500
888	13, 600, 580	976	64, 561, 000	1090	112, 010, 000
889	47, 599, 580	977	64, 079, 500	1091	118, 470, 000
890	53, 766, 510	978	63, 388, 000	1092	102, 230, 000
891	54, 193, 580	979	62, 285, 000	1093	102, 410, 000
892	20, 264, 580	980	57, 492, 610	1094	84, 054, 400
893	13, 726, 580	981	99, 190, 000	1095	126, 266, 000
894	46, 497, 400	982	104, 790, 000	1096	39, 489, 600
895	47, 700, 000	983	108, 805, 000	1097	122, 990, 000
896	50, 618, 150	984	107, 340, 000	1098	174, 372, 800
897	50, 034, 400	985	117, 020, 000.	1099	114, 365, 000
898	60, 943, 700	986	122, 633, 000	1100	122, 765, 200
902	44, 389, 550	987	130, 960, 000	1104	113, 660, 200
903	54, 574, 550	988	128, 478, 000	1105	120, 196, 580
904	63, 558, 400	989	132, 090, 000	1106	120, 805, 200
906	21, 272, 800	990	130, 050, 000	1107	125, 815, 200
907	1, 671, 564, 200	991	131, 350, 000	1108	108, 415, 200
908	1, 227, 334, 200	992	129, 980, 000	1109	107, 195, 200
909	19, 999, 646	993	122, 315, 000	1110	115, 745, 280
910	19, 999, 646	994	122, 170, 000	1111	39, 743, 640
911	19, 999, 646	995	131, 635, 000	1112	114, 570, 200
912	19, 999, 646	996	121, 860, 000	1113	120, 400, 200
913	19, 999, 646	997	121, 120, 000	1114	91, 160, 200
914	19, 999, 646	998	119, 120, 000	1115	114, 860, 200
915	19, 999, 646	999	112, 125, 000	1116	126, 500, 000
916	14, 999, 646	1000	114, 140, 000	1117	120, 561, 280
917	14, 999, 646	1001	114, 490, 000	1118	44, 064, 576
918	14, 999, 646	1002	117, 200, 000	1119	118, 390, 200
919	14, 999, 646	1003	116, 130, 000	1120	125, 770, 200
920	14, 999, 646	1004	116, 175, 000	1121	114, 114, 280
921	14, 999, 646	1005	115, 945, 000	1122	156, 600, 200
922	61, 303, 000	1006	112, 540, 000	1123	124, 200, 200
923	61, 001, 450	1007	117, 415, 000	1124	120, 740, 200
924	60, 605, 000	1008	2, 899, 580, 000	1125	133, 623, 280
925	50, 129, 350	1009	114, 540, 000	1126	45, 569, 088
926	53, 479, 400	1010	113, 135, 000	1127	122, 493, 280
927	61, 617, 350	1011	116, 255, 000	1128	131, 260, 200
928	75, 500, 000	1012	113, 860, 000	1129	47, 125, 200
929	137, 321, 000	1013	124, 260, 000	1130	123, 105, 000
930	128, 140, 000	1014	115, 735, 000	1131	126, 105, 050
931	67, 255, 000	1015	115, 430, 000	1132	209, 170, 000
932	133, 870, 000	1016	136, 220, 000	1133	120, 835, 000
933	76, 455, 400	1017	114, 894, 600	1134	115, 715, 000
934	128, 357, 750	1018	118, 706, 000	1135	118, 445, 000
935	138, 863, 000	1019	114, 190, 000	1136	111, 685, 000
936	111, 616, 700	1020	113, 990, 000	1137	43, 099, 200
937	308, 587, 700	1021	89, 289, 600	1138	115, 444, 000
938	170, 640, 000	1022	114, 865, 000	1139	126, 470, 000
939	135, 927, 000	1023	115, 780, 000	1140	124, 560, 000
940	260, 339, 100	1024	115, 244, 600	1141	115, 455, 000

Cat. No.	Quantity	Cat. No.	Quantity	Cat. No.	Quantity
1142	122,060,000	1248	122,825,000	1382	139,055,000
1143	120,540,000	1249	453,090,000	1383	150,611,200
1144	113,075,000	1250	123,245,000	1384	1,709,795,000
1145	139,325,000	1251	123,355,000	1385	127,545,000
1146	124,445,000	1252	126,970,000	1386	145,788,800
1147	113,792,000	1253	121,250,000	1387-1390	201,794,200
1148	44,215,200	1254-1257	1,407,760,000	1391	171,850,000
1149	113,195,000	1258	120,005,000	1392	142,205,000
1150	121,805,000	1259	125,800,000	1405	137,660,000
1151	115,353,000	1260	122,230,000	1406	135,125,000
1152	111,080,000	1261	115,695,000	1407	135,895,000
1153	153,025,000	1262	115,095,000	1408	132,675,000
1154	119,665,000	1263	119,560,000	1409	134,795,000
1155	117,855,000	1264	125,180,000	1410-1413	161,600,000
1156	118,185,000	1265	120,135,000	1414-1418	1,950,000,000
1157	112,260,000	1266	115,405,000	1419	127,610,000
1158	125,010,000	1267	115,855,000	1420	129,785,000
1159	119,798,000	1268	115,340,000	1421-1422	134,380,000
1160	42,696,000	1269	114,840,000	1423	136,305,000
1161	106,610,000	1270	116,140,000	1424	134,840,000
1162	109,695,000	1271	116,900,000	1425	130,975,000
1163	123,690,000	1272	114,085,000	1426	161,235,000
1164	123,970,000	1273	114,880,000	1427-1430	175,679,600
1165	124,796,000	1274	26,995,000	1431	138,700,000
1166	42,076,800	1275	128,495,000	1432	138,165,000
1167	116,210,000	1276	1,139,930,000	1433	152,125,000
1168	126,252,000	1306	116,835,000	1434-1435	176,295,000
1169	42,746,400	1307	117,470,000	1436	142,845,000
1170	124,117,000	1308	123,770,000	1437	148,755,000
1171	119,840,000	1309	131,270,000	1438	139,080,000
1172	117,187,000	1310	122,285,000	1439	130,755,000
1173	124,390,000	1311	14,680,000	1440-1443	170,208,000
1174	112,966,000	1312	114,160,000	1444	1,074,350,000
1175	41,644,200	1313	128,475,000	1445	979,540,000
1176	110,850,000	1314	119,535,000	1446	137,355,000
1177	98,616,000	1315	125,110,000	1447	150,400,000
1178	101,125,000	1316	114,853,200	1448-1451	172,730,000
1179	124,865,000	1317	124,290,000	1452	104,090,000
1180	79,905,000	1318	128,460,000	1453	164,096,000
1181	125,410,000	1319	127,585,000	1454	53,920,000
1182	112,845,000	1320	115,875,000	1455	153,025,000
1183	106,210,000	1321	1,173,547,420	1456-1459	201,890,000
1184	110,810,000	1322	114,015,000	1460	67,335,000
1185	116,995,000	1323	121,105,000	1461	179,675,000
1186	121,015,000	1324	132,045,000	1462	46,340,000
1187	111,600,000	1325	118,780,000	1463	180,155,000
1188	110,620,000	1326	121,985,000	1464-1467	198,364,800
1189	109,110,000	1327	111,850,000	1468	185,490,000
1190	145,350,000	1328	117,225,000	1469	162,335,000
1191	112,870,000	1329	111,515,000	1470	162,789,950
1192	121,820,000	1330	114,270,000	1471	1,003,475,000
1193	289,240,000	1331-1332	120,865,000	1472	1,017,025,000
1194	120,155,000	1333	110,675,000	1473	165,895,000
1195	124,595,000	1334	110,670,000	1474	166,508,000
1196	147,310,000	1335	113,825,000	1475	328,440,000
1197	118,690,000	1336	1,208,700,000	1476	166,005,000
1198	122,730,000	1337	113,330,000	1477	162,800,000
1199	126,515,000	1339	141,350,000	1478	158,880,000
1200	130,960,000	1340	144,345,000	1479	146,545,000
1201	120,055,000	1342	147,120,000	1480-1483	195,470,000
1202	120,715,000	1343	130,125,000	1484	139,152,000
1203	121,440,000	1344	158,700,000	1485	128,048,000
1204	40,270,000	1345-1354	228,040,000	1486	146,008,000
1205	861,970,000	1355	153,015,000	1487	139,608,000
1206	120,035,000	1356	132,560,000	1488	159,475,000
1207	117,870,000	1357	130,385,000	1489-1498	486,020,000
1230	129,945,000	1358	132,265,000	1499	157,052,800
1231	135,620,000	1359	128,710,000	1500	53,005,000
1232	137,540,000	1360	124,775,000	1501	159,775,000
1233	132,435,000	1361	128,295,000	1502	39,005,000
1234	135,520,000	1362	142,245,000	1503	152,624,000
1235	131,420,000	1363	1,410,580,000	1504	145,840,000
1236	133,170,000	1364	125,100,000	1507	885,160,000
1237	130,195,000	1365-1368	192,570,000	1508	939,835,000
1238	128,450,000	1369	148,770,000	1525	143,930,000
1239	118,665,000	1370	139,475,000	1526	140,150,000
1240	1,291,250,000	1371	187,165,000	1527	127,116,000
1241	175,175,000	1372	125,555,000	1528	141,740,000
1242	125,995,000	1373	144,425,000	1529	160,280,000
1243	128,025,000	1374	135,875,000	1530-1537	157,398,400
1244	145,700,000	1375	151,110,000	1538-1541	148,065,000
1245	120,310,000	1376-1379	159,195,000	1542	136,575,000
1246	511,750,000	1380	129,540,000	1543-1546	139,615,000
1247	123,845,000	1381	130,925,000		

HISTORY OF FLIGHT

The desire to fly has long been a wish of man. Some of the earliest references to flight have appeared in ancient Greek, Egyptian and Oriental mythologies. In 1250, English philosopher Roger Bacon made the earliest recorded plan for a gas-filled balloon. By 1505 Leonardo da Vinci had published his essay and sketched detailed diagrams on human flight and various potential flying machines (one of which was a forerunner of the modern helicopter).

Man finally reached the sky in 1783 when Joseph and Etienne Montgolfier built and flew the first successful balloon. They crossed Paris, a distance of 6 miles at an altitude of 6,000 feet within 25 minutes. The first successful air venture marked the beginning of the balloon era, which was to flourish and gain popularity over the next hundred years.

The wish to be one with the sky took another turn by the late 19th century. Alberto Santos-Dumont, a Brazilian living in Paris, was experimenting with different flight techniques, and in 1898 introduced the motor-powered lighter-than-airship, a vehicle more balloon than ship-like in appearance. Santos-Dumont built sixteen airships altogether, most of them operated by small lightweight cooled-by-air motors, very much like motorcycle engines. Around the same time, other attempts were made to launch workable gliders, such as those by Otto Lilienthal of Germany and Octave Chanute of the United States.

Finally on December 17, 1903, after countless attempts, Wilbur and Orville Wright made their first successful airplane flight at Kitty Hawk, South Carolina. Their plane flew 825 feet in only 59 seconds, and airplane flying as we know it today, was born. Within two years, the Wright brothers developed a more sophisticated plane, the "Flyer No. 3" which could easily fly for half an hour, and perform such feats as turning, circling and flying in a figure-eight pattern.

European aviation was greatly stimulated in 1908 by the public air show given at LeMans, France by Wilbur Wright (brother Orville stayed home making acceptance flights for the U.S. Army). Two years earlier, the first European flight had been achieved by veteran Santos-Dumont in a box-kite style biplane.

Other European aviation pioneers included Louis Blériot and Henri Farman both of France.

Airplane flying became more and more widespread as well as sophisticated. Air racing contests were frequently held, with new records constantly being set... Louis Blériot made the first flight across the English Channel in 1909...the following year Glen Curtiss flew 152 miles from Albany to New York City in 2 hours and 46 minutes. Charles Lindbergh made his famous non-stop 33 hour 20 minute flight from New York City to Paris on May 20th-May 21st, 1927.

By World War I, the United States Army had an airsquadron, which consisted of eight aircraft and sixteen officers. In 1930, the Ford Tri-Motor, which could carry twelve passengers, began transcontinental service, and by 1933, United States commercial air travel was increasing at a rapid rate.

In 1959, the first jet to be used commercially in the United States, the Boeing 707, made its debut. Today, the huge 747 jumbo jet can carry over 300 passengers, while the U.S. Air Force XB-70A can fly three times the speed of sound.

157

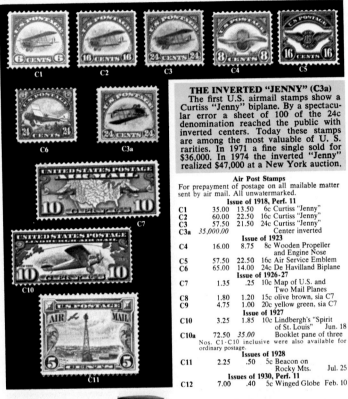

THE INVERTED "JENNY" (C3a)

The first U.S. airmail stamps show a Curtiss "Jenny" biplane. By a spectacular error a sheet of 100 of the 24c denomination reached the public with inverted centers. Today these stamps are among the most valuable of U. S. rarities. In 1971 a fine single sold for $36,000. In 1974 the inverted "Jenny" realized $47,000 at a New York auction.

Air Post Stamps

For prepayment of postage on all mailable matter sent by air mail. All unwatermarked.

Issue of 1918, Perf. 11			
C1	35.00	13.50	6c Curtiss "Jenny"
C2	60.00	22.50	16c Curtiss "Jenny"
C3	57.50	21.50	24c Curtiss "Jenny"
C3a	35,000.00		Center inverted
Issue of 1923			
C4	16.00	8.75	8c Wooden Propeller and Engine Nose
C5	57.50	22.50	16c Air Service Emblem
C6	65.00	14.00	24c De Havilland Biplane
Issue of 1926-27			
C7	1.35	.25	10c Map of U.S. and Two Mail Planes
C8	1.80	1.20	15c olive brown, sia C7
C9	4.75	1.00	20c yellow green, sia C7
Issue of 1927			
C10	3.25	1.85	10c Lindbergh's "Spirit of St. Louis" Jun. 18
C10a	72.50	*35.00*	Booklet pane of three

Nos. C1-C10 inclusive were also available for ordinary postage.

Issues of 1928			
C11	2.25	.50	5c Beacon on Rocky Mts. Jul. 25
Issues of 1930, Perf. 11			
C12	7.00	.40	5c Winged Globe Feb. 10

CHARLES A. LINDBERGH
(1902-   )

In 1927 at the age of twenty-five the "Lone Eagle", Charles A. Lindbergh, captured the world's imagination when he made the first solo non-stop New York to Paris flight in his single-engine *Spirit of St. Louis.*

The historic flight began at Roosevelt Field, New York, on May 20, at 7:53 A. M. and ended in Paris at 10 P. M. French time on May 21. It made Lindbergh a hero overnight. The recipient of medals from Great Britain, France, and the United States, Lindbergh received $250,000 from *The New York Times* for the rights to the story of his flight. His autobiography, *We,* was a national best seller. It was followed in 1953 by *The Spirit of St. Louis.*

See Scott Stamp No. C10

C12

C13

C14

C15

C18

C20

C21

			Graf Zeppelin Issue, Apr. 19
C13	175.00	110.00	65c Zeppelin Over Atlantic Ocean
C14	300.00	175.00	$1.30 Zeppelin Between Continents
C15	450.00	285.00	$2.60 Zeppelin Passing Globe

Issued for use on mail carried on the first Europe-Pan-America round trip flight of Graf Zeppelin, May, 1930.

			Issues of 1931–32, Perf. 10½ x 11
C16	3.00	.35	5c violet, sia C12
C17	1.00	.22	8c olive bistre, sia C12
			Issue of 1933, Perf. 11
C18	60.00	40.00	50c Century of Progress Oct. 2

Issued in connection with the flight of the "Graf Zeppelin" in October, 1933 to Miami, Akron, and Chicago, and from the last city to Europe.

			Issue of 1934, Perf. 10½ x 11
C19	.80	.10	6c dull orange, sia C12 Jun. 30
			Issue of 1935, Perf. 11
C20	1.50	1.10	25c Transpacific Nov. 22

Issued to pay postage on mail carried on the Transpacific air post service inaugurated Nov. 22, 1935.

			Issue of 1937
C21	4.50	2.00	20c The "China Clipper," Over the Pacific Feb. 15
C22	6.00	3.00	50c carmine, sia C21

Germany
Scott No. C35

"GRAF ZEPPELIN"

In 1929 the *Graf Zeppelin* became the first airship to fly around the world. Eight hundred feet long and one hundred feet wide, the giant dirigible held fifty passengers and could travel faster than 70 mph. The *Graf Zeppelin* made 590 flights before it was decommissioned in 1937. The developer of the dirigible, Count ("Graf" in German) Ferdinand von Zeppelin (1838-1917), was a retired German army officer.

Germany dominated the manufacture and commerce of airships until May 6, 1937, when the spectacular *Hindenburg* disaster by hydrogen fire ended passenger flights. In 1938, however, a second *Graf Zeppelin* which operated on noninflammable helium was completed. But also in 1938 the United States refused to export helium to Germany, and the new *Zeppelin* made no commercial flights. In April 1940 both *Graf Zeppelins* were dismantled by Nazi directive.

See Scott Stamp Nos. C13-C15, C18

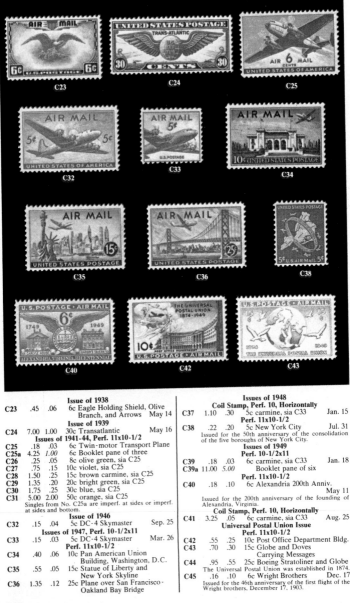

		Issue of 1938	
C23	.45	.06	6c Eagle Holding Shield, Olive Branch, and Arrows May 14
		Issue of 1939	
C24	7.00	1.00	30c Transatlantic May 16
		Issues of 1941-44, Perf. 11x10-1/2	
C25	.18	.03	6c Twin-motor Transport Plane
C25a	4.25	1.00	6c Booklet pane of three
C26	.25	.05	8c olive green, sia C25
C27	.75	.15	10c violet, sia C25
C28	1.50	.25	15c brown carmine, sia C25
C29	1.35	.20	20c bright green, sia C25
C30	1.75	.25	30c blue, sia C25
C31	5.00	2.00	50c orange, sia C25

Singles from No. C25a are imperf. at sides or imperf. at sides and bottom.

		Issue of 1946	
C32	.15	.04	5c DC-4 Skymaster Sep. 25
		Issues of 1947, Perf. 10-1/2x11	
C33	.15	.03	5c DC-4 Skymaster Mar. 26
		Perf. 11x10-1/2	
C34	.40	.06	10c Pan American Union Building, Washington, D.C.
C35	.55	.05	15c Statue of Liberty and New York Skyline
C36	1.35	.12	25c Plane over San Francisco-Oakland Bay Bridge

		Issues of 1948	
		Coil Stamp, Perf. 10, Horizontally	
C37	1.10	.30	5c carmine, sia C33 Jan. 15
		Perf. 11x10-1/2	
C38	.22	.20	5c New York City Jul. 31

Issued for the 50th anniversary of the consolidation of the five boroughs of New York City.

		Issues of 1949	
		Perf. 10-1/2x11	
C39	.18	.03	6c carmine, sia C33 Jan. 18
C39a	11.00	5.00	Booklet pane of six
		Perf. 11x10-1/2	
C40	.18	.10	6c Alexandria 200th Anniv. May 11

Issued for the 200th anniversary of the founding of Alexandria, Virginia.

		Coil Stamp, Perf. 10, Horizontally	
C41	3.25	.05	6c carmine, sia C33 Aug. 25
		Universal Postal Union Issue	
		Perf. 11x10-1/2	
C42	.55	.25	10c Post Office Department Bldg.
C43	.70	.30	15c Globe and Doves Carrying Messages
C44	.95	.55	25c Boeing Stratoliner and Globe

The Universal Postal Union was established in 1874.

C45	.16	.10	6c Wright Brothers Dec. 17

Issued for the 46th anniversary of the first flight of the Wright brothers, December 17, 1903.

C44

C45

C46

C47

C49

C54

C48

C51

C53

			Issue of 1952					Issues of 1958	
C46	4.75	1.00	80c Diamond Head, Honolulu, Hawaii Mar. 26		C50	.22	.08	5c rose red, sia C48	
			Issue of 1953					Perf. 10½ x 11	
C47	.16	10	6c Powered Flight May 29		C51	.22	.03	7c Silhouette of Jet Liner Jul. 31	
			Issued for the 50th anniversary of powered flight.		C51a	15.00	6.50	Booklet pane of six	
			Issue of 1954					Coil Stamp, Perf. 10 Horizontally	
C48	.12	.08	4c Eagle in Flight Sep. 3		C52	5.00	.18	7c blue, sia C51	
			Issue of 1957					Issues of 1959, Perf. 11 x 10½	
C49	.20	.10	6c Air Force Aug. 1		C53	.25	.12	7c Alaska Statehood Jan. 3	
			Issued for the 50th anniversary of the U.S. Air Force.						

THE WRIGHT BROTHERS AT KITTY HAWK

If you are looking for perfect safety, you will do well to sit on a fence and watch the birds ... Wilbur Wright

At 10:30 A.M. on December 17, 1903, Orville (1871-1948) and Wilbur Wright (1867-1912) made the first successful airplane flight. The scene was Kitty Hawk, North Carolina, where steady winds and high sand dunes had long been ideal for the gliding hobby of the Wright brothers, two young bicycle repairmen from Dayton, Ohio.

Plane and pilot weighed 750 pounds. The wings were wooden frames strung together with piano wire and spanned forty feet, six inches. The biplane, propelled by a twelve horsepower, four-cylinder gasoline engine, stayed aloft twelve seconds and flew 120 feet. On this first historic journey Orville piloted the brothers' revolutionary vehicle. At noon Wilbur set the record for the day, a flight of 852 feet in 59 seconds.

See Scott Stamp Nos. 649-650, C45

		Perf. 11	
C54	.25	.12	7c Balloon Jupiter	Aug. 17

Issued for the 100th anniversary of the carrying of mail by the balloon Jupiter from Lafayette to Crawfordsville, Indiana.

Perf. 11 x 10½

| C55 | .25 | .12 | 7c Hawaii Statehood | Aug. 21 |

Hawaii became a state in 1959.

Perf. 11

| C56 | .40 | .25 | 10c Pan–American Games | Aug. 27 |

Issued for the 3rd Pan-American Games, held at Chicago from Aug. 27-Sep. 7, 1959.

Issue of 1959–66

C57	1.75	.25	10c Liberty Bell
C58	.75	.06	15c Statue of Liberty
C59	.65	.06	25c Abraham Lincoln

Issue of 1960, Perf. 10½ x 11

| C60 | .28 | .05 | 7c Jet Airliner | Aug. 12 |
| C60a | 22.50 | 7.00 | Booklet pane of six |

Coil Stamp, Perf. 10 Horizontally

| C61 | 6.50 | .25 | 7c carmine, sia C60 | Oct. 22 |

Issue of 1961–67, Perf. 11

| C62 | .35 | .10 | 13c Liberty Bell |
| C63 | .35 | .08 | 15c Statue of Liberty |

No. C63 has a gutter between the two parts of the design; No. C58 does not.

AMELIA EARHART (1898-1937)

The bravest thing I did was to try to drop a bag of oranges and a note on the head of an ocean liner's captain — and I missed the whole ship!

Thus remarked Amelia Earhart on June 17, 1928, when she became the first woman passenger to fly the Atlantic Ocean. In spite of such protests, her courage and daring made her an international celebrity. In 1932 she soloed across the Atlantic and in 1935 conquered the Pacific (Hawaii to California). In 1937, she began a 27,000 mile round-the-world flight. With Fred Noonan navigating, Miss Earhart completed the next-to-last leg of her journey in late June. In July radio contact was lost. Their bodies were never found, and their deaths remain shrouded in mystery.

See Scott Stamp No. C68

Surinam Scott No. 346

Issue of 1962–64
Perf. 10½ x 11

C64 .18 .03 8c Jetliner over Capitol Dec. 5
C64b 5.00 .75 Booklet pane of 5 + label
Coil Stamp, Perf. 10 Horizontally
C65 .45 .08 8c carmine, sia C64 Dec. 5
Nos. C64 and C65 were issued on Dec. 5, 1962.

Issue of 1963, Perf. 11
C66 1.35 .50 15c Montgomery Blair May 3
Montgomery Blair (1813-1883), was Postmaster General from 1861-1864. In 1863 he called the first International Postal Conference, which was a forerunner of the Universal Postal Union.

Issues of 1963–67
C67 .15 .08 6c Bald Eagle Jul. 12, 1963
Perf. 11
C68 .30 .10 8c Amelia Earhart Jul. 24
Amelia Earhart (1898-1937), was the first woman to fly across the Atlantic.

Issue of 1964
C69 .90 .15 8c Robert H. Goddard Oct. 5
Dr. Robert H. Goddard (1882-1945), was a physicist and a pioneer rocket researcher.

1962-68

Issues of 1967
C70 .65 .12 8c Alaska Purchase Mar. 30
Issued for the 100th anniversary of the Alaska Purchase, this stamp shows a Tlingit totem from southern Alaska.
C71 .70 .15 20c "Columbia Jays"
by Audubon Apr. 26
See note after 1241.

Issues of 1968, Perf. 11 x 10½
C72 .20 .03 10c carmine Jan. 5
C72b 2.25 .75 Booklet pane of eight
C72c 2.00 .75 Booklet pane of 5 + label

Coil Stamp, Perf. 10
C73 .25 .04 10c carmine, sia C72
The $1 Air Lift stamp is listed as No. 1341.

Air Mail Service Issue
Perf. 11
C74 .60 .10 10c Curtiss Jenny May 15
Issued for the 50th anniversary of regularly scheduled U.S. air mail service.
C75 .60 .06 20c U.S.A. and Jet Nov. 22

MONTGOMERY BLAIR (1813-1883)
United States Postmaster General — 1861-1864

At the time President Lincoln appointed Montgomery Blair as Postmaster General, mailing a letter to a foreign country was not a simple matter. The cost of postage to any one country could vary from 5c to $1.02, depending on the steamship route or the country owning the ship. Postal administrations the world over were bogged down with complex accounting systems. Very few people, including many postal clerks, were able to figure out the complicated rate charts.

Montgomery Blair proposed an international conference of postal officials to discuss mutual problems and prepared the way for the Paris Conference, which convened May 11, 1863 with fifteen nations represented. The thirty-one principles resulting from the Conference laid the groundwork for the formation of the General Postal Union in 1874. At the Paris Congress of 1878, the membership agreed to change the name to the Universal Postal Union in order to reflect the world wide scope of the organization.

"Sir: Many embarrassments to foreign correspondence exist in this and probably in other postal departments which can be remedied only by international convert of action."
Montgomery Blair to the
Secretary of State August 4, 1862
See Scott Nos. C42-C44, C66, 1530-1537

C67   C69   C70   C71   C72   C74   C75

AIR MAIL IN AMERICA

The development of the airplane and the accelerated growth of aviation in the first half of the twentieth century revolutionized the delivery of mail. Parts of the world that once were weeks away from the United States can now be reached in hours.

The pioneer in the use of the airplane as a commercial carrier was the Post Office Department. Regularly scheduled domestic air mail service was introduced in 1918, overseas service began in the 1930's, and after World War II direct air mail service to every continent was established. Today, American planes cover over 300,000 miles of foreign routes, carrying mail from the United States to the most distant points on the globe.

Issue of 1969

C76	.25	.10	10c Moon Landing	Sep. 9

Issues of 1971–73
Perf. 10½ x 11, 11 x 10½

C77	.18	.06	9c Plane	May 15, 1971
C78	.22	.03	11c Silhouette of Jet	May 7, 1971
C78a	.90	.40	Booklet pane of 4 + 2 labels	
C79	.26	.13	13c Winged Airmail Envelope	Nov. 16, 1973
C79a	1.35	.70	Booklet pane of 5 + label	Dec. 27, 1973

Perf. 11

C80	.34	.15	17c Statue of Liberty	Jul. 13, 1971

Perf. 11 x 10½

C81	.42	.21	21c red, blue and black. sia C75	May 21, 1971

Coil Stamp, Perf. 10 Vertically

C82	.22	.06	11c Silhouette of Jet	May 7, 1971
C83	.26	.13	13c red, sia C79	Dec. 27, 1973

Issues of 1972, Perf. 11

C84	.22	.11	11c City of Refuge	May 3

The City of Refuge National Park, 180 acres on island of Hawaii, preserves Polynesian temples royal tombs.

Perf. 11 x 10½

C85	.22	.11	11c Skiing and Olympic Rings	Aug. 17

Issued in honor of the 1972 Olympic Games.

Issue of 1973

C86	.30	.11	11c De Forest Audions	Jul. 10

Issued to note the progress of electronics from Marconi to the space age.

Issues of 1974, Perf. 11

C87	.36	.18	18c Statue of Liberty	Jan. 11
C88	.52	.26	26c Mt. Rushmore National Memorial	Jan. 2

Air Post Special Delivery Stamps

To provide for the payment of both the postage and the special delivery of one stamp.

Issue of 1934, Perf. 11

. CE1	.60	.55	16c dark blue, sia CE2

For imperforate variety, see No. 771.

Issue of 1936

CE2	.45	.18	16c Great Seal of United States

Special Delivery Stamps

When affixed to any letter or mailable article, ordinarily secures separate, speedy delivery.

Unwmkd.
Issue of 1885, Perf. 12

E1	57.50	11.50	10c Messenger Running

Issue of 1888

E2	52.50	3.00	10c blue, sia E3

Issue of 1893

E3	20.00	5.25	10c Messenger Running

Issue of 1894, Line under "Ten Cents"

E4	135.00	6.50	10c Messenger Running

Issue of 1895
Wmkd. USPS **(191)**

E5	14.00	1.00	10c blue, sia E4

Issue of 1902

E6	12.00	1.00	10c Messenger on Bicycle

Issue of 1908

E7	8.75	8.00	10c Mercury Helmet and Olive Branch

Issue of 1911
Wmkd. USPS **(190)**

E8	14.00	1.20	10c ultramarine, sia E6

Issue of 1914, Perf. 10

E9	40.00	1.85	10c ultramarine, sia E6

Unwmkd.
Issue of 1916

E10	70.00	8.50	10c ultramarine, sia E6

Issue of 1917, Perf. 11

E11	4.25	.18	10c ultramarine, sia E6

Issue of 1922

E12	6.25	.10	10c Postman and Motorcycle

Issue of 1925

E13	3.75	.20	15c Postman and Motorcycle
E14	1.25	.60	20c Post Office Truck

Issues of 1927, Perf. 11 x 10½

E15	.35	.04	10c Postman and Motorcycle

Issue of 1931

E16		.50	.08	15c orange, sia E12

Issue of 1944

E17	.35	.06	13c Postman and Motorcycle
E18	1.30	.65	17c Postman and Motorcycle

Issue of 1951

E19	.65	.12	20c black, sia E14

Issue of 1954–57

E20	.55	.08	20c Delivery of Letter
E21	.75	.04	30c Delivery of Letter

Issue of 1969–71, Perf. 11

E22	1.50	.08	45c Arrows
E23	1.20	.12	60c Arrows

F1

FA1

Registration Stamp

Issued for the prepayment of registry; not usable for postage. Sales discontinued May 28, 1913.

Issue of 1911, Perf. 12
Wmkd. USPS (190)

F1	30.00 2.00	10c Bald Eagle

Certified Mail Stamp

For use on first–class mail for which no indemnity value is claimed, but for which proof of mailing and proof of delivery are available at less cost than registered mail.

Issue of 1955, Perf. 10½ x 11

FA1	.50 .30	15c Letter Carrier

Postage Due Stamps

For affixing by a postal clerk to any mail to denote amount to be collected from addressee because of insufficient prepayment of postage.

Printed by American Bank Note Company
Issue of 1879, Design of J2, Perf. 12 Unwmkd.

J1	3.25	1.25	1c brown
J2	27.50	1.75	2c Figure of Value
J3	1.35	.60	3c brown
J4	22.50	6.00	5c brown
J5	65.00	3.00	10c brown
J6	12.00	6.00	30c brown
J7	30.00	12.00	50c brown

Special Printing

J8	1600.00		1c deep brown
J9	800.00		2c deep brown
J10	800.00		3c deep brown
J11	600.00		5c deep brown
J12	600.00		10c deep brown
J13	450.00		30c deep brown
J14	450.00		50c deep brown

Regular Issue of 1884–89 Design of J19, Perf.12

J15	2.50	.90	1c red brown
J16	1.50	.80	2c red brown
J17	55.00	20.00	3c red brown
J18	15.00	2.50	5c red brown
J19	15.00	1.35	10c Figure of Value
J20	15.00	7.25	30c red brown
J21	165.00	40.00	50c red brown

Issue of 1891–93 Design of J25, Perf. 12

J22	.50	.15	1c bright claret
J23	.75	.10	2c bright claret
J24	1.35	1.00	3c bright claret
J25	2.00	1.00	5c Figure of Value
J26	4.75	2.00	10c bright claret
J27	30.00	17.50	30c bright claret
J28	32.50	20.00	50c bright claret

Printed by the Bureau of Engraving and Printing
Issue of 1894 Design of J33, Perf. 12

J29	55.00	17.50	1c vermilion
J30	17.50	9.50	2c vermilion
J31	1.25	1.00	1c deep claret
J32	1.00	.50	2c deep claret
J33	6.00	4.75	3c Figure of Value
J34	9.00	5.50	5c deep claret
J35	5.25	3.50	10c deep rose
J36	27.50	13.50	30c deep claret
J37	57.50	32.50	50c deep claret

Issue of 1895, Design of J33, Perf. 12

Wmkd. USPS (191)

J38	.30	.12	1c deep claret
J39	.30	.08	2c deep claret
J40	1.60	.45	3c deep claret
J41	1.60	.35	5c deep claret
J42	2.00	.55	10c deep claret
J43	30.00	5.00	30c deep claret
J44	9.50	5.75	50c deep claret

Issue of 1910–12 Design of J33, Perf. 2

Wmkd. USPS (190)

J45	1.25	.75	1c deep claret
J46	.80	.08	2c deep claret
J47	37.50	4.00	3c deep claret
J48	3.75	.65	5c deep claret
J49	3.75	1.50	10c deep claret
J50	85.00	16.00	50c deep claret

Issue of 1914–15, Design of J33, Perf. 10

J52	4.75	2.50	1c carmine lake
J53	1.50	.12	2c carmine lake
J54	45.00	2.50	3c carmine lake
J55	1.50	.75	5c carmine lake
J56	2.50	.30	10c carmine lake
J57	8.50	5.50	30c carmine lake
J58	550.00	125.00	50c carmine lake

Issue of 1916, Design of J33, Perf. 10
Unwmkd.

J59	150.00	50.00	1c rose
J60	4.00	.60	2c rose

Issue of 1917, Design of J33, Perf. 11

J61	.08	.05	1c carmine rose
J62	.15	.04	2c carmine rose
J63	.45	.08	3c carmine rose
J64	.45	.08	5c carmine rose
J65	.55	.20	10c carmine rose
J66	2.75	.30	30c carmine rose
J67	3.50	.08	50c carmine rose

Issue of 1925, Design of J33, Perf. 11

J68	.12	.06	½c dull red

Issue of 1930–31, Design of J69, Perf. 11

J69	.40	.18	½c Figure of Value
J70	.35	.10	1c carmine
J71	.45	.10	2c carmine
J72	2.25	.40	3c carmine
J73	2.00	.50	5c carmine
J74	2.75	.30	10c carmine
J75	6.00	.50	30c carmine
J76	6.00	.12	50c carmine

Design of J78

J77	3.75	.12	$1 carmine
J78	13.00	.18	$5 "FIVE" on $

Issue of 1931–56, Design of J69
Perf. 11 x 10½

J79	.10	.08	½c dull carmine
J80	.05	.03	1c dull carmine
J81	.06	.03	2c dull carmine
J82	.10	.03	3c dull carmine
J83	.15	.03	5c dull carmine
J84	.30	.03	10c dull carmine
J85	1.20	.08	30c dull carmine
J86	1.75	.06	50c dull carmine

Perf. 10½ x 11

J87	3.75	.20	$1 scarlet, same design as J78

Issue of 1959, Perf. 11 x 10½
Design of J88 and J98

J88	.50	.30	½c Figure of Value
J89	.04	.04	1c carmine rose
J90	.06	.05	2c carmine rose
J91	.07	.04	3c carmine rose
J92	.08	.04	4c carmine rose
J93	.10	.04	5c carmine rose
J94	.12	.05	6c carmine rose
J95	.14	.05	7c carmine rose
J96	.16	.05	8c carmine rose
J97	.20	.04	10c carmine rose
J98	.70	.05	30c Figure of Value
J99	1.10	.06	50c carmine rose

Design of J101

J100	2.00	.05	$1 carmine rose
J101	8.00	.15	$5 Outline Figure of Value

Parcel Post Postage Due Stamps

For affixing by a postal clerk, to any parcel post package, to denote the amount to be collected from the addressee because of insufficient prepayment of postage.
Beginning July 1, 1913, these stamps were valid for use as regular postage due stamps.

Issue of 1912

Wmkd. USPS (190)

Design of JQ1 and JQ5
Perf. 12

JQ1	2.00	1.25	1c Figure of Value
JQ2	12.50	6.00	2c dark green
JQ3	2.35	1.85	5c dark green
JQ4	30.00	15.00	10c dark green
JQ5	12.50	1.50	25c Figure of Value

United States Offices in China

Issued for sale by the postal agency at Shanghai, China, at their surcharged value in local currency. Valid to the amount of their original values for the prepayment of postage on mail dispatched from the United States postal agency at Shanghai to addresses in the United States.

Issue of 1919, Perf. 11
K1–K7: Washington, sia K1

K1	3.00	3.50	2c on 1c Washington
K2	3.00	3.50	4c on 2c rose
K3	4.25	4.75	6c on 3c violet
K4	5.50	6.75	8c on 4c brown
K5	7.25	9.00	10c on 5c blue
K6	7.75	9.50	12c on 6c red orange
K7	7.75	9.50	14c on 7c black

K8–K16: Franklin, sia K8

K8	7.00	9.00	16c on 8c Franklin
K9	7.00	8.50	18c on 9c salmon red
K10	5.75	6.00	20c on 10c orange yellow
K11	7.50	9.50	24c on 12c brown carmine
K12	9.00	10.00	30c on 15c gray
K13	9.00	10.00	40c on 20c deep ultramarine
K14	10.00	12.50	60c on 30c orange red
K15	80.00	80.00	$1 on 50c light violet
K16	32.50	32.50	$2 on $1 violet brown

Issue of 1922

K17	12.50	12.50	2c on 1c Washington
K18	13.50	13.50	4c on 2c Washington

U.S. Stamps of 1917-19 Surcharged:

U.S. Stamp Nos. 498 and 528B Surcharged:

1873

Official Stamps

The franking privilege having been abolished, as of July 1, 1873, these stamps were provided for each of the departments of Government for the prepayment on official matter.

These stamps were supplanted on May 1, 1879 by penalty envelopes and on July 5, 1884 were declared obsolete.

Designs are as follows: Post Office officials, figures of value and department name; all other departments, various portraits and department names.

O6   **O7**

Issues of 1873
Printed by the Continental Bank Note Co.
Thin Hard Paper
Dept. of Agriculture: Yellow

O1	12.00	10.00	1c Franklin
O2	4.25	4.25	2c Jackson
O3	3.50	1.10	3c Washington
O4	6.00	4.00	6c Lincoln
O5	15.00	13.00	10c Jefferson
O6	27.50	20.00	12c Clay
O7	15.00	13.00	15c Webster
O8	17.50	15.00	24c Winfield Scott
O9	22.50	18.50	30c Hamilton

Executive Dept.

O10	55.00	40.00	1c carmine, Franklin
O11	32.50	27.50	2c Jackson
O12	40.00	20.00	3c carmine, Washington
O13	57.50	45.00	6c carmine, Lincoln
O14	55.00	40.00	10c Jefferson

Dept. of the Interior: Vermilion

O15	1.35	1.20	1c Franklin
O16	1.00	.80	2c Jackson
O17	5.00	.75	3c Washington
O18	3.00	.80	6c Lincoln

O11   **O14**

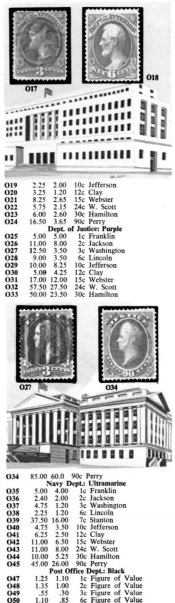

O17   **O18**

O19	2.25	2.00	10c Jefferson
O20	3.25	1.20	12c Clay
O21	8.25	2.65	15c Webster
O22	5.75	2.15	24c W. Scott
O23	6.00	2.60	30c Hamilton
O24	16.50	3.65	90c Perry

Dept. of Justice: Purple

O25	5.00	5.00	1c Franklin
O26	11.00	8.00	2c Jackson
O27	12.50	3.50	3c Washington
O28	9.00	3.50	6c Lincoln
O29	10.00	8.25	10c Jefferson
O30	5.00	4.25	12c Clay
O31	17.00	12.00	15c Webster
O32	57.50	27.50	24c W. Scott
O33	50.00	23.50	30c Hamilton

O27   **O34**

O34	85.00	60.0	90c Perry

Navy Dept.: Ultramarine

O35	5.00	4.00	1c Franklin
O36	2.40	2.00	2c Jackson
O37	4.75	1.20	3c Washington
O38	2.25	1.20	6c Lincoln
O39	37.50	16.00	7c Stanton
O40	4.75	3.50	10c Jefferson
O41	6.25	2.50	12c Clay
O42	11.00	6.50	15c Webster
O43	11.00	8.00	24c W. Scott
O44	10.00	5.25	30c Hamilton
O45	45.00	26.00	90c Perry

Post Office Dept.: Black

O47	1.25	1.10	1c Figure of Value
O48	1.35	1.00	2c Figure of Value
O49	.55	.30	3c Figure of Value
O50	1.10	.85	6c Figure of Value

O51	7.25	6.25	10c Figure of Value
O52	3.25	2.00	12c Figure of Value
O53	3.50	2.65	15c Figure of Value
O54	5.00	3.25	24c Figure fo Value
O55	4.00	2.25	30c Figure of Value
O56	4.50	2.65	90c Figure of Value

Dept. of State

O57	4.25	3.50	1c dark green Franklin
O58	9.25	7.00	2c dark green Jackson
O59	3.00	2.65	3c bright green Washington
O60	2.65	2.50	6c bright green Lincoln
O61	7.00	5.25	7c dark green Stanton

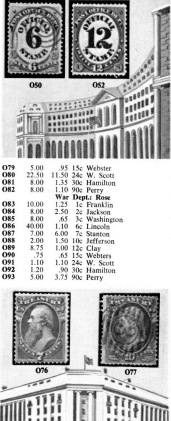

O50   O52

O57

O71

O62	4.75	4.00	10c dark green Jefferson
O63	11.00	10.00	12c dark green Clay
O64	6.25	5.75	15c dark green Webster
O65	24.00	18.00	24c dark green W. Scott
O66	20.00	16.50	30c Hamilton
O67	45.00	31.50	90c dark green Perry
O68	100.00	60.00	$2 green and black Seward
O69	850.00	465.00	$5 green and black Seward
O70	500.00	350.00	$10 green and black Seward
O71	425.00	300.00	$20 Seward

Treasury Dept.: Brown

O72	2.00	.75	1c Franklin
O73	2.50	.70	2c Jackson
O74	1.50	.35	3c Washington
O75	1.75	.40	6c Lincoln
O76	5.00	3.00	7c Stanton
O77	4.25	1.25	10c Jefferson
O78	4.25	.65	12c Clay

O44   O91

O79	5.00	.95	15c Webster
O80	22.50	11.50	24c W. Scott
O81	8.00	1.35	30c Hamilton
O82	8.00	1.10	90c Perry

War Dept.: Rose

O83	10.00	1.25	1c Franklin
O84	8.00	2.50	2c Jackson
O85	8.00	.65	3c Washington
O86	40.00	1.10	6c Lincoln
O87	7.00	6.00	7c Stanton
O88	2.00	1.50	10c Jefferson
O89	8.75	1.00	12c Clay
O90	.75	.65	15c Webters
O91	1.10	1.10	24c W. Scott
O92	1.20	.90	30c Hamilton
O93	5.00	3.75	90c Perry

O76   O77

Issues of 1879
Printed by the American Bank Note Co.
Soft, Porous Paper
Dept. of Agriculture: Yellow

O94	375.00		1c Franklin, issued without gum
O95	35.00	7.00	3c Washington

Dept. of the Interior: Vermilion

O96	20.00	16.00	1c Franklin
O97	.55	.55	2c Jackson
O98	.45	.35	3c Washington
O99	.55	.55	6c Lincoln
O100	5.75	5.25	10c Jefferson
O101	10.00	8.00	12c Clay
O102	22.50	18.50	15c Webster
O103	285.00		24c W. Scott

Dept. of Justice: Bluish Purple

O106	7.50	6.00	3c Washington
O107	20.00	15.00	6c Lincoln

Post Office Dept.
O108	1.35	.90	3c black, Figure of Value

Treasury Dept.: Brown
O109	3.75	1.00	3c Washington
O110	7.50	5.00	6c Lincoln
O111	11.00	3.00	10c Jefferson
O112	160.00	40.00	30c Hamilton
O113	160.00	50.00	90c Perry

War Dept.
O114	.45	.45	1c Franklin
O115	.70	.65	2c rose red, Jackson
O115a	.80	.75	2c dull vermilion, Jackson
O116	.55	.35	3c rose red, Washington
O116a	425.00		3c Imperf. (pair)
O117	.45	.40	6c rose red, Lincoln
O118	2.75	3.00	10c rose red, Jefferson
O119	1.40	1.00	12c rose red, Clay
O120	6.50	6.50	30c rose red, Hamilton

O93   O95

O101   O114

O121   O122   O123

O124   O125   O126

Official Postal Savings Mail
Perf. 12
These stamps were used to prepay postage on official correspondence of the Postal Savings Division of the Post Office Department.
Discontinued Sept. 23, 1914

Issues of 1911

Wmkd. **USPS** (191)

O121	2.00	.55	2c Official Postal Savings
O122	20.00	8.50	50c Official Postal Savings
O123	11.00	3.25	$1 Official Postal Savings

Wmkd. **USPS** (190)

O124	1.35	.50	1c Official Postal Savings
O125	5.00	1.25	2c Official Postal Savings
O126	2.00	.50	10c Official Postal Savings

NEWSPAPER STAMPS

The spread of popular education and improved production methods in the mid-1800's led to the rise of the mass penny press. Because the mails were used for bulk shipments of newspapers, the U.S. Post Office issued special stamps for them beginning in 1865. Many of these stamps were not used on mail, but were cancelled by postal clerks and kept on file. Because the stamps did not circulate, used copies are quite rare and valuable. Newspaper issues also include the largest U.S. stamps and denominations are quite high—up to $100. When the stamps were discontinued, on July 1, 1898, collectors persuaded the post office to sell the remainders. Sold at $5 a set, this is the only time in history that the post office has sold stamps at a discount.

Newspaper Stamps
Perf. 12
Issues of 1865
Printed by the National Bank Note Co.
Thin, Hard Paper, No Gum, Unwmkd.
Colored Borders
PR1	52.50		5c Washington
PR2	20.00		10c Franklin
PR3	20.00		25c Lincoln

White Border, Yellowish Paper
PR4	13.00	11.00	5c light blue, sia PR1

Reprints of 1875
Printed by the Continental Bank Note Co.
Hard, White Paper, No Gum
PR5	25.00		5c dull blue, sia PR1, white border
PR6	16.50		10c dark bluish green, sia PR2, colored border
PR7	25.00		25c dark carmine, sia PR3, colored border

Issue of 1880
Printed by the American Bank Note Co.
Soft, Porous Paper, White Border
PR8	37.50		5c dark blue, sia PR1

Issue of 1875
Printed by the Continental Bank Note Co.
Thin, Hard Paper
PR9–PR15: "Statue of Freedom", sia PR15

PR9	2.50	1.75	2c black
PR10	4.25	2.75	3c black
PR11	3.50	2.50	4c black
PR12	4.75	3.75	6c black
PR13	5.50	5.00	8c black
PR14	8.00	7.00	9c black
PR15	4.25	3.25	10c Statue of Freedom

PR16–PR23: "Justice", sia PR18

PR16	6.00	5.00	12c rose
PR17	10.50	8.00	24c rose
PR18	12.00	10.00	36c "Justice"
PR19	25.00	12.50	48c rose
PR20	12.00	9.00	60c rose
PR21	32.50	25.00	72c rose
PR22	35.00	25.00	84c rose
PR23	27.50	20.00	96c rose
PR24	21.00	12.50	$1.92 Ceres
PR25	30.00	17.00	$3 "Victory"
PR26	75.00	42.50	$6 Clio
PR27	87.50	50.00	$9 Minerva
PR28	87.50	55.00	$12 Vesta
PR29	90.00	55.00	$24 "Peace"
PR30	125.00	90.00	$36 "Commerce"

PR31	200.00	135.00	$48.00 red brown Hebe, sia PR78
PR32	190.00	125.00	$60.00 violet Indian Maiden, sia PR79

Special Printing, Hard, White Paper, Without Gum
PR33–PR39: Statue of Freedom, sia PR15

PR33	15.00	2c gray black
PR34	15.00	3c gray black
PR35	15.00	4c gray black
PR36	16.00	6c gray black
PR37	16.00	8c gray black
PR38	16.00	9c gray black
PR39	25.00	10c gray black

PR40–PR47: "Justice", sia PR18

PR40	47.50	12c pale rose
PR41	65.00	24c pale rose
PR42	75.00	36c pale rose
PR43	95.00	48c pale rose
PR44	120.00	60c pale rose
PR45	175.00	72c pale rose
PR46	185.00	84c pale rose
PR47	210.00	96c pale rose
PR48	*850.00*	$1.92 dark brown Ceres, sia PR24
PR49	*1200.00*	$3 vermilion "Victory", sia PR25

PR1   PR2   PR3

PR15   PR18   PR24   PR25   PR26

PR27   PR28   PR29   PR30   PR78   PR79

PR50		$6 ultra. Clio, sia PR26
PR51		$9 yel. Minerva, sia PR27
PR52		$12 bl. grn. Vesta, sia PR28
PR53		$24 dark gray violet "Peace", sia PR29
PR54		$36 brown rose "Commerce", sia PR30
PR55		$48 red brown Hebe, sia PR78
PR56		$60 violet Indian Maiden, sia PR79

All values of this issue Nos. PR33 to PR56 exist imperforate but were not regularly issued. (See Scott's U.S. Specialized Catalogue.)

Issue of 1879
Printed by the American Bank Note Co.
Soft, Porous Paper
PR57–PR62: Statue of Freedom, sia PR15

PR57	1.35	1.20	2c black
PR58	1.65	1.30	3c black
PR59	1.75	1.75	4c black
PR60	4.25	4.00	6c black
PR61	4.25	4.00	8c black
PR62	4.00	2.75	10c black

PR63–PR70: "Justice", sia PR18

PR63	11.00	7.75	12c red
PR64	11.00	6.00	24c red
PR65	47.50	25.00	36c red
PR66	32.50	20.00	48c red
PR67	67.50	45.00	60c red
PR68	45.00	35.00	72c red
PR69	45.00	35.00	84c red
PR70	35.00	25.00	96c red
PR71	20.00	15.00	$1.92 pale brown Ceres, sia PR24
PR72	21.50	16.00	$3 red vermilion "Victory", sia PR25
PR73	42.50	30.00	$6 blue Clio, sia PR26
PR74	27.50	20.00	$9 org. Minerva, sia PR27
PR75	37.50	25.00	$12 yellow green Vesta, sia PR28
PR76	57.50	35.00	$24 dark violet "Peace", sia PR29
PR77	67.50	45.00	$36 Indian red, "Commerce", sia PR30
PR78	75.00	50.00	$48 Hebe

PR79	75.00	50.00	$60 Indian Maiden

All values of the 1879 issue except Nos. PR63 to PR66 and PR68 to PR70 exist imperforate but were not regularly issued.

Issue of 1883
Special Printing

PR80	50.00	2c intense black Statue of Freedom, sia PR15

Regular Issue of 1885

PR81	1.25	1.10	1c black Statue of Freedom, sia PR15

PR82–PR89: "Justice", sia PR18

PR82	4.50	3.50	12c carmine
PR83	5.75	5.00	24c carmine
PR84	7.50	6.00	36c carmine
PR85	10.00	8.00	48c carmine
PR86	15.00	11.50	60c carmine
PR87	20.00	13.00	72c carmine
PR88	40.00	27.50	84c carmine
PR89	25.00	20.00	96c carmine

All values of the 1885 issue exist imperforate but were not regularly issued.

Issue of 1894
Printed by the Bureau of Engraving and Printing
Soft Wove Paper
PR90–PR94: Statue of Freedom, sia PR90

PR90	2.50	1c Statue of Freedom
PR91	2.75	2c intense black
PR92	4.50	4c intense black
PR93	375.00	6c intense black
PR94	7.00	10c intense black

PR95–PR99: "Justice", sia PR18

PR95	40.00	12c pink
PR96	25.00	24c pink
PR97	250.00	36c pink
PR98	250.00	60c pink
PR99	350.00	96c pink
PR100	*750.00*	$3 scarlet "Victory" sia PR25
PR101	*1200.00*	$6 pale blue Clio, sia PR26

Issue of 1895, Unwmkd.
PR102–PR105: Statue of Freedom, sia PR116

PR102	2.50	1.35	1c black
PR103	2.75	1.75	2c black
PR104	3.00	2.25	5c black
PR105	8.50	5.75	10c black

PR90   PR116   PR118   PR119   PR120

GROWTH OF A FREE PRESS

Were it left to me to decide whether we should have a government without newspapers, or newspapers without a government, I should not hesitate to prefer the latter. Thomas Jefferson

The first newspaper in the American colonies, published in 1690, promptly came under government attack. But by the time of the American Revolution the right to freedom of the press was firmly established and since then journalists have been among our most influential citizens. Most important of the early printers was Benjamin Franklin who in 1729 bought the *Pennsylvania Gazette.* In 1737 Franklin was appointed postmaster of Pennsylvania and began the practice of cheap and fast distribution of the news through the mails. Later editors such as Horace Greeley and Frederick Douglass helped institute social reforms including the abolition of slavery. Such men began the traditions of modern journalism. In addition to dispensing the news, newspapers began to include informational and educational features. Directed at the masses, newspapers spread education and culture, creating an enlightened citizenry to lead the growth and direction of the nation.

See Scott Stamp Nos. 946, 1073, 1119, 1177, 1290, 1476

PR106	9.00	6.50	25c carmine "Justice", sia PR118
PR107	25.00	15.00	50c carmine "Justice", sia PR119
PR108	18.50	6.00	$2 scarlet "Victory", sia PR120
PR109	40.00	21.50	$5 ultra. Clio, sia PR121
PR110	37.50	19.00	$10 green Vesta, sia PR122
PR111	72.50	37.50	$20 slate "Peace", sia PR123
PR112	72.50	25.00	$50 dull rose "Commerce", sia PR124
PR113	85.00	47.50	$100 purple Indian Maiden, sia PR125

Issue of 1895–97

Wmkd. **USPS** (191)

Yellowish Gum

PR114	.80	.70	1c black, Statue of Freedom, sia PR116

PR115	.75	.60	2c black, Statue of Freedom, sia PR116
PR116	1.60	1.40	5c Statue of Freedom
PR117	.85	.65	10c black, Statue of Freedom, sia PR116
PR118	1.50	1.20	25c "Justice"
PR119	1.75	1.10	50c "Justice"
PR120	2.50	1.85	$2 "Victory"
PR121	5.00	5.00	$5 Clio
PR122	3.00	4.75	$10 Vesta
PR123	3.00	5.50	$20 "Peace"
PR124	4.00	5.50	$50 "Commerce"
PR125	5.00	6.50	$100 Indian Maiden

In 1889 the Government sold 26,989 sets of these stamps, but, as the stock of the high values was not sufficient to make up the required number, the $5, $10, $20, $50 and $100 were reprinted. These are virtually indistinguishable from earlier printings.

PR121 PR122 PR123 PR124 PR125

Q1 Q2 Q3
Q4 Q5 Q6
Q7 Q8 Q9
Q10 Q11 Q12
QE1 QE2 QE3 QE4

PARCEL POST STAMPS

Issued for the prepayment of postage on parcel post packages only.

Beginning July 1, 1913, these stamps were valid for all postal purposes.

Wmkd. USPS (190)

Issue of 1912–13, Perf. 12

Q1	1.10	.55	1c Post Office Clerk
Q2	1.15	.40	2c City Carrier
Q3	3.00	2.00	3c Railway Postal Clerk
Q4	7.25	.95	4c Rural Carrier
Q5	5.50	.50	5c Mail Train
Q6	9.00	.80	10c Steamship and Mail Tender
Q7	14.00	4.50	15c Automobile Service
Q8	25.00	5.50	20c Airplane Carrying Mail
Q9	10.00	1.75	25c Manufacturing
Q10	57.50	18.50	50c Dairying
Q11	11.50	7.25	75c Harvesting
Q12	80.00	7.25	$1 Fruit Growing

SPECIAL HANDLING STAMPS

For use on parcel post packages to secure the same expeditious handling accorded to first class mail matter.

Issue of 1925–29, Design of QE3
Perf. 11

QE1	.50	.25	10c Special Handling
QE2	.70	.35	15c Special Handling
QE3	1.00	.65	20c Special Handling
QE4	4.75	3.75	25c Special Handling

UNITED STATES POST OFFICE
& U.S.P.S.
SOUVENIR CARDS

These cards were issued as souvenirs of the philatelic gatherings at which they were distributed by the United States Postal Service, its predecessor the United States Post Office Department, or the Bureau of Engraving and Printing. They were not valid for postage.

Most of the cards bear reproductions of United States stamps with the design enlarged or altered. The U.S. reproductions are engraved except stamps Nos. 914, 1396, 1460-1462 and C85. The cards are not perforated.

Cards for international exhibitions were issued by the U.S.P.O.D. or U.S.P.S. and were given to visitors without charge. Cards for national exhibitions were issued by the Bureau which usually sold them for $1 at the event. Most of the Postal Service cards were available for $1 from the Philatelic Sales Unit, Washington, D.C.

A forerunner of the souvenir cards is the 1938 Philatelic Truck souvenir sheet which the Post Office Department issued and distributed in various cities visited by the Philatelic Truck. It shows the White House, printed in blue on white paper. Issued with and without gum. Price, with gum, $25; without gum, $10.

1960

200.00 Barcelona, 1st International Philatelic Congress, Mar. 26-Apr. 5, 1960. Enlarged vignette, Landing of Columbus from No. 231. Printed in black.

1968

7.50 EFIMEX, International Philatelic Exhibition, Nov. 1-9, 1968, Mexico City. No. 292 enlarged to 58x37½ mm. Card inscribed in Spanish.

5.00 PHILYMPIA, London International Stamp Exhibition, Sept. 18-26, 1970. Card of 3. Nos. 548-550 enlarged 1½ times.

1971

2.00 EXFILIMA 71, 3rd Inter-American Philatelic Exhibition, Nov. 6-14, 1971, Lima, Peru. Card of 3. Nos. 1111 and 1126 with "8c" and "Postage" removed. Reproduction of Peru No. 360. Card inscribed in Spanish.

1972

2.50 BELGICA 72, Brussels International Philatelic Exhibition, June 24-July 9, 1972, Brussels, Belgium. Card of 3. No. 914 enlarged to 56x34mm. Nos. 1026 and 1104 with denomination, etc. removed. Card inscribed in Flemish and French.

2.00 Olympia Philatelie München 72, Aug. 18-Sept. 10, 1972, Munich, Germany. Card of 4. Nos. 1460-1462 and C85 enlarged to 54x32mm. Card inscribed in German.

2.00 EXFILBRA 72, 4th Inter-American Philatelic Exhibition, Aug. 26-Sept. 2, 1972, Rio de Janeiro, Brazil. Card of 3. No. C14 enlarged to 69½x28½ mm. and reproductions of Brazil Nos. C18-C19. Card inscribed in Portuguese.

175

INTERNATIONALE BRIEFMARKEN AUSSTELLUNG
IBRA 73

MÜNCHEN

11.-20. MAI 1973

Diese Andenkenkarte wird zu Ehren der Internationalen Briefmarkenausstellung IBRA 73 in München ausgegeben. Auf der Karte ist die 65 cent-Luftpostbriefmarke, die in einer Sonderserie anlässlich des ersten Fluges des Luftpostschiffs "Graf Zeppelin" von Europa nach Nord- und Südamerika im Mai 1930 herausgegeben wurde, abgebildet. Die Briefmarke zeigt "Graf Zeppelin" auf seinem Rückflug über den Atlantik.

E. T. Klassen
Postmaster General

THE COPYING OF THIS PRINT IS RESTRICTED BY TITLE 18 U. S. C. WHICH PROHIBITS THE UNAUTHORIZED REPRODUCTION, IN WHOLE OR IN PART, OF CURRENCY, POSTAGE STAMPS, OR OTHER SECURITIES OF THE UNITED STATES.

2.00 National Philatelic Forum VI, Aug. 28-30, 1972, Washington, D.C. Card of 4 No. 1396 enlarged to 26x31mm.

1973

2.00 IBRA 73 Internationale Briefmarken Ausstellung, Munich, May 11-20, 1973, with one No. C13 enlarged to 70x29mm.

2.00 APEX 73, International Airmail Exhibition, Manchester, England, July 4-7, 1973. Card of 3. Reproductions of Newfoundland No. C4, U.S. No. C3a and Honduras No. C12.

2.00 POLSKA 73, Swiatowa Wystawa Filatelisyczna, Poznan, Poland, Aug. 19-Sept. 2, 1973.

INTERNATIONAL AIRMAIL EXHIBITION
APEX 73

MANCHESTER, ENGLAND

JULY 4-7, 1973

This souvenir card is issued in compliment to the 50th anniversary of the Aero Philatelic Club of London, and its Exhibition at Manchester APEX 73. Depicted on the card is the United States 24-cent airmail stamp of 1918 showing the Curtis "Jenny" vignette inverted. On the left of this stamp is the rare De Pinedo Newfoundland airmail of 1927; and on the right the very rare Honduras airmail surcharge of 1925.

E. T. Klassen
Postmaster General

THE COPYING OF THIS PRINT IS RESTRICTED BY TITLE 18 U. S. C. WHICH PROHIBITS THE UNAUTHORIZED REPRODUCTION, IN WHOLE OR IN PART, OF CURRENCY, POSTAGE STAMPS, OR OTHER SECURITIES OF THE UNITED STATES.

176

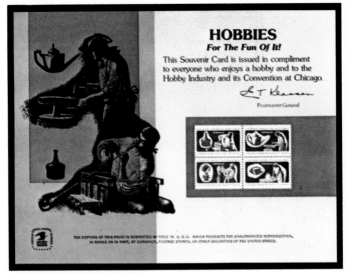

2.00   HOBBY, The Hobby Industry Association of America Convention and Trade Show, February 3-6, 1974. Chicago, Illinois. Reproduction of American Revolution Bicentennial Issue, Colonial Craftsman Block of Four.

2.00   INTERNABA, International Philatelic Exhibition, June 7-16, 1974. Basel, Switzerland. Reproduction (photogravure) of Nos. 1530-1537. Se-tenant strip of eight. Card inscribed in 4 languages.

1974

2.00   STOCKHOLMIA '74, International frimarksustallning, September 21-29, 1974. Stockholm, Sweden. Card of 3. No. 836, Sweden Nos. 300 and 765.

2.00   EXFILMEX 74 UPU, Philatelic Exposition Interamericana, October 26-November 3, 1974. Mexico City, Mexico. Card of 2. No. 1157 and Mexico No. 910. Card inscribed in Spanish and English.

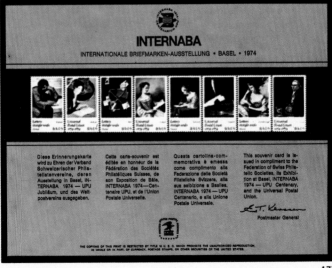

BUREAU OF ENGRAVING
& PRINTING

SOUVENIR CARDS

1954

600.00 Postage Stamp Design Exhibition, National Philatelic Museum, Mar. 13, 1954, Philadelphia. Card of 4. Monochrome views of Washington, D.C. Inscribed: "Souvenir sheet designed, engraved and printed by members, Bureau, Engraving and Printing. / Reissued by popular request".

1966

85.00 SIPEX, 6th International Philatelic Exhibition, May 21-30, 1966, Washington, D.C. Card of 3. Multicolored views of Washington, D.C. Inscribed: "Sixth International Philatelic Exhibition / Washington, D.C. / Designed, Engraved, and Printed by Union Members of Bureau of Engraving and Printing".

1969

40.00 SANDIPEX, San Diego Philatelic Exhibition, July 16-20, 1969, San Diego, Cal. Card of 3. Multicolored views of Washington, D.C. Inscribed: "Sandipex — San Diego 200th Anniversary — 1769-1969".

15.00 A.S.D.A. National Postage Stamp Show, Nov. 21-23, 1969, New York. Card of 4. No. E4 reengraved. Denomination and "United States" removed.

1970

35.00 INTERPEX, Mar. 20-22, 1970, New York. Card of 4. Nos. 1027, 1035, C35 and C38 reengraved. Denomination, country name and "Postage" or "Air Mail" removed.

15.00 COMPEX, Combined Philatelic Exhibition of Chicagoland, May 29-31, 1970, Chicago. Card of 4 No. C18 reengraved. Denomination and "United States Postage" removed.

17.50 HAPEX, American Philatelic Society Convention, Nov. 5-8, 1970, Honolulu, Hawaii. Card of 3. Nos. 799, C46 and C55 reengraved. Denomination, etc. removed.

1971

5.00 INTERPEX, Mar. 12-14, 1971, New York. Card of 4 No. 1193 reengraved. "4c" removed. Background tint includes enlargements of Nos. 1331-1332, 1371 and C76.

4.00 WESTPEX, Western Philatelic Exhibition, Apr. 23-25, 1971, San Francisco. Card of 4. Nos. 740, 852, 966 and 997. Denomination, etc. removed.

2.50 NAPEX 71, National Philatelic Exhibition, May 21-23, 1971, Washington, D.C. Card of 3. Nos. 990, 991, 992. Denomination, etc. removed.

2.50 TEXANEX 71, Texas Philatelic Association and American Philatelic Society conventions, Aug. 26-29, 1971, San Antonio, Tex. Card of 3. Nos. 938, 1043 and 1242. Denomination, etc. removed.

2.00 A.S.D.A. National Postage Stamp Show, Nov. 19-21, 1971, New York. Card of 3. Nos. C13-C15. Denomination, etc. removed.

2.00 ANPHILEX '71, Anniversary Philatelic Exhibition, Nov. 26-Dec. 1, 1971, New York. Card of 2. Nos. 1-2. Denomination, etc. removed.

1972

2.50 INTERPEX, Mar. 17-19, 1972, New York. Card of 4 No. 1173. Denomination, etc. removed. Background tint includes enlargements of Nos. 976, 1434-1435 and C69.

2.50 NOPEX, Apr. 6-9, 1972, New Orleans. Card of 4 No. 1020. Denomination, etc. removed. Background tint includes enlargements of Nos. 323-327.

2.00 SEPAD '72, Oct. 20-22, 1972, Philadelphia. Card of 4 No. 1044 with denomination, etc. removed.

2.00 A.S.D.A. National Postage Stamp Show, Nov. 17-19, 1972, New York. Card of 4. Nos. 883, 863, 868 and 888 with denominations, etc. removed.

2.00 STAMP EXPO, Nov. 24-26, 1972, San Francisco. Card of 4 No. C36 with denomination, etc. removed.

1973

2.00 INTERPEX, March 9-11, 1973, New York. Card of 4 No. 976 with denomination, etc. removed.

2.00 COMPEX 73, May 25-27, 1973, Chicago. Card of 4 No. 245 with denomination, etc. removed.

1974

2.00 MILCOPEX, March 8-10, 1974, Milwaukee, Wisconsin. Card of 4, No. C43. Denomination, etc. removed. Background tint depicts U.P.U. monument at Berne, Switzerland.

POSTAL STATIONERY

Another category of collectibles available at post offices is a group of three items of postal stationery — stamped envelopes, postal cards and aerogrammes. The number of postal stationery enthusiasts in the United States continues to grow each year as many collectors discover that more than stamps are available in this fascinating hobby.

STAMPED ENVELOPES

An increasing number of commemorative stamped envelopes have been issued by the United States in recent years. The most recent of these is the envelope issued in 1974 marking the 100th anniversary of the introduction of lawn tennis into the United States.

Stamped envelopes were first issued in June 1853 and are, by law, manufactured for the Postal Service under private contract, let to the lowest bidder for a term of 4 years.

The largest number of stamped envelopes manufactured in a single day was 19,168,000 in 1932. The contractor was working at full speed to produce the large quantity of envelopes needed for initial distribution to post offices throughout the country to conform to a new rate.

Envelopes bearing the purchaser's printed return card were authorized by law in 1865. Today, envelopes bearing the buyer's printed return address are very popular.

The average yearly issues of stamped envelopes are in excess of 1.2 billion, having a sales value of about $120 million.

Stamped envelopes are issued in a number of sizes and styles, including the window type, to meet the general requirements of the public. Envelopes with distinctive red, white, and blue borders have been provided for airmail letters. The colored border enables the detection of airmail letters more readily when mixed with other mail.

The variety of recent themes of postal cards has made them extremely attractive to collectors. For example, three cards have been issued in a series saluting colonial patriots as a part of the commemoration of the Bicentennial of the American Revolution. The latest of these was the 8-cent card honoring Samuel Adams, issued in 1973.

The first U.S. commemorative postal card was issued in 1956. The first pictorial postal card was issued in 1966 with a "Visit the USA" theme. In 1972, a series of five picture postal cards focused attention on "Tourism Year of the Americas." Twenty different scenic attractions in the U.S. appeared on the backs of the cards.

Regular type one-color Government postal cards were first issued May 1, 1873. They are now manufactured at the Government Printing Office in Washington, D.C., by means of four high-speed rotary web presses with a capacity of 250,000 completed cards an hour per press. Approximately 2,500 tons of paper are consumed in printing the normal yearly supply of about 800 million postal cards required for issuance by the Postal Service. Two-color air mail and multi-color commemorative postal cards are also manufactured at the Government Printing Office by means of two-color sheet-fed offset presses.

AEROGRAMMES

An aerogramme is a mailing piece which folds to normal letter size and carries a message by air to any place in the world at a rate lower than regular airmail.

Similar to other items of postal stationery, the issuance of commemorative aerogrammes has increased recently. During the past year, for example, a commemorative aerogramme was issued marking the 25th anniversary of the signing of the North Atlantic Treaty and the formation of NATO.

Aerogrammes are produced by the Bureau of Engraving and Printing on the Andreotti press which can execute multi-color stamp designs as well as applying a phosphor tag and gumming the sealing flaps.

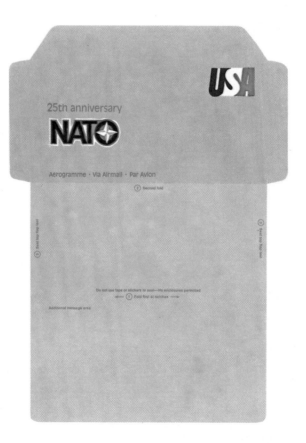

AEROGRAMME • VIA AIRMAIL • PAR AVION

② Second fold

③ Seal top flap last

JEFFERSON DAVIS (1808-89)

While Grant and Lee fought on the bloody battlefields of the Civil War, Jefferson Davis waged an insurmountable war to provide food and guns for his troops. Early in the war Davis, the first and only president of the Confederate States of America, had seen that it would be a long fight and had chosen his military leaders well—such as Robert E. Lee and Stonewall Jackson. But in spite of tactical victories, the agricultural South could not hold out against the industrial North, and Davis was faced with a crumbling economy and a short-sighted congress in Richmond, Virginia. Despite such odds Davis managed to keep the South together for four long years. Following the Confederacy's collapse, he was imprisoned on treason charges for two years but was released after the amnesty proclamation of 1868.

Confederate States
Postmasters' Provisionals

On June 1, 1861, the Confederate States of America stopped using U. S. stamps. Between that date and the first issue of Confederate Government stamps on October 16, 1861, postmasters in different cities issued provisional stamps for use on Southern mail.

11X2	350.00	175.00	5c Baton Rouge, Louisiana
47X2		450.00	5c Knoxville, Tennessee
56X1	20.00	300.00	2c Memphis, Tennessee
58X2	110.00	40.00	5c Mobile, Alabama
62X1	25.00	90.00	2c New Orleans, Louisiana
62X2	30.00	200.00	2c New Orleans, Louisiana
62X3	35.00	22.50	5c New Orleans, Louisiana

General Issues, All Imperf.
Issue of 1861: Lithographed Unwatermarked

1	30.00	17.30	5c Jefferson Davis
2	30.00	22.50	10c Thomas Jefferson

Issues of 1862

3	110.00	140.00	2c Andrew Jackson
4	17.50	14.50	5c blue J. Davis, sia 6

5	175.00	65.00	10c Thomas Jefferson

Typographed

6	2.25	3.25	5c J. Davis (London print)
7	4.00	4.50	5c blue, sia 6 (local print)

Issues of 1863, Engraved

8	10.00	37.50	2c Andrew Jackson

Thick or Thin Paper

9	110.00	90.00	10c Jefferson Davis
10	800.00	450.00	10c blue, sia 9, (with rectangular frame)

Prices of No.10 are for copies showing parts of lines on at least two sides of frame.

11	2.50	3.25	10c Jefferson Davis, die A
12	2.75		3.25	10c blue J. Davis die B, sia 11

Dies A and B differ in that B has an extra line outside its corner ornaments.

13	7.00	40.00	20c George Washington

Issue of 1862, Typographed

14	27.50		1c John C. Calhoun (This stamp was never put in use.)

UNITED STATES POSSESSIONS AND ADMINISTRATIVE AREAS

The Spanish American War Peace Treaty of December 10, 1898 ceded Guam, the Philippine Is—lands and Puerto Rico to the United States. Under the terms of the same treaty, Cuba was to be held in trust by the United States for the Cuban people. The territories were under the jurisdiction of the War Department, except for Guam, which was administered by the Navy Department. All four areas were temporarily furnished regular U. S. postage stamps overprinted with the name of the ter—ritory in which they were to be used.

When regular mail service under the jurisdiction of the U. S. Post Office Department was established on Guam and Puerto Rico, the overprinted stamps were replaced with regular U. S. postage stamps. The Bureau of Engraving and Printing printed stamps especially for use in Cuba in 1899. Although U. S. military administration of the islands ended in May 1902, the Bureau continued to furnish stamps for the Republic of Cuba until 1905.

Stamps overprinted "Philippines" were replaced in 1906 by a special issue peculiar to the Islands. The Bureau continued to produce Philippine postage stamps until the Islands became an independent republic on July 4, 1946.

For the Canal Zone, excepting for three U. S. stamps of 1904, all stamps issued in the U. S. Admin—istrative Area through 1924, were Panama stamps overprinted "Canal Zone." Since 1924 Canal Zone postage stamps have been prepared by the Bureau of Engraving and Printing in Washington, D. C.

CANAL ZONE
(kå•năl′zōn)

LOCATION — A strip of land ten miles wide, extending through the Republic of Panama, from the Atlantic to the Pacific Ocean.

GOVT. — A United States Government Reservation.

AREA — 552.8 sq. mi.

The Canal Zone, site of the Panama Canal, was leased in perpetuity to the United States for a cash payment of $10,000,000 and a yearly rental ($1,900,000 a year since 1955). The cities of Panama and Colon remain under the authority of Panama, subject to certain U.S. jurisdiction.

100 Centavos = 1 Peso   100 Cents = 1 Dollar
100 Centesimos = 1 Balboa

Issues of 1904
Blue-black Handstamp, "CANAL ZONE," on Panama Nos. 72, 72c, 78 and 79.
Perf. 12, Unwmkd.

1	130.00	130.00	2c Map of Panama
2	70.00	55.00	5c Map of Panama
3	100.00	90.00	10c Map of Panama

Counterfeit "CANAL ZONE" overprints exist.

United States Nos. 300, 319, 304, 306 and 307 Overprinted in Black

Wmkd. USPS (191)

4	7.00	6.25	1c Franklin
5	6.50	5.00	2c Washington
6	20.00	20.00	5c blue Lincoln, sia U.S. 304
7	35.00	35.00	8c violet black M. Wash—ington, sia U.S. 306
8	37.50	37.50	10c Webster

Issues of 1904-06 Unwmkd.

Black Overprint on Stamps of Panama **CANAL ZONE**

9	1.00	.65	1c Map of Panama
10	1.25	1.00	2c rose, sia 9

Overprinted "CANAL ZONE" in Black, "PANAMA" 15 mm. long and Bar in Red.

11	2.25	1.75	2c rose, sia 13

THE PANAMA CANAL

Today they call it one of mankind's greatest works, this fifty-mile canal. But less than a century ago Isthmus jungle stood where the canal now flows. Its tangled mass blocked the efforts of far-sighted men who sensed the time had come for a change; that sailing from Atlantic to Pacific by the route Magellan used (around Cape Horn) was too slow for the needs of a modern age.

The first country to try its hand at digging a canal was France (1882). This attempt met with failure. When Theodore Roosevelt became president of the United States in 1901 he correctly sensed that a U. S. built canal would add to American prestige and might. Roosevelt moved to complete the project but was faced with mossback Congressmen who held back badly needed funds.

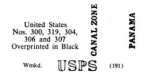

12	1.75	1.00	5c blue, sia 13
13	5.00	3.50	10c Map of Panama
14	5.00	4.00	8c in red on 50c Map of Panama, "PANAMA" reading up and down

Nos. 11, 12 and 13 are overprinted, and 14 is surcharged on Panama Nos. 77, 78, 79 and 81.

While politicians haggled over where and how to dig the canal, Roosevelt acted to achieve his goal. He picked Panama, then a part of Colombia, as the site. When Colombia failed to ratify the project Panama revolted, gained its independence (1903) and gave the United States permanent use of a ten-mile-wide canal zone for which America now pays $1.93 million annually.

Panama No. 74 Overprinted "CANAL ZONE" in Regular Type and Surcharged. 13mm long "PANAMA" reading up on both sides.
Issue of 1905

15	600.00	600.00	8c in red on 50c bistre brown, sia 14

Issues of 1906

16	.35	.35	1c in black on 20c violet, sia 17
17	.55	.55	2c in black on 1p Map of Panama

Issues of 1905–06

18	16.00	15.00	8c in red on 50c Map of Panama
19	12.00	12.00	8c without period in red on 50c bistre brown, sia 20
20	5.50	5.00	8c in red on 50c Map of Panama, "PANAMA" reading up and down

Stamps of Panama Overprinted "CANAL ZONE" in Black
Issue of 1906, Overprint Reading Up

21	4.50	4.00	2c Francisco de Córdoba

Issue of 1906–07, Overprint Reading Down

22	.75	.50	1c Vasco Núñez de Balboa
23	.75	.60	2c red and black. Córdoba, sia 21
24	1.50	.65	5c Justo Arosemena
25	4.00	1.65	8c Manuel J. Hurtado
26	4.00	1.50	10c José de Obaldía

Overwhelming obstacles, including mud, earth slides, and disease faced the men who built the canal. Opened in 1914, it remains one of the United States greatest technological achievements. Roosevelt, often questioned about his alleged role in the Panamanian revolt that helped make it possible, once said, "If I had followed conventional, conservative methods, I should have submitted a dignified state paper...to the Congress and the debate would have been going on yet..."

Issue of 1909, Overprint Reading Down

27	4.00	1.75	2c vermilion and black Córdoba, sia 32
28	9.50	2.50	5c Arosemena
29	7.00	2.50	8c Hurtado
30	8.00	2.75	10c Obaldía

Issues of 1909–10
Type I Black Overprint Reading Up*

31	.75	.50	1c Balboa
31c	150.00		Booklet pane of six, handmade, perf. margins
32	1.00	.50	2c Córdoba
32c	100.00		Booklet pane of six, handmade, perf. margins

*Canal Zone overprints, types I-V, are shown in the Appendix.

185

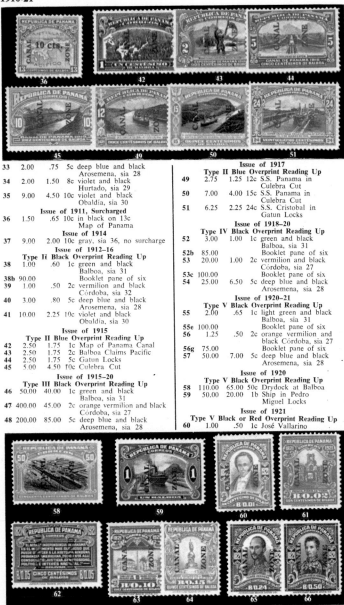

33	2.00	.75	5c deep blue and black Arosemena, sia 28
34	2.00	1.50	8c violet and black Hurtado, sia 29
35	9.00	4.50	10c violet and black Obaldía, sia 30

Issue of 1911, Surcharged

36	1.50	.65	10c in black on 13c Map of Panama

Issue of 1914

37	9.00	2.00	10c gray, sia 36, no surcharge

Issue of 1912–16
Type II Black Overprint Reading Up

38	1.00	.60	1c green and black Balboa, sia 31
38b	90.00		Booklet pane of six
39	1.00	.50	2c vermilion and black Córdoba, sia 32
40	3.00	.80	5c deep blue and black Arosemena, sia 28
41	10.00	2.25	10c violet and black Obaldía, sia 30

Issue of 1915
Type II Blue Overprint Reading Up

42	2.50	1.75	1c Map of Panama Canal
43	2.50	1.75	2c Balboa Claims Pacific
44	2.50	1.75	5c Gatun Locks
45	5.00	4.50	10c Culebra Cut

Issue of 1915–20
Type III Black Overprint Reading Up

46	50.00	40.00	1c green and black Balboa, sia 31
47	400.00	45.00	2c orange vermilion and black Córdoba, sia 27
48	200.00	85.00	5c deep blue and black Arosemena, sia 28

Issue of 1917
Type II Blue Overprint Reading Up

49	2.75	1.25	12c S.S. Panama in Culebra Cut
50	7.00	4.00	15c S.S. Panama in Culebra Cut
51	6.25	2.25	24c S.S. Cristobal in Gatun Locks

Issue of 1918–20
Type IV Black Overprint Reading Up

52	3.00	1.00	1c green and black Balboa, sia 31
52b	85.00		Booklet pane of six
53	20.00	1.00	2c vermilion and black Córdoba, sia 27
53c	100.00		Booklet pane of six
54	25.00	6.50	5c deep blue and black Arosemena, sia 28

Issue of 1920–21
Type V Black Overprint Reading Up

55	2.00	.65	1c light green and black Balboa, sia 31
55e	100.00		Booklet pane of six
56	1.25	.50	2c orange vermilion and black Córdoba, sia 27
56g	75.00		Booklet pane of six
57	50.00	7.00	5c deep blue and black Arosemena, sia 28

Issue of 1920
Type V Black Overprint Reading Up

58	110.00	65.00	50c Drydock at Balboa
59	50.00	20.00	1b Ship in Pedro Miguel Locks

Issue of 1921
Type V Black or Red Overprint Reading Up

60	1.00	.50	1c José Vallarino

68	69	70	71	73	74

60b	110.00		Booklet pane of six
61	1.00	.45	2c "Land Gate"
61f	*300.00*		Booklet pane of six
62	2.75	1.20	5c Bolivar's Tribute
63	4.00	1.50	10c Municipal Building—
			1821 and 1921
64	7.00	2.75	15c Balboa
65	15.00	6.00	24c Tomás Herrera
66	40.00	24.00	50c José de Fabrega

Issue of 1924
Type III Black Overprint Reading Up

67	200.00	55.00	1c green Vallarino, sia 60

Issue of 1924, Black Overprint

68	2.75	1.65	1c Coat of Arms
69	2.00	.95	2c Coat of Arms

The 5c to 1b values were prepared but never issued.

Issue of 1924–25, Perf. 11
CANAL
United States
Nos. 551 to 554, 557,
562, 564, 565, 566,
569, 570 and 571a
Overprinted
ZONE in Red or Black
Type A. Letters "A" with Flat Tops.

70	.20	.20	½c Nathan Hale
71	.30	.20	1c Franklin
71e	20.00		Booklet pane of six
72	.30	.30	1½c yellow brown Harding,
			sia U.S. 553
73	1.35	.35	2c Washington
73a	25.00		Booklet pane of six

THEODORE ROOSEVELT (1858-1919)

I wish to preach, not the doctrine of ignoble ease, but the doctrine of the strenuous life. An 1899 speech

Tough, aggressive, and adventurous, Teddy Roosevelt lived the "strenuous life". He transformed himself from a frail and asthmatic child into the man who climbed the Matterhorn during his honeymoon and led the Rough Riders in the charge of San Juan Hill. The latter episode made him a popular hero, and as president he fought for the rights of the people against industrial monopolies and moneyed trusts. A fighter, Roosevelt was also a diplomat. His personal mediation ending the Russo-Japanese War in 1905 won him a Nobel Peace Prize. In 1912 he ran for a third term, saying "I feel as fit as a Bull Moose," and gave his maverick party its name. In that year, however, Woodrow Wilson was the new hero.

See Canal Zone Scott Nos. 74, 138, 150

74	3.50	2.00	5c Theodore Roosevelt
75	11.00	7.00	10c James Monroe
76	6.50	5.75	12c Grover Cleveland
77	4.50	4.00	14c American Indian
78	11.00	9.00	15c Statue of Liberty
79	6.00	5.00	30c Buffalo
80	8.75	7.50	50c Amphitheater,
			sia U.S. 570
81	75.00	35.00	$1 Lincoln Memorial

Issues of 1925–26
CANAL
United States
Nos. 554, 555, 557, 562,
564, 565, 566, 567, 569,
570, 571a and 623
Overprinted
ZONE in Black or Red
Type B. Letters "A" with Sharp Pointed Tops

75	76	77	78	79	81

Stamp illustrations with catalog numbers: 105, 106, 107, 108, 109, 110, 111, 112, 113, 114, 115, 116, 117

84	6.00	2.00	2c carmine Washington, sia U.S. 554
84d	40.00		Booklet pane of six
85	1.00	.80	3c violet Lincoln, sia U.S. 555
86	.90	.60	5c dark blue T. Roosevelt, sia U.S. 557
87	8.00	1.40	10c orange Monroe, sia U.S. 562
88	4.00	3.75	12c brown violet Cleveland, sia U.S. 564
89	4.50	4.00	14c dark blue Indian, sia U.S. 565
90	1.25	1.00	15c gray Statue of Liberty, sia U.S. 566
91	1.00	.75	17c black Wilson (red overprint), sia U.S. 623
92	1.10	.90	20c carmine rose Golden Gate, sia U.S. 567
93	1.35	1.00	30c olive brown Buffalo, sia U.S. 569
94	75.00	40.00	50c lilac Amphitheater, sia U.S. 570
95	23.50	11.00	$1 violet brown Lincoln Memorial, sia U.S. 571

Issues of 1926
Type B Overprint in Black on U.S. 627

96	1.75	1.35	2c carmine rose Liberty Bell, sia U.S. 627

Issues of 1927, Perf. 10
Type B Overprint in Black on U.S. Nos. 583, 584, 591

97	7.50	2.50	2c carmine Washington sia U.S. 554
97b	65.00		Booklet pane of six
98	1.50	1.40	3c violet Lincoln, sia U.S. 555
99	3.25	2.75	10c orange Monroe, sia U.S. 562

Issues of 1927–31, Perf. 11x10½
Type B Overprint in Black on U.S. Nos. 632, 634 (Type I), 635, 637, 642

100	.40	.40	1c green Franklin, sia U.S. 552
101	.35	.20	2c carmine Washington, sia U.S. 554
101a	22.50		Booklet pane of six
102	1.50	.70	3c violet Lincoln, sia U.S. 555
102a	250.00		Booklet pane of six, handmade, perf. margs.
103	3.00	2.75	5c dark blue T. Roosevelt, sia U.S. 557
104	3.50	2.50	10c orange Monroe, sia U.S. 562

Issues of 1928–40, Perf. 11

105	.08	.05	1c Gen. William Crawford Gorgas
106	.10	.06	2c Gen. George Washington Goethals

BUILDERS OF THE PANAMA CANAL

Theodore Roosevelt needed men like himself to build the Panama Canal, tough men who would stick to the job. But before construction could begin, Panama, infested with yellow fever and malaria, had to be made safe for the workers. From 1904-06 Col. William Gorgas (1854-1920) made medical history with mosquito control in Panama. Breeding spots were found, oil poured on water, swamp grass burned, and in two years the diseases were under control.

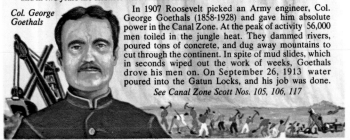

Col. George Goethals

In 1907 Roosevelt picked an Army engineer, Col. George Goethals (1858-1928) and gave him absolute power in the Canal Zone. At the peak of activity 56,000 men toiled in the jungle heat. They dammed rivers, poured tons of concrete, and dug away mountains to cut through the continent. In spite of mud slides, which in seconds wiped out the work of weeks, Goethals drove his men on. On September 26, 1913 water poured into the Gatun Locks, and his job was done.

See Canal Zone Scott Nos. 105, 106, 117

106a	2.50	1.50	Booklet pane of six
107	.40	.20	5c Gaillard Cut
108	.30	.15	10c Harry Foote Hodges
109	.35	.25	12c Col. David D. Gaillard
110	.50	.40	14c Gen. William L. Sibert
111	.40	.20	15c Jackson Smith
112	.50	.20	20c Admiral Harry H. Rousseau
113	.90	.75	30c Col. Sydney B. Williamson
114	1.10	.25	50c J.C.S. Blackburn

Issues of 1933, Perf. 11x10-1/2
Type B Overprint in Black on U.S. 720, 695

115	.75	.12	3c Washington
115c	35.00		Booklet pane of six, handmade, perf. margins
116	.90	.75	14c American Indian

Issue of 1934, Perf. 11

117	.10	.06	3c Gen. Goethals	Aug. 15
117a	2.50	2.00	Booklet pane of six	

Issued for the twentieth anniversary of the opening of the Panama Canal. Also see No. 153.

120 · 121 · 122 · 123 · 124 · 125 · 126 · 127 · 128 · 129 · 130 · 131 · 132 · 133 · 134 · 135

Issues of 1939

United States
Nos. 803 and 805
Overprinted in Black

CANAL ZONE

Perf. 11x10-1/2

118	.06	.06	½ c deep orange Franklin, sia 803 Sep. 1
119	.08	.08	1½ c bistre brown M. Washington, sia 805 Sep. 1

Panama Canal 25th Anniversary Issue
Perf. 11, Aug. 15

120	.20	.20	1c Balboa — Before Canal
121	.25	.25	2c Balboa — After Canal
122	.20	.08	3c Gaillard Cut — Before Canal
123	.55	.55	5c Gaillard Cut — After Canal
124	.90	.90	6c Bas Obispo — Before Canal
125	.90	.90	7c Bas Obispo — After Canal
126	1.50	1.35	8c Gatun Locks — Before Canal
127	1.50	1.35	10c Gatun Locks — After Canal
128	2.75	2.75	11c Canal Channel — Before 1914
129	2.75	2.75	12c Canal Channel — After 1914
130	3.00	3.00	14c Gamboa — Before Canal
131	4.00	1.65	15c Gamboa — After Canal
132	3.00	3.00	18c Pedro Miguel Locks — Before Canal
133	4.00	1.85	20c Pedro Miguel Locks — After Canal
134	7.50	5.50	25c Gatun Spillway — Before Canal
135	9.00	1.50	50c Gatun Spillway — After Canal

The Panama Canal was opened in 1914.

Issue of 1946-49

136	.08	.06	½c Maj. Gen. George W. Davis
137	.08	.06	1½c Gov. Charles E. Magoon
138	.08	.06	2c T. Roosevelt
139	.15	.10	5c John F. Stevens
140	.70	.60	25c John F. Wallace

Issue of 1948

141	.70	.55	10c Biological Area Issue Apr. 17

The Canal Zone Biological Area on Barro Colorado Island was established in 1923.

Issue of 1949
Gold Rush 100th Anniv. Issue, Jun. 1

142	.25	.17	3c "Forty-niners" Arriving at Chagres
143	.30	.20	6c Journey in Bungo to Las Cruces
144	.60	.45	12c Las Cruces Trail to Panama
145	.85	.75	18c Departure for San Francisco

The gold rush of 1849 brought 90,000 settlers to California.

Issue of 1951

146	1.00	.85	10c West Indian Laborers Aug. 15

Construction of the Panama Canal was accomplished with the aid of 31,071 West Indian laborers.

Issue of 1955

147	.30	.25	3c Panama Railroad Jan. 28

The Panama Railroad, completed in 1855, was the first transcontinental railroad across the Americas.

Issue of 1957

148	.18	.15	3c Gorgas Hospital Issue Nov. 17

In 1957, Gorgas Hospital, named for Gen. William Gorgas, celebrated its 75th anniversary.

Issues of 1958

149	.18	.15	4c S.S. Ancon Aug. 30
150	.20	.15	4c T. Roosevelt Issue Nov. 15

1958 marked the 100th anniversary of the birth of Theodore Roosevelt, the U.S. President instrumental in the building of the Panama Canal.

Issues of 1960

151	.40	.30	4c Boy Scout Issue Feb. 8

The Boy Scouts of America was founded in 1910.

152	.10	.08	4c Administration Bldg. Nov. 1

Coil Stamps
Perf. 10 Vertically

153	.15	.12	3c deep violet Goethals, sia 117

Perf. 10 Horizontally

154	.18	.15	4c dull rose lilac Administration Building, sia 152

Issues of 1962
Coil Stamp, Perf. 10 Vertically

155	.25	.18	5c deep blue Stevens, sia 139

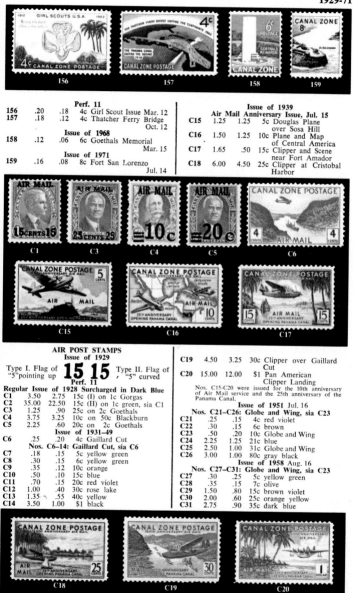

	Perf. 11		
156	.20	.18	4c Girl Scout Issue Mar. 12
157	.18	.12	4c Thatcher Ferry Bridge Oct. 12
	Issue of 1968		
158	.12	.06	6c Goethals Memorial Mar. 15
	Issue of 1971		
159	.16	.08	8c Fort San Lorenzo Jul. 14

Issue of 1939
Air Mail Anniversary Issue, Jul. 15

C15	1.25	1.25	5c Douglas Plane over Sosa Hill
C16	1.50	1.25	10c Plane and Map of Central America
C17	1.65	.50	15c Clipper and Scene near Fort Amador
C18	6.00	4.50	25c Clipper at Cristobal Harbor

AIR POST STAMPS
Issue of 1929

Type I. Flag of "5" pointing up **15 15** Type II. Flag of "5" curved

Perf. 11
Regular Issue of 1928 Surcharged in Dark Blue

C1	3.50	2.75	15c (I) on 1c Gorgas
C2	35.00	22.50	15c (II) on 1c green, sia C1
C3	1.25	.90	25c on 2c Goethals
C4	3.75	3.25	10c on 50c Blackburn
C5	2.25	.60	20c on 2c Goethals

Issue of 1931–49

C6	.25	.20	4c Gaillard Cut

Nos. C6–14: Gaillard Cut, sia C6

C7	.18	.15	5c yellow green
C8	.30	.15	6c yellow green
C9	.35	.12	10c orange
C10	.50	.10	15c blue
C11	.70	.15	20c red violet
C12	1.00	.40	30c rose lake
C13	1.35	.55	40c yellow
C14	3.50	1.00	$1 black

C19	4.50	3.25	30c Clipper over Gaillard Cut
C20	15.00	12.00	$1 Pan American Clipper Landing

Nos. C15-C20 were issued for the 10th anniversary of Air Mail service and the 25th anniversary of the Panama Canal.

Issue of 1951 Jul. 16
Nos. C21–C26: Globe and Wing, sia C23

C21	.25	.15	4c red violet
C22	.30	.15	6c brown
C23	.50	.20	10c Globe and Wing
C24	2.25	1.25	21c blue
C25	2.50	1.00	31c Globe and Wing
C26	3.00	1.00	80c gray black

Issue of 1958 Aug. 16
Nos. C27–C31: Globe and Wing, sia C23

C27	.30	.25	5c yellow green
C28	.35	.15	7c olive
C29	1.50	.80	15c brown violet
C30	2.00	.60	25c orange yellow
C31	2.75	.90	35c dark blue

	Issue of 1961		
C32	.75	.50	15c Emblem of U.S. Army, Caribbean School Nov. 21
	Issue of 1962		
C33	.30	.25	7c Malaria Eradication Issue Sep. 24

World Health Organization's drive to eradicate malaria.

	Issues of 1963		
	Perf. 10½x11		
C34	.30	.15	8c carmine, sia C23 Jan. 7
	Perf. 11		
C35	.75	.55	15c Alliance for Progress Aug. 17

The Alliance for Progress, founded in 1961, aims to stimulate economic growth in Latin America.

"PANAMA CANAL" 19–20 mm. long
Issues of 1941–42, Perf. 11
Nos. CO1–CO14: Gaillard Cut, sia C6

CO1	1.50	.60	5c yellow green
CO2	2.25	.90	10c orange
CO3	2.50	1.00	15c blue
CO4	3.25	2.75	20c red violet
CO5	3.85	2.40	30c rose lake
CO6	5.00	2.75	40c yellow
CO7	6.25	3.65	$1 black

"PANAMA CANAL" 17 mm. long

CO8	90.00	5c light green
CO9	200.00	10c orange
CO10	80.00	20c red violet
CO11	35.00	30c rose lake

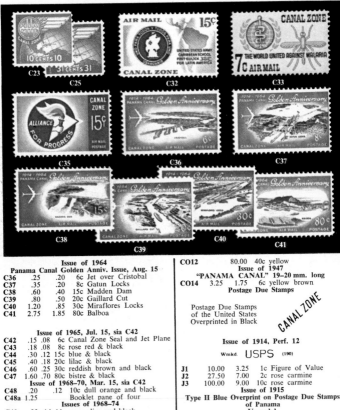

C23   C25   C32   C33

C35   C36   C37

C38   C39   C40   C41

	Issue of 1964		
	Panama Canal Golden Anniv. Issue, Aug. 15		
C36	.25	.20	6c Jet over Cristobal
C37	.35	.20	8c Gatun Locks
C38	.60	.40	15c Madden Dam
C39	.80	.50	20c Gaillard Cut
C40	1.20	.85	30c Miraflores Locks
C41	2.75	1.85	80c Balboa

	Issue of 1965, Jul. 15, sia C42		
C42	.15	.08	6c Canal Zone Seal and Jet Plane
C43	.18	.08	8c rose red & black
C44	.30	.12	15c blue & black
C45	.40	.18	20c lilac & black
C46	.60	.25	30c reddish brown and black
C47	1.60	.70	80c bistre & black
	Issue of 1968–70, Mar. 15, sia C42		
C48	.20	.12	10c dull orange and black
C48a	1.25		Booklet pane of four
	Issues of 1968–74		
C49	.22	.14	11c gray olive and black
C49a	1.25		Booklet pane of four
C50	.26	.15	13c emerald & black, sia C42
C50a	1.10		Booklet pane of 4
C51	.50	.20	25c pale yellow green & black, sia C42

Air Post Official Stamps

Air Post Stamps
of 1931–41
Overprinted in Black

OFFICIAL

PANAMA CANAL

CO12	80.00		40c yellow
	Issue of 1947		
	"PANAMA CANAL" 19–20 mm. long		
CO14	3.25	1.75	6c yellow brown

Postage Due Stamps

Postage Due Stamps
of the United States
Overprinted in Black

CANAL ZONE

Issue of 1914, Perf. 12

Wmkd. USPS (190)

J1	10.00	3.25	1c Figure of Value
J2	27.50	7.00	2c rose carmine
J3	100.00	9.00	10c rose carmine
	Issue of 1915		

Type II Blue Overprint on Postage Due Stamps of Panama

Unwmkd.

J4	3.00	1.10	1c olive brown, sia J7
J5	20.00	5.00	2c olive brown, sia J10
J6	10.00	4.00	10c Pedro J. Sosa
	Surcharged in Red		
J7	20.00	3.25	1c on 1c San Geronimo Castle Gate

No. J7 was intended to show a gate of San Lorenzo Castle, Chagres, and is so labeled. By error the stamp actually shows the main gate of San Geronimo Castle, Portobelo.

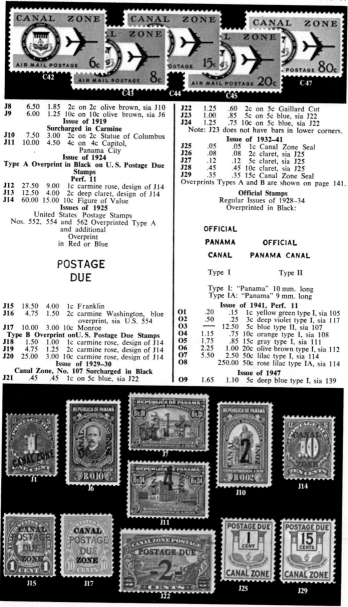

J8	6.50	1.85	2c on 2c olive brown, sia J10
J9	6.00	1.25	10c on 10c olive brown, sia J6

Issue of 1919
Surcharged in Carmine

J10	7.50	3.00	2c on 2c Statue of Columbus
J11	10.00	4.50	4c on 4c Capitol, Panama City

Issue of 1924
Type A Overprint in Black on U. S. Postage Due Stamps
Perf. 11

J12	27.50	9.00	1c carmine rose, design of J14
J13	12.50	4.00	2c deep claret, design of J14
J14	60.00	15.00	10c Figure of Value

Issues of 1925
United States Postage Stamps
Nos. 552, 554 and 562 Overprinted Type A
and additional
Overprint
in Red or Blue

POSTAGE
DUE

J15	18.50	4.00	1c Franklin
J16	4.75	1.50	2c carmine Washington, blue overprint, sia U.S. 554
J17	10.00	3.00	10c Monroe

Type B Overprint on U. S. Postage Due Stamps

J18	1.50	1.00	1c carmine rose, design of J14
J19	4.75	1.25	2c carmine rose, design of J14
J20	25.00	3.00	10c carmine rose, design of J14

Issue of 1929–30
Canal Zone, No. 107 Surcharged in Black

J21	.45	.45	1c on 5c blue, sia J22

J22	1.25	.60	2c on 5c Gaillard Cut
J23	1.00	.85	5c on 5c blue, sia J22
J24	1.25	.75	10c on 5c blue, sia J22

Note: J23 does not have bars in lower corners.

Issue of 1932–41

J25	.05	.05	1c Canal Zone Seal
J26	.08	.08	2c claret, sia J25
J27	.12	.12	5c claret, sia J25
J28	.45	.45	10c claret, sia J25
J29	.35	.35	15c Canal Zone Seal

Overprints Types A and B are shown on page 141.

Official Stamps
Regular Issues of 1928–34
Overprinted in Black:

OFFICIAL		
PANAMA	OFFICIAL	
CANAL	PANAMA CANAL	
Type I	Type II	

Type I: "Panama" 10 mm. long
Type IA: "Panama" 9 mm. long

Issue of 1941, Perf. 11

O1	.20	.15	1c yellow green type I, sia 105
O2	.50	.25	3c deep violet type I, sia 117
O3	—	12.50	5c blue type II, sia 107
O4	1.15	.75	10c orange type I, sia 108
O6	1.75	.85	15c gray type I, sia 111
O7	2.25	1.00	20c olive brown type I, sia 112
O7	5.50	2.50	50c lilac type I, sia 114
O8		250.00	50c rose lilac type IA, sia 114

Issue of 1947

O9	1.65	1.10	5c deep blue type I, sia 139

GUAM
(gwäm)

LOCATION—One of the Mariana Islands in the Pacific Ocean, about 1450 miles east of the Philippines.

GOVT.—United States Possession.

AREA—206 sq. mi.

CAPITAL—Agaña.

Formerly a Spanish possession. Guam was ceded to the United States in 1898 following the Spanish–American War.

100 Cents = 1 Dollar

Issues of 1899, Perf. 12
United States Stamps Nos. 279, 267, 268, 280a, 281a, 282, 272, 282C, 283a, 284, 275, 275a, 276 and 276A.

Overprinted **GUAM**

Wmkd. **USPS** (191)

Black Overprint

1	7.50	9.00	1c Benjamin Franklin
2	7.00	8.50	2c George Washington
3	37.50	47.50	3c purple Jackson, sia U.S. 253
4	35.00	47.50	4c Abraham Lincoln
5	11.00	12.50	5c blue Grant, sia U.S. 255
6	35.00	40.00	6c James A. Garfield
7	25.00	35.00	8c General Sherman
8	17.50	20.00	10c Daniel Webster, type I
9	*1100.00*		10c brown Webster, type II, sia 8
10	40.00	50.00	15c Henry Clay
11	62.50	70.00	50c orange Jefferson, sia U.S. 260

Red Overprint

12	100.00	110.00	$1 black Perry type I, sia U.S. 261
13	750.00		$1 black Perry type II, sia U.S. 261A

Special Delivery Stamps
United States Stamps No. E5
Overprinted in Red **GUAM**

Wmkd. **USPS** (191)

E1	60.00	60.00	10c Messenger Running

Stamps overprinted "Guam" were superseded by the regular postage stamps of the United States in 1901.

Guam Guard Mail
Local Postal Service
Issues of 1930
Perf. 11, Unwmkd.
Philippines
Nos. 290b and 291
Overprinted

M1	125.00	125.00	2c green Rizal, sia M7	Apr.
M2	125.00	125.00	4c car. McKinley, sia M6	Apr.

Perf. 12, Without Gum

M3	55.00	55.00	1c Seal of Guam	Jul.
M4	40.00	45.00	2c Seal of Guam	Jul.

Perf. 11, Unwmkd.
Philippines
Nos. 290b, 290 and 291
Overprinted in Black

M5	2.75	3.50	2c green Rizal, sia M7	Aug. 10
M6	.60	2.75	4c William McKinley	Aug. 10

Red Overprint

M7	.95	.95	2c José Rizal	Dec.
M8	.95	.95	4c car. McKinley, sia M6	Dec.
M9	2.50	2.50	6c deep violet Magellan, sia P1243	Dec.
M10	1.80	1.80	8c orange brown Legaspi, sia P1244	Dec.
M11	2.00	2.00	10c Gen. Henry W. Lawton	Dec.

The local postal service was discontinued on April 8th, 1931, and replaced by the service of the United States Post Office Department.

HAWAII
(hä—wī̇́)

LOCATION—A group of twenty islands in the Pacific Ocean, about two thousand miles southwest of San Francisco.
GOVT.—Former Kingdom and Republic.
AREA—6,435 sq. mi.
CAPITAL—Honolulu.
Until 1893 an independent kingdom, from 1893 to 1898 a republic, the Hawaiian Islands were annexed to the United States in 1898 at the request of the inhabitants. The Territory of Hawaii achieved statehood in 1959.

100 Cents = 1 Dollar

Prices of early Hawaii stamps vary according to condition. Quotations for Nos. 1–18 are for fine copies. Very fine to superb specimens sell at much higher prices, and inferior or poor copies sell at reduced prices, depending on the condition of the individual specimen.

HAWAII: FROM KINGDOM TO STATEHOOD

Long ago Polynesians in sea-faring canoes migrated to Hawaii and evolved a feudal society. By the time Captain Cook arrived in 1778, six of the main islands were united under the monarchy of King Kamehameha I. His descendants and other Hawaiians continued to rule until 1893. During this period a great many foreigners immigrated to Hawaii, making it a melting pot. The first company of Protestant missionaries arrived in 1820 from New England. Others followed and churches, schools, and newspapers were soon established. By 1893 the growth of American interests in the sugar and pineapple industries had led to the annexation movement. When Queen Liliuokalani assumed the throne the powerful "Committee of Safety" abolished the monarchy and appealed to the United States for annexation. When this failed the Republic of Hawaii was established (in 1894) with Sanford B. Dole as its leader. Following the Spanish-American War the United States recognized the strategic value of Hawaii for naval installations. Hawaii was annexed in 1898 and made a territory in 1900. In 1959 it became the 50th state.

799

Issue of 1851–52
Imperf.
Type–set, Pelure Paper, Unwmkd.

1	65,000.00	37,500.00	2c Figure of Value
2	20,000.00	9000.00	5c Figure of Value
3	10,000.00	6500.00	13c Figure of Value
4	20,000.00	12,500.00	13c Figure of Value

Issue of 1853
Thick White Wove Paper

5	550.00	400.00	5c King Kamehameha III
6	225.00	250.00	13c dark red King Kamehamha III. sia 7
7	2000,00	2250.00	5c on 13c King Kamehameha III

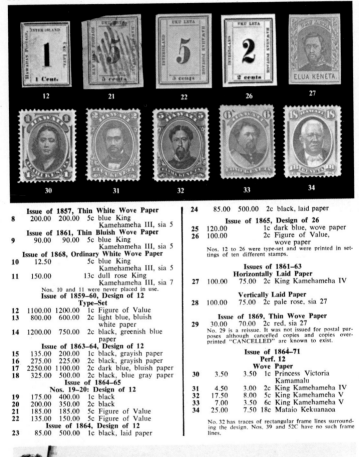

Issue of 1857, Thin White Wove Paper
8   200.00   200.00   5c blue King Kamehameha III, sia 5

Issue of 1861, Thin Bluish Wove Paper
9   90.00   90.00   5c blue King Kamehameha III, sia 5

Issue of 1868, Ordinary White Wove Paper
10   12.50   5c blue King Kamehameha III, sia 5
11   150.00   13c dull rose King Kamehameha III, sia 7

Nos. 10 and 11 were never placed in use.

Issue of 1859–60, Design of 12
Type–Set
12   1100.00 1200.00 1c Figure of Value
13   800.00   600.00 2c light blue, bluish white paper
14   1200.00 750.00 2c black, greenish blue paper

Issue of 1863–64, Design of 12
15   135.00   200.00 1c black, grayish paper
16   275.00   225.00 2c black, grayish paper
17   2250.00 1100.00 2c dark blue, bluish paper
18   325.00   500.00 2c black, blue gray paper

Issue of 1864–65
Nos. 19–20: Design of 12
19   175.00   400.00 1c black
20   200.00   350.00 2c black
21   185.00   185.00 5c Figure of Value
22   135.00   150.00 5c Figure of Value

Issue of 1864, Design of 12
23   85.00   500.00 1c black, laid paper

24   85.00   500.00 2c black, laid paper

Issue of 1865, Design of 26
25   120.00   1c dark blue, wove paper
26   100.00   2c Figure of Value, wove paper

Nos. 12 to 26 were type-set and were printed in settings of ten different stamps.

Issues of 1861–63
Horizontally Laid Paper
27   100.00   75.00 2c King Kamehameha IV

Vertically Laid Paper
28   100.00   75.00 2c pale rose, sia 27

Issue of 1869, Thin Wove Paper
29   30.00   70.00 2c red, sia 27

No. 29 is a reissue. It was not issued for postal purposes although cancelled copies and copies overprinted "CANCELLED" are known to exist.

Issue of 1864–71
Perf. 12
Wove Paper
30   3.50   3.50 1c Princess Victoria Kamamalu
31   4.50   3.00 2c King Kamehameha IV
32   17.50   8.00 5c King Kamehameha V
33   7.00   3.50 6c King Kamehameha V
34   25.00   7.50 18c Mataio Kekuanaoa

No. 32 has traces of rectangular frame lines surrounding the design. Nos. 39 and 52C have no such frame lines.

HAWAII, TROPICAL PARADISE

From historic Diamond Head and Waikiki to Hawaii's western bird sanctuary the Aloha State is a tropic wonderland. Snow-capped volcanoes roll into lush green hills cut by mountain streams and waterfalls; spraying surf abounds in its Pacific waters. Hawaii's balmy climate, sand, and sea make it a mecca for tourists; its plant and marine life make it a laboratory for scientists.

Issue of 1875

35	2.75	1.50	2c King David Kalakaua
36	17.50	10.00	12c Prince William Pitt Leleiohoku

See also Nos. 38, 43, 46.

Issue of 1882

37	2.25	2.25	1c Princess Likelike (Mrs. Archibald Cleghorn)
38	22.50	10.00	2c King David Kalakaua
39	5.00	1.40	5c ultramarine, sia 32
40	10.00	7.50	10c King David Kalakaua
41	17.50	11.00	15c Queen Kapiolani

Issue of 1883–86

42	1.25	1.00	1c green, sia 37
43	2.00	.65	2c rose, sia 35
44	7.00	2.75	10c red brown, sia 40
45	9.00	7.00	10c vermilion, sia 40
46	20.00	15.00	12c red lilac, sia 36
47	25.00	16.00	25c Statue of King Kamehameha I
48	50.00	32.50	50c King William Lunalilo
49	60.00	40.00	$1 Queen Emma Kaleleonalani

Reproduction and Reprint, Yellowish Wove Paper
Issue of 1886–89, Imperf.

50	100.00		2c orange vermilion, sia 27
51	15.00		2c carmine, sia 27

For reprint information, refer to the Appendix.

Issue of 1890–91, Perf. 12

52	2.00	1.00	2c dull violet, sia 57
52C	20.00	22.50	5c deep indigo, sia 32

Issues of 1893

Issues of 1864 to 1891 Overprinted

Provisional GOVT. 1893

Red Overprint

53	2.00	2.00	1c purple, sia 30
54	2.00	2.25	1c blue, sia 37
55	.80	.80	1c green, sia 37
56	2.75	4.50	2c brown, sia 35
57	.75	.75	2c Queen Liluokalani, (Mrs. John Dominis)
58	2.75	5.50	5c deep indigo, sia 32
59	2.00	1.75	5c ultramarine, sia 32
60	4.50	6.00	6c green, sia 33
61	3.50	3.25	10c black, sia 40
61B	*2000.00*		10c red brown, sia 40
62	3.50	3.50	12c black, sia 36
63	55.00	75.00	12c Prince William Pitt Leleiohoku
64	7.50	8.50	25c dark violet, sia 47

Black Overprint

65	17.00	16.00	2c rosy vermilion, sia 31
66	.80	1.00	2c rose, sia 35
66C	*2250.00*	——	6c green, sia 33
67	5.00	10.00	10c vermilion, sia 40
68	3.00	3.75	10c King David Kalakaua
69	100.00	115.00	12c red lilac, sia 36
70	8.00	10.00	15c red brown, sia 41
71	8.50	9.00	18c dull rose, sia 34
72	16.50	18.50	50c red, sia 48
73	35.00	40.00	$1 rose red, sia 49

The islands' 900 species of flowering plants include violets which grow six feet tall. The sea also yields exotic treasure: 650 species of bright tropical fish swim in the waters around Hawaii. Sugar cane and pineapples are the chief export products, although coffee, rice, sisal, and cotton are also grown. The seven main islands are Hawaii, Maui, Oahu, Kauai, Molokai, Lanai, Niihau, and the uninhabited Kahooawe. Honolulu, the capital, is on Oahu.

74   75

76   77

78   79

80   81

O1   O6

Issue of 1894
74	1.10	.75	1c Coat of Arms
75	1.25	.50	2c View of Honolulu
76	2.35	1.00	5c Statue of King Kamehameha I
77	2.75	2.25	10c Star and Palms
78	4.25	4.00	12c S. S. Arawa
79	6.25	6.25	25c Pres. Sanford Ballard Dole

Issue of 1899
80	1.20	1.10	1c Coat of Arms
81	1.00	.60	2c View of Honolulu
82	2.50	1.50	5c blue, sia 76

Official Stamps, 1896
Perf. 12
O1	8.50	8.50	2c Lorrin Andrews Thurston Nos. O2–O5, sia O1
O2	8.50	.50	5c black brown
O3	8.50	8.50	6c deep ultramarine
O4	8.50	8.50	10c bright rose
O5	8.50	8.50	12c orange
O6	8.50	8.50	25c Lorrin Andrews Thurston

The stamps of Hawaii have been replaced by those of the United States.

PHILIPPINES
(fil–i–penz;–pinz)

LOCATION—A group of 7,100 islands and islets in the Malaya Archipelago, north of Borneo, in the North Pacific Ocean.
GOVT.—U. S. Administration, 1898–1946.
AREA—115,748 sq. mi.
CAPITAL — Quezon City

The islands were ceded to the United States by Spain in 1898. On November 15, 1935, they were given their independence, subject to a transition period which ended July 4, 1946. On that date the Commonwealth became the "Republic of the Philippines."

100 Cents=1 Dollar (1899)
100 Centavos=1 Peso (1906)
Issued under American Dominion.

Regular Issues of the United States Overprinted **PHILIPPINES**

Issue of 1899–1900, Perf. 12
Unwmkd.
Blk. Overprint on U. S. 260
212	85.00	57.50	50c Thomas Jefferson

Wmkd. **USPS** (191)

Blk. Overprint on U. S. Nos. 279a, 279d, 268, 281a 282C, 283, 284, 275
213	1.00	.50	1c yellow green Franklin, sia U.S. 246
214	.75	.50	2c orange red Washington sia U.S. 248
214b	85.00	45.00	Booklet pane of six
215	1.50	1.10	3c Jackson, sia U.S. 253
216	1.75	.75	5c blue Grant, sia U.S. 255
217	4.00	2.50	10c brown Webster type I, sia U.S. 282C
217A	37.50	5.00	10c orange brown Webster, type II, sia U.S. 283
218	5.00	3.00	15c ol. gr. Clay, sia U.S. 259
219	20.00	14.00	50c orange Jefferson, sia U.S. 260

Issue of 1901
Blk. Overprint on U.S. Nos. 280b, 282 and 272
220	3.25	2.00	4c orange brown Lincoln, sia U.S. 254
221	4.00	3.75	6c lake Garfield, sia U.S. 256
222	4.50	2.50	8c violet brown Sherman, sia U.S. 257

Red Overprint on U. S. Nos. 276, 276A, 277a, 278
223	135.00	75.00	$1 black Perry type I, sia U.S. 276
223A	350.00	200.00	$1 black Perry type II, sia U.S. 276A
224	150.00	80.00	$2 dark blue Madison, sia U.S. 262
225	275.00	175.00	$5 dark green Marshall, sia U.S. 263

Issue of 1903–04
Black Overprint on U. S. Nos. 300–310
226	.90	.30	1c blue green Franklin, sia U.S. 300
227	1.85	1.85	2c carmine Washington, sia U.S. 301
227a			Booklet pane of six
228	7.25	5.75	3c Andrew Jackson
229	11.00	8.00	4c br. Grant, sia U.S. 303
230	2.25	.75	5c bl. Lincoln, sia U.S. 304
231	6.50	6.00	6c brownish lake Garfield, sia U.S. 305
232	6.00	5.25	8c violet black M. Washington, sia U.S. 306
233	4.50	2.00	10c pale red brown Webster, sia U.S. 307
234	7.00	6.00	13c purple black Harrison, sia U.S. 308
235	11.50	4.50	15c olive green Clay, sia U.S. 309
236	27.50	9.00	50c orange Jefferson, sia U.S. 310

THE SPANISH-AMERICAN WAR

As a result of this brief war the United States acquired Guam, Puerto Rico, and the Philippines from Spain. On April 24, 1898, after relations with Spain had been strained by disagreements over the government of Cuba and the blow-up of the *Maine* in the Havana harbor, the United States declared war. One week later Commodore George Dewey destroyed the Spanish fleet in the Battle of Manila Bay, and in the months that followed U. S. forces captured Guantanamo, San Juan Hill, and Santiago. On August 12, during the invasion of Puerto Rico, an armistice was declared.

Philippines Scott No. 422

Red Overprint on U.S. Nos. 311–313
237	100.00	65.00	$1 black Farragut, sia U.S. 311
238	225.00	155.00	$2 dark blue Madison, sia U.S. 312
239	325.00	200.00	$5 dark green Marshall, sia U.S. 313

Issue of 1904
Black Overprint on U.S. 319
240	2.00	1.00	2c carmine Washington sia U.S. 319
240a	125.00		Booklet pane of six

Issues of 1906–10
Wmkd. Double–lined PIPS (191PI)
241	.25	.06	2c José Rizal
241b	32.50		Booklet pane of six

José Rizal (1861-96), Philippine patriot and author was exiled in 1887 and executed by the Spanish in 1896.

242	.40	.06	4c William McKinley
242b	35.00		Booklet pane of six
243	1.10	.15	6c Fernando Magellan
244	1.25	.70	8c Miguel Lopez de Legaspi
245	1.65	.10	10c Gen. Henry W. Lawton
246	2.75	1.85	12c Abraham Lincoln
247	3.00	.25	16c Adm. William T. Sampson
248	3.25	.40	20c George Washington
249	2.75	2.35	26c Francisco Carriedo
250	4.00	1.60	30c Benjamin Franklin
251	11.00	8.25	1p Arms of Manila
252	10.00	1.00	2p black, sia 251
253	24.00	9.50	4p dark blue, sia 251
254	67.50	30.00	10p Arms of Manila

Issue of 1909–13
255	4.00	2.65	12c red orange Lincoln, sia 246
256	1.10	.40	16c ol. gr. Sampson, sia 247
257	5.00	1.35	20c yellow Washington, sia 248
258	.90	.80	26c blue green Carriedo, sia 249
259	7.25	3.85	30c ultramar. Franklin, sia 250
260	13.50	3.85	1p pale violet Manila Arms, sia 251
260A	32.50	1.35	2p violet brown Manila Arms, sia 251

Issue of 1911
Wmkd. Single–lined PIPS (190PI)
261	.60	.10	2c green Rizal, sia 241
261a	27.50		Booklet pane of six
262	2.75	.12	4c car. lake McKinley, sia 242
262b	37.50		Booklet pane of six
263	1.50	.10	6c dp. violet Magellan, sia 243
264	4.50	.30	8c brown Legaspi, sia 244
265	1.75	.08	10c blue Lawton, sia 245
266	1.35	.18	12c orange Lincoln, sia 246
267	2.00	.15	16c olive grn. Sampson, sia 247
268	1.75	.15	20c yellow Washington, sia 248
269	2.50	.30	26c blue green Carriedo, sia 250
270	2.50	.50	30c ultramar. Franklin, sia 250
271	10.00	.40	1p pale violet Manila Arms, sia 251
272	13.50	.70	2p violet brown Manila Arms, sia 251
273	185.00	15.00	4p deep blue Manila Arms, sia 251
274	75.00	10.00	10p deep green Manila Arms, sia 254

Wmk. 190

Wmk. 191

319-325

354   355   356

Issue of 1914			
275	5.50	.40	30c gray Franklin, sia 250
Issue of 1914–23, Perf. 10			
276	1.00	.12	2c green Rizal, sia 241
276a	22.50		Booklet pane of six
277	1.00	.15	4c carm. McKinley, sia 242
277a	27.50		Booklet pane of six
278	9.00	6.00	6c lt. vio. Magellan, sia 243
279	9.00	4.00	8c brown Legaspi, sia 244
280	7.00	.25	10c dark blue Lawton, sia 245
281	20.00	1.85	16c ol. gr. Sampson, sia 247
282	6.00	1.00	20c or. Washington, sia 248
283	14.00	1.30	30c gray Franklin, sia 250
284	30.00	1.30	1p pale violet Manila Arms, sia 251
Issue of 1918–26, Perf. 11			
285	4.00	1.35	2c green Rizal, sia 241
285a	100.00		Booklet pane of six
286	7.25	1.10	4c carm. McKinley, sia 242
286a	110.00		Booklet pane of six
287	10.00	.55	6c dp. vio. Magellan, sia 243
287A	55.00	10.00	8c lt. br. Legaspi, sia 244
288	12.00	1.00	10c dk. blue Lawton, sia 245
289	25.00	1.00	16c ol. gr. Sampson, sia 247
289A	13.50	3.75	20c or. Washington, sia 248
289C	10.00	5.25	30c gray Franklin, sia 250
289D	20.00	5.50	1p pale violet Manila Arms, sia 251
Issue of 1917–25			
Perf. 11, Unwmkd.			
290	.10	.05	2c yel. green Rizal, sia 241
290e	6.50		Booklet pane of six
291	.10	.05	4c carm. McKinley, sia 242
291b	2.50	1.50	Booklet pane of six
292	.30	.08	6c dp. vio. Magellan, sia 243
292c	37.50		Booklet pane of six

293	.20	.12	8c yellow brown Legaspi, sia 244
294	.20	.08	10c deep blue Lawton, sia 245
295	.30	.15	12c red orange Lincoln, sia 246
296	9.00	.15	16c light olive green Sampson, sia 247
297	.35	.10	20c orange yellow Washington, sia 248
298	.55	.50	26c green Carriedo, sia 249
299	.50	.10	30c gray Franklin, sia 250
300	17.00	1.00	1p pale violet Manila Arms, sia 251
301	15.00	.60	2p violet brown Manila Arms, sia 251
302	9.00	.25	4p blue Manila Arms, sia 251
Issue of 1923–26			
303	.75	.15	16c Adm. George Dewey
304	30.00	3.65	10p deep green Manila Arms, sia 254
Issue of 1926			
Perf. 12, Unwmkd.			
319	.35	.25	2c Legislative Palace
320	.35	.35	4c Legislative Palace
321	.80	.75	6c Legislative Palace
322	.85	.65	18c Legislative Palace
323	1.25	1.10	20c Legislative Palace
324	1.00	.70	24c Legislative Palace
325	15.00	12.50	1p Legislative Palace

This issue commemoraties the opening of the Legislative Palace at Manila.

Coil Stamp of 1928			
Perf. 11 Vertically			
326	2.00	2.00	2c green Rizal, sia 241
Issue of 1925–31			
Imperf., Unwmkd.			
340	.12	.12	2c green Rizal, sia 241
341	.20	.20	4c carmine McKinley, sia 242

358   359

360   368   369

342	1.75	1.75	6c deep violet Magellan, sia 243
343	1.50	1.50	8c yellow brown Legaspi, sia 244
344	2.00	2.00	10c deep blue Lawton, sia 245
345	2.75	2.75	12c red orange Lincoln, sia 246
346	2.00	2.00	16c olive bistre Dewey, sia 303
347	2.00	2.00	20c yellow Washington, sia 248
348	2.00	2.00	26c blue green Carriedo, sia 249
349	2.25	2.25	30c gray Franklin, sia 250
350	6.00	6.00	1p violet Manila Arms, sia 251
351	13.00	13.00	2p violet brown Manila Arms, sia 251

368	2.25	.50	1p (in orange) on 4p Arms of Manila
369	4.00	.90	2p (in red) on 4p Arms of Manila

Issue of 1934, Perf. 11-1/2, 12

380	.18	.18	2c Baseball Players
381	.35	.35	6c Tennis Player
382	.70	.70	16c Basketball Players

The issue honors the Tenth Far Eastern Championship Games.

Issues of 1935, Perf. 11

383	.05	.04	2c José Rizal
384	.05	.05	4c Woman and Carabao
385	.09	.06	6c La Filipina
386	.12	.12	8c Pearl Fishing
387	.22	.20	10c Fort Santiago
388	.18	.15	12c Salt Spring
389	.18	.12	16c Magellan's Landing
390	.25	.06	20c "Juan de la Cruz"
391	.35	.35	26c Rice Terraces
392	.35	.35	30c "Blood Compact", 1565

352	22.50	22.50	4p deep blue Manila Arms, sia 251
353	**55.00**	50.00	10p deep green Manila Arms, sia 251

Issue of 1932, Perf. 11

354	.75	.35	2c Mayon Volcano
355	.50	.35	4c Post Office, Manila
356	.75	.75	12c Pier No. 7, Manila Bay

No. 357 was intended to show a view of Pagsanjan Falls, and is so labeled. By error the stamp actually shows a view of Vernal Falls in Yosemite National Park, California.

357	12.50	8.50	18c Vernal Falls
358	1.00	.80	20c Rice Planting
359	1.50	1.00	24c Rice Terraces
360	1.50	1.15	32c Baguio Zigzag

Stamps of 1917-25, Surcharged.

393	2.00	1.85	1p Barasoain Church, Malolos
394	3.75	1.75	2p Battle of Manila, 1898
395	3.75	3.75	4p Montalban Gorge
396	8.00	2.25	5p George Washington

Commonwealth Issue

397	.10	.08	2c "The Temples of Human Progress"
398	.15	.12	6c "The Temples of Human Progress"
399	.25	.20	16c "The Temples of Human Progess"
400	.45	.45	36c "The Temples of Human Progress"
401	.70	.70	50c "The Temples of Human Progress"

The Philippine Commonwealth was inaugurated on Nov. 15, 1935.

Issues of 1936
Perf. 12

402	.10	.10	2c José Rizal
403	.15	.15	6c José Rizal
404	.60	.60	36c José Rizal

1936 marked the 75th anniversary of the birth of José Rizal.

Perf. 11

408	.06	.06	2c Pres. Manuel L. Quezon
409	.12	.10	6c Pres. Manuel L. Quezon
410	.18	.15	12c Pres. Manuel L. Quezon

Issued for the first anniversary of the Commonwealth. Stamps show Manuel L. Quezon (1878-1944), first President of the Philippines.

Issue of 1936-37
Stamps of 1935 Overprinted in Black:

COMMON-
WEALTH **COMMONWEALTH**

a **Perf. 11** *b*

Nos. 411, 413, and 418 are overprinted
with type "a".
Nos. 412, 414-417, 419-424 are overprinted
with type "b".

411	.06	.04	2c rose Rizal, sia 383
411a	1.00	.90	Booklet pane of six
412	.75	.40	4c yellow green Woman, sia 384
413	.25	.10	6c dark brn. La Filipina, sia 385

414	.35	.30	8c violet Pearl Fishing, sia 386
415	.18	.06	10c rose carmine Ft. Santiago, sia 387
416	.18	.08	12c black Salt Spring, sia 388
417	.25	.20	16c dark blue Magellan's Landing, sia 389
418	.70	.50	20c light olive green "Juan de la Cruz", sia 390
419	.60	.45	26c indigo Rice Terraces, sia 391
420	.25	.15	30c orange red "Blood Compact", sia 392
421	.90	.30	1p red orange and black Church, sia 393
422	5.00	2.50	2p bistre brown and black Manila Bay, sia 394
423	10.00	2.00	4p blue and black Montalban Gorge, sia 395
424	1.75	1.65	5p green and black Washington, sia 396

Issues of 1937

425	.06	.06	2c Map of Philippines
426	.15	.10	6c Map of Philippines
427	.20	.10	12c Map of Philippines
428	.30	.12	20c Map of Philippines
429	.50	.50	36c Map of Philippines
430	.65	.35	50c Map of Philippines

Issue commemorates the 33rd Eucharistic Congress.

Perf. 11

431	3.75	2.50	10p Arms of Manila
432	2.00	1.85	20p Arms of Manila

Issues of 1938-40, Perf. 11

Stamps of 1935 Overprinted in Black

COMMON-WEALTH	COMMONWEALTH
a	b

Nos. 433, 435, and 440 are overprinted with type "a". Nos. 434, 436-439, 441-446 are overprinted with type "b".

433	.08	.05	2c rose Rizal, sia 383
433a	1.00	.90	Booklet pane of six
434	.60	.50	4c yellow green Woman, sia 384
435	.08	.08	6c dk. brown La Filipina, sia 385
436	.10	.10	8c violet Pearl Fishing, sia 386
437	.10	.06	10c rose car. Ft. Santiago, sia 387
438	.10	.09	12c black Salt Spring, sia 388
439	.18	.10	16c dark blue Magellan's Landing, sia 389
440	.20	.10	20c light olive green "Juan de la Cruz", sia 390
441	.25	.30	26c indigo Rice Terraces, sia 391
442	1.45	.85	30c orange red "Blood Compact", sia 392
443	.50	.25	1p red orange and black Church, sia 393
444	3.00	1.00	2p bistre brown and black Manila Bay, sia 394
445	30.00	25.00	4p blue and black Montalban Gorge, sia 395
446	4.00	4.00	5p green and black Washington, sia 396

Foreign Trade Week Issue

Stamps of 1917-37 Surcharged in Red, Violet or Black:

FIRST FOREIGN   **TRADE WEEK**

MAY 21-27, 1939   **2** CENTAVOS

Type a: on 449

FIRST FOREIGN TRADE WEEK   **50**CENTAVOS**50**

FIRST FOREIGN TRADE WEEK

MAY 21-27, 1939   **MAY 21-27, 1939**

6 CENTAVOS**6**

Type b: on 450   Type c: on 451

449	.10	.08	2c (in red) on 4c yellow green, sia 384
450	.20	.20	6c (in violet) on 26c blue green, sia 249
451	1.00	.90	50c (in black) on 20p henna brown, sia 432

Commonwealth Fourth Anniv. Issue, 1939-40

1939

452	.10	.08	2c Triumphal Arch
453	.15	.10	6c Triumphal Arch
454	.25	.10	12c Triumphal Arch
455	.10	.06	2c Malacañan Palace
456	.15	.10	6c Malacañan Palace
457	.25	.08	12c Malacañan Palace

1940

458	.10	.08	2c Quezon Inauguration
459	.15	.12	6c Quezon Inauguration
460	.30	.15	12c Quezon Inauguration

Nos. 452-460 were issued to commemorate the fourth anniversary of the Commonwealth.

Issue of 1941, Perf. 11x10-1/2

461	.05	.04	2c José Rizal

Issue of 1941-43, Perf. 11

462	.12	.06	2c apple green Rizal, sia 461

452 453 454
453

455 457
456

458 460
459

461

462b	.80	.70	Booklet pane of six

This stamp was issued in booklet panes and all copies have straight edges.

Further printings were made in 1942 and 1943 in different shades from the first supply of stamps sent to the islands.

No. 462 was privately overprinted in red or black "PPC V-PEX Oct. 20, 21, 22, 1945 To Commemorate First Anniv. Leyte D-Day" in seven lines by the Philippine Philatelic Club.

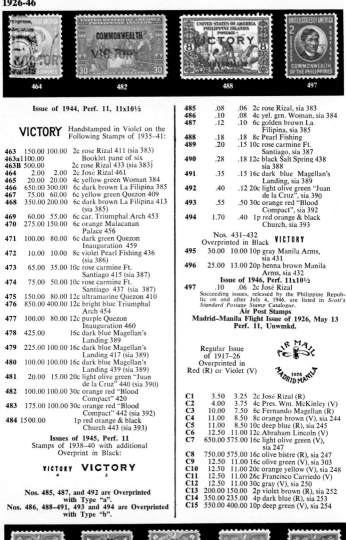

464 482 488 497

Issue of 1944, Perf. 11, 11x10½

VICTORY Handstamped in Violet on the Following Stamps of 1935–41:

463	150.00	100.00	2c rose Rizal 411 (sia 383)
463a	1100.00		Booklet pane of six
463B	500.00		2c rose Rizal 433 (sia 383)
464	2.00	2.00	2c José Rizal 461
465	20.00	20.00	4c yellow green Woman 384
466	650.00	300.00	6c dark brown La Filipina 385
467	75.00	60.00	6c yellow green Quezon 409
468	350.00	200.00	6c dark brown La Filipina 413 (sia 385)
469	60.00	55.00	6c car. Triumphal Arch 453
470	275.00	150.00	6c orange Malacanan Palace 456
471	100.00	80.00	6c dark green Quezon Inauguration 459
472	10.00	10.00	8c violet Pearl Fishing 436 (sia 386)
473	65.00	35.00	10c rose carmine Ft. Santiago 415 (sia 387)
474	75.00	50.00	10c rose carmine Ft. Santiago 437 (sia 387)
475	150.00	80.00	12c ultramarine Quezon 410
476	850.00	400.00	12c bright blue Triumphal Arch 454
477	100.00	80.00	12c purple Quezon Inauguration 460
478	425.00		16c dark blue Magellan's Landing 389
479	225.00	100.00	16c dark blue Magellan's Landing 417 (sia 389)
480	100.00	100.00	16c dark blue Magellan's Landing 439 (sia 389)
481	20.00	15.00	20c light olive green "Juan de la Cruz" 440 (sia 390)
482	100.00	100.00	30c orange red "Blood Compact" 420
483	175.00	100.00	30c orange red "Blood Compact" 442 (sia 392)
484	1500.00		1p red orange & black Church 443 (sia 393)

Issues of 1945, Perf. 11
Stamps of 1938–40 with additional Overprint in Black:

VICTORY *a* **VICTORY** *b*

Nos. 485, 487, and 492 are Overprinted with Type "a".
Nos. 486, 488–491, 493 and 494 are Overprinted with Type "b".

485	.08	.06	2c rose Rizal, sia 383
486	.10	.08	4c yel. grn. Woman, sia 384
487	.12	.10	6c golden brown La Filipina, sia 385
488	.18	.18	8c Pearl Fishing
489	.20	.15	10c rose carmine Ft. Santiago, sia 387
490	.28	.18	12c black Salt Spring 438 sia 388
491	.35	.15	16c dark blue Magellan's Landing, sia 389
492	.40	.12	20c light olive green "Juan de la Cruz", sia 390
493	.55	.50	30c orange red "Blood Compact", sia 392
494	1.70	.40	1p red orange & black Church, sia 393

Nos. 431–432
Overprinted in Black **VICTORY**

495	30.00	10.00	10p gray Manila Arms, sia 431
496	25.00	13.00	20p henna brown Manila Arms, sia 432

Issue of 1946, Perf. 11x10½

497	.10	.06	2c José Rizal

Succeeding issues, released by the Philippine Republic on and after July 4, 1946, are listed in *Scott's Standard Postage Stamp Catalogue.*

Air Post Stamps
Madrid–Manila Flight Issue of 1926, May 13
Perf. 11, Unwmkd.

Regular Issue of 1917–26 Overprinted in Red (R) or Violet (V)

C1	3.50	3.25	2c José Rizal (R)
C2	4.00	3.75	4c Pres. Wm. McKinley (V)
C3	10.00	7.50	6c Fernando Magellan (R)
C4	11.00	8.50	8c orange brown (V), sia 244
C5	11.00	8.50	10c deep blue (R), sia 245
C6	12.50	11.00	12c Abraham Lincoln (V)
C7	650.00	575.00	16c light olive green (V), sia 247
C8	750.00	575.00	16c olive bistre (R), sia 247
C9	12.50	11.00	16c olive green (V), sia 303
C10	12.50	11.00	20c orange yellow (V), sia 248
C11	12.50	11.00	26c Francisco Carriedo (V)
C12	12.50	11.00	30c gray (V), sia 250
C13	200.00	150.00	2p violet brown (R), sia 252
C14	350.00	235.00	4p dark blue (R), sia 253
C15	550.00	400.00	10p deep green (V), sia 254

C1 C2 C3 C6 C11

REPUBLIC OF THE PHILIPPINES, ASIA'S YOUNG DEMOCRACY

The Philippine islands, discovered by Magellan in 1521, were controlled by Spain for three hundred years before the islanders revolted and declared their independence in 1898. The Spanish-American War of that year, however, doomed this first attempt at becoming a republic. During that brief conflict Spain was driven out of the archipelago and control of the Philippines fell to the United States.

Guerilla war broke out again in 1899, this time against the United States. Led by Emilio Aguinaldo, it continued until 1905.

Even with the cessation of hostilities the Philippines continued to demand independence and in 1934 the United States declared 1946 as freedom year. The Japanese occupation of World War II failed to halt freedom plans and on July 4, 1946 the Philippines became an independent nation.

The Republic consists of more than 7,000 mountainous islands. The official languages are Filipino (taken from Tagalog), English, and Spanish. The native people are mainly of Malay stock, but Spanish, Chinese, American and other immigrants have produced an ethnically mixed population.

		Wmkd. Single-lined PIPS (190PI)	
		Perf. 12	
		Same Overprint on No. 269	
C16	750.00		26c blue green (V), sia 249
		Perf. 10	
		Same Overprint on No. 284	
C17	75.00	50.00	1p pale violet (V), sia 251

This issue honors the flight of Spanish aviators Gallarza and Loriga from Madrid to Manila.

London-Orient Flight Issue of 1928, Nov. 9
Perf. 11
Unwmkd.

Regular Issue
of 1917-25
Overprinted in Red

L.O.F.

1928

C18	.40	.40	2c green, sia 241
C19	.50	.50	4c carmine, sia 242
C20	1.75	1.75	6c violet, sia 243
C21	1.85	1.85	8c orange brown, sia 244
C22	1.85	1.85	10c deep blue, sia 245
C23	2.50	2.50	12c red orange, sia 246
C24	2.25	2.25	16c olive green, sia 303
C25	3.00	3.00	20c George Washington
C26	6.25	6.25	26c blue green, sia 249
C27	6.25	6.25	30c gray, sia 250

Perf. 12
Same Overprint on No. 271
Wmkd. Single-lined PIPS (190PI)

C28	18.00	18.00	1p Arms of Manila

Stamp honors air flight from London to Manila.

Issue of 1932, Sep. 27
Perf. 11, Unwmkd.
Nos. 354-360 Overprinted

ROUND-THE-WORLD FLIGHT
VON GRONAU

1932

C29	.45	.45	2c yellow green, sia 354
C30	.50	.50	4c Post Office, Manila
C31	.80	.80	12c orange, sia 356
C32	4.00	4.00	18c red orange, sia 357
C33	2.25	2.25	20c Rice Planting
C34	2.25	2.25	24c Rice Terraces
C35	2.25	2.25	32c olive brown, sia 360

In 1932, Captain Wolfgang von Gronau visited the Philippines during his historic round-the-world flight.

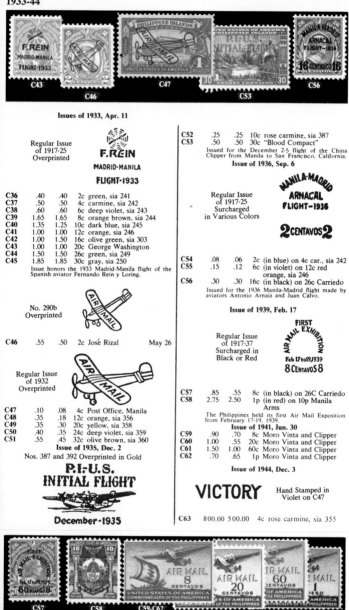

C43   C46   C47   C53   C56

Issues of 1933, Apr. 11

Regular Issue
of 1917-25
Overprinted

F.REIN

MADRID-MANILA

FLIGHT-1933

C36	.40	.40	2c green, sia 241
C37	.50	.50	4c carmine, sia 242
C38	.60	.60	6c deep violet, sia 243
C39	1.65	1.65	8c orange brown, sia 244
C40	1.35	1.25	10c dark blue, sia 245
C41	1.00	1.00	12c orange, sia 246
C42	1.00	1.50	16c olive green, sia 303
C43	1.00	1.00	20c George Washington
C44	1.50	1.50	26c green, sia 249
C45	1.85	1.85	30c gray, sia 250

Issue honors the 1933 Madrid-Manila flight of the Spanish aviator Fernando Rein y Loring.

No. 290b
Overprinted

AIR MAIL

C46	.55	.50	2c José Rizal	May 26

Regular Issue
of 1932
Overprinted

AIR MAIL

C47	.10	.08	4c Post Office, Manila
C48	.35	.18	12c orange, sia 356
C49	.35	.30	20c yellow, sia 358
C50	.40	.35	24c deep violet, sia 359
C51	.55	.45	32c olive brown, sia 360

Issue of 1935, Dec. 2

Nos. 387 and 392 Overprinted in Gold

P.I.-U.S.
INITIAL FLIGHT

December-1935

C52	.25	.25	10c rose carmine, sia 387
C53	.50	.50	30c "Blood Compact"

Issued for the December 2-5 flight of the China Clipper from Manila to San Francisco, California.

Issue of 1936, Sep. 6

Regular Issue
of 1917-25
Surcharged
in Various Colors

MANILA-MADRID
ARNACAL
FLIGHT-1936

2 CENTAVOS 2

C54	.08	.06	2c (in blue) on 4c car., sia 242
C55	.15	.12	6c (in violet) on 12c red orange, sia 246
C56	.30	.30	16c (in black) on 26c Carriedo

Issued for the 1936 Manila-Madrid flight made by aviators Antonio Arnaiz and Juan Calvo.

Issue of 1939, Feb. 17

Regular Issue
of 1917-37
Surcharged in
Black or Red

FIRST
AIR MAIL EXHIBITION
Feb 17 to 19, 1939
8 CENTAVOS 8

C57	.85	.55	8c (in black) on 26C Carriedo
C58	2.75	2.50	1p (in red) on 10p Manila Arms

The Philippines held its first Air Mail Exposition from February 17-19, 1939.

Issue of 1941, Jun. 30

C59	.90	.70	8c Moro Vinta and Clipper
C60	1.00	.55	20c Moro Vinta and Clipper
C61	1.50	1.00	60c Moro Vinta and Clipper
C62	.70	.65	1p Moro Vinta and Clipper

Issue of 1944, Dec. 3

VICTORY   Hand Stamped in Violet on C47

C63	800.00	500.00	4c rose carmine, sia 355

C57   C58   C59-C62

THE SIEGE OF THE PHILIPPINES: 1941-45

Japan's World War II invasion of the Philippines began ten hours after the surprise attack on Pearl Harbor of December 7, 1941. On January 2, 1942 Manila fell before a Japanese land invasion and Allied forces under the command of General Douglas A. MacArthur retreated to Bataan and Corregidor.

On February 22 MacArthur transferred his headquarters to Australia by order of President Franklin D. Roosevelt. In April Bataan succumbed, but troops under General Jonathan Wainwright remained at Corregidor, an island fortress in Manila Bay. Though vastly outnumbered and low on supplies, the heroic army kept Japan's navy out of Manila Bay until May 6, 1942 when the fall of Corregidor ended all organized Philippine resistance to the Japanese.

925

More than two years after this defeat, on October 9, 1944, MacArthur returned to the Philippines and invaded Leyte. The Battle of Leyte Gulf (October 23-25) ended with three Japanese units in retreat. Soon afterward the Allies were victorious at Mindoro and Luzon. When Manila was liberated on February 25, 1945 the general had fulfilled his famous promise, "I shall return."

See U.S. Scott Stamp Nos. 925, 1424

Special Delivery Stamps
Issue of 1901, Perf. 12

United States No. E5 **PHILIPPINES**
Overprinted in Red

Wmkd. Double–lined USPS (191)
E1   30.00   30.00   10c dark blue, sia U.S. E5
Issue of 1906
Wmkd. Double–lined PIPS (191PI)
E2   9.00   5.50   20c ultramarine, sia E3
Special Printing of 1907
Red Overprint of E1 on U.S. No. E6
E2A   475.00   10c ultramarine, sia U.S. E6
Issue of 1911
Wmkd. Single–lined PIPS (190PI)
E3   7.00   1.25   20c Special Delivery Messenger
Issue of 1916, Perf. 10
E4   45.00   12.50   20c deep ultramarine, sia E3
Issue of 1919, Perf. 11, Unwmkd.
E5   .45   .25   20c ultramarine, sia E3
Issue of 1931, Imperf.
E6   6.50   6.50   20c Special Delivery Messenger
Issue of 1939, Perf. 11
type of 1919

Overprinted **COMMONWEALTH**
in Black

E7   .30   .30   20c blue violet, sia E3

Issue of 1944

VICTORY   Handstamped in Violet on E5b and E7

E8   125.00   90.00   20c dull violet, sia E3
E9   75.00   60.00   20c blue violet, sia E3

Issue of 1945

No. E7
with additional **VICTORY**
Overprint
in Black

E10   .60   .60   20c Special Delivery Messenger

Official Special Delivery Stamp
Perf. 11, Unwmkd.

E5b Overprinted **O.B.**

EO1   .65   .55   20c dull violet, sia E3

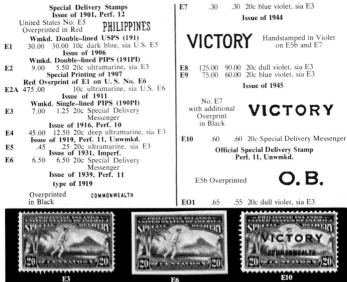

E3   E6   E10

Postage Due Stamps

Issue of 1899, Design of U. S. J33
Perf. 12

Postage Due Stamps
of the United States
Nos. J38 to J44
Overprinted in Black

PHILIPPINES

Wmkd. USPS (191)

J1	1.75	1.10	1c deep claret
J2	1.75	1.10	2c deep claret
J3	2.00	1.65	5c deep claret
J4	3.75	3.25	10c deep claret
J5	35.00	32.50	50c deep claret

Issue of 1901

J6	3.50	3.50	3c deep claret
J7	37.50	32.50	30c deep claret

Issue of 1928, sia J10
Perf. 11, Unwmkd.

J8	.12	.12	4c brown red
J9	.15	.15	6c brown red
J10	.15	.15	8c Post Office Clerk
J11	.18	.18	10c brown red
J12	.20	.20	12c brown red
J13	.25	.25	16c brown red
J14	.18	.18	20c brown red

Issue of 1937

No. J8
Surcharged in Blue   **3 CVOS. 3**

J15	.20	.12	3c (3 cvos. 3 in blue) on 4c brown red, sia J10

Issue of 1944, sia J10

VICTORY   Handstamped in Violet
on Nos. J8–J14

J16	40.00	4c brown red
J17	30.00	6c brown red
J18	35.00	8c brown red
J19	30.00	10c brown red
J20	30.00	12c brown red
J21	30.00	16c brown red
J22	35.00	20c brown red

Official Stamps

Regular Issue
of 1926   **OFFICIAL**
Overprinted in Red

Issue of 1926, Perf. 12
Unwmkd.

O1	1.75	1.75	2c green and black, sia 319
O2	1.75	1.60	4c carmine and black, sia 320
O3	4.50	3.25	18c lt. brown and black, sia 322
O4	3.50	1.75	20c orange and black, sia 323

Note: Prior to 1926, stamps used for official business
handstamped "OB" or "Official Business." For information on these stamps, refer to the Appendix.

Regular Issue
of 1917–26   **O. B.**
Overprinted

Issue of 1931, Perf. 11

O5	.06	.04	2c green, sia 241

O6	.08	.05	4c carmine, sia 242
O7	.10	.08	6c deep violet, sia 243
O8	.10	.08	8c yellow brown, sia 244
O9	.40	.12	10c deep blue, sia 245
O10	.25	.15	12c red orange, sia 246
O11	.25	.15	16c light olive green, sia 303
O12	.30	.10	20c orange yellow, sia 248
O13	.45	.45	26c green, sia 249
O14	.40	.35	30c gray, sia 250

Issues of 1935
Same Overprint on Regular Issue of 1935

O15	.06	.04	2c rose, sia 383
O16	.06	.05	4c yellow green, sia 384
O17	.10	.06	6c dark brown, sia 385
O18	.12	.12	8c Pearl Fishing
O19	.15	.06	10c rose carmine, sia 387
O20	.20	.15	12c black, sia 388
O21	.20	.15	16c dark blue, sia 389
O22	.20	.15	20c light olive green, sia 390
O23	.40	.35	26c indigo, sia 391
O24	.45	.40	30c orange red, sia 392

Same Overprint on Overprinted Issue of 1936-37

O25	.08	.04	2c rose, sia 383
O26	1.00	.75	20c light olive green, sia 390

Issue of 1938-40, Perf. 10
Regular Issue of 1935
Overprinted in Black:

O. **B.**   **O.** **B.**

COMMON-   COMMONWEALTH
WEALTH
a   *b*

Nos. O27, O29, and O34 are overprinted
with type "a".
Nos. O28, O30-O33, O35 and O36 are
overprinted with type "b".

O27	.08	.04	2c rose, sia 383
O28	.10	.08	4c yellow green, sia 384
O29	.15	.06	6c dark brown, sia 385
O30	.15	.10	8c violet, sia 386
O31	.17	.10	10c rose carmine, sia 387
O32	.18	.18	12c black, sia 388
O33	.25	.12	16c dark blue, sia 389
O34	.35	.35	20c light olive green, sia 390
O35	.45	.45	26c indigo, sia 391
O36	.40	.40	30c "Blood Compact"

Issue of 1941, Perf. 11x10-1/2
Unwmkd.

Regular Stamp of 1941   **O.** **B.**
Overprinted in Black
c

O37	.04	.04	2c Rizal

Issue of 1944, Perf. 11, 11x10-1/2

VICTORY   Handstamped in Violet
on the Following:

O38	160.00	75.00	2c rose O27 (sia 383)
O39	5.00	3.00	2c apple green O37
O40	20.00	17.50	4c yellow green O16 (sia 384)
O40A	2000.00		6c dark brown O29 (sia 385)
O41	200.00		10c rose carmine O31 (sia 387)
O42	1000.00		20c lt. olive green O22 (sia 390)
O43	2000.00		20c lt. olive green O26 (sia 390)

Issue of 1946, Perf. 11x10-1/2
Black Overprint of O37 on No. 497

O44	.06	.05	2c sepia, sia 497

J10   O18   O34   O36   O37

PUERTO RICO
(pwěr' tǔ rē' kō)
(Porto Rico)

When Christopher Columbus discovered this island of green mountains and fertile valleys in 1493, it was the only time he set foot on what is now U. S. territory. Soon afterwards gold was found in the Puerto Rican mountains, and in 1508 Juan Ponce de León brought settlers to the island and became its first governor. The gold, however, was soon exhausted and the colonists were plagued by hurricanes and pirates. Finally, at the islanders' request, Spain fortified the island with impregnable fortresses that withstood foreign attack until the United States invaded Puerto Rico during the Spanish-American War of 1898. At this short war's conclusion Puerto Rico became an American possession. Since 1917 its people have been U. S. citizens.

LOCATION—A large island in the West Indies, east of Hispaniola.
GOVT.—Former Spanish possession.
AREA—3,435 sq. mi.
POP.—2,689,932 (1970).
CAPITAL—San Juan.
Spanish issues of 1855-71 for Puerto Rico were also used by Cuba.

Issued Under U. S. Administration

CORREOS

5 CTS.

COAMO

Issues of 1898, Imperf
Unwmkd.

200	1200.00	—	5c Ponce Issue

Counterfeits of Nos. 200-201 exist.

201	150.00	175.00	5c Coamo Issue

There are ten varieties in the setting. The stamps bear the control mark "F. Santiago" in violet.

Issue of 1899, Perf. 12

United States
Nos. 279a, 267, 281a,
272 and 282C
Overprinted in Black
at 36 degree angle

Wmkd. USPS (191)

210	2.00	.75	1c Benjamin Franklin
211	2.00	.35	2c George Washington

212	2.25	1.25	5c Ulysses S. Grant
213	7.50	6.00	8c William T. Sherman
214	4.50	2.50	10c Daniel Webster

Issue of 1900

United States Stamps
Nos. 279a and 267
Overprinted Diagonally
in Black

215	1.35	.75	1c yellow grn. Franklin, sia 210
216	1.35	.60	2c carmine Washington, sia 211

Postage Due Stamps
Issue of 1899, Perf. 12

United States
Nos. J38, J39 and J42
Overprinted in Black
at 36 degree angle

Wmkd. USPS (191)

J1	5.00	3.25	1c deep clearet, design of J2
J2	4.50	3.25	2c Figure of Value
J3	35.00	20.00	10c deep claret, design of J2

Stamps of Puerto Rico have been replaced by those of the United States.

210	211	212	213	214	J2

Major U.S. Philatelic Publications and Societies

Catalogues

Minkus New World Wide Stamp Catalogue
New York, 1973.

Scott Standard Postage Stamp Catalogue.
New York, 1973.

First Day Cover Catalogue (U.S.-U.N.)
Washington Press
Maplewood, New Jersey 07040

United States Stamps & Stories,
published for the U.S.P.S.
by Scott Publishing Co., 1973.

Magazines and Newspapers

Linn's Stamp News
Box 29
Sidney, Ohio 45365

Mekeel's Weekly Stamp News
Box 1660
Portland, Maine 04104

Minkus Stamp Journal
116 West 32nd Street
New York, New York 10001

Scott Monthly Journal
10102 F Street
Omaha, Nebraska 68127

Stamps
153 Waverly Place
New York, New York 45365

Western Stamp Collector
Box 10
Albany, Oregon 97321

Philatelic Literature

Brookman, Lester G. *The 19th Century Postage Stamps of the United States.* (3 volumes). New York, 1968.

Chase, Carroll C. *The 3c Stamps of the United States.* Springfield, Massachusetts, 1942.

Johl, Max G. *The United States Commemorative Stamps of the Twentieth Century.* New York, 1947.

Kimble, Ralph A. *Commemorative Postage Stamps of the United States.* New York, 1933.

Lidman, David. *The New York Times Guide to Collecting Stamps.* New York, 1970.

Luff, John N. *The Postage Stamps of the United States.* New York, 1907.

Mueller, Barbara R. *United States Postage Stamps.* Princeton, 1958.

Patrick, Douglas and Mary. *The Musson Stamp Dictionary.* Toronto, 1972.

Sampson, E.N. *The American Stampless Cover Catalog.* Albany, Oregon, 1971.

Scheele, Carl H. *A Short History of the Mail Service.* Washington, D.C., 1970.

Scott's New Handbook for Philatelists. New York, 1967.

Thorp, Prescott H. *The Complete Guide to Stamp Collecting.* New York, 1953.

United Postal Stationery Society. *United States Postal Card Catalog.* Albany, Oregon, 1970.

United States Postal Service. *United States Postage Stamps.* Washington, D.C., 1972.

Many of the books listed above, while not currently in print, are available at public libraries.

Philatelic Societies

American First Day Cover Society
626 Woodward Building
Washington, D.C. 20005

American Philatelic Society
Box 800
State College, Pennsylvania 16801

American Stamp Dealers Association
595 Madison Avenue
New York, New York 10022

American Topical Association
3308 North 50th
Milwaukee, Wisconsin 53216

Bureau Issues Association
19 Maple Street
Arlington, Massachusetts 02174

Society of Philatelic Americans
P.O. Box 42060
Cincinnati, Ohio 45242

For the name of the stamp dealer nearest you, consult your Yellow Pages under the listing "Stamps" or "Stamps for Collectors."

UNITED STATES STAMP PRODUCTION

Creation of a Postage Stamp

Stamp designed by Stevan Dohanos

Letters requesting commemorative and other postage stamps originate with individuals and organizations, and are sent to the Postmaster General. A Citizens' Stamp Advisory Committee makes recommendations for new stamp issues from the thousands of requests on file. The Postmaster General makes the final determination based on the Committee's recommendations.

When a new postage stamp is approved for issuance, the U. S. Postal Service commissions an artist to provide a design. Outstanding American artists, such as Norman Rockwell, Stevan Dohanos, Bradbury Thompson, Robert Geissmann and Jamie Wyeth have designed United States postage stamps.

Stamps designed by
Norman Rockwell, Jamie Wyeth.

Stamps designed by
Bradbury Thompson, Robert Geissmann.

The Bureau of Engraving and Printing of the Treasury Department then prepares a model for the proposed stamp, following the artist's design and other suggestions the Postal Service may furnish. Additional models may be called for until one is found to be satisfactory. An acceptable model is approved and returned to the Bureau of Engraving and Printing for the engraving of the master die. This consists of cutting the design into a piece of soft steel from which completed prints, known as die proofs, are pulled in various colors and presented to the Postmaster General for final approval of the design and color of ink to be used in the printing. After approval of the die proof, the master die is hardened by heating to a very high degree. The hardened master die is then impressed into a soft steel roll, thereby transferring the master impression. The roll is then hardened and subsequently impressed into a soft steel plate the desired number of times. When the plate is hardened, it is attached to a press to begin its role in stamp printing.

Proof

Proof

Postage stamp plates are also produced by the electrolytic process (electroplating). A master plate is produced as described earlier. The master plate is immersed in a plating tank and metallic plating is deposited on the master. After the desired thickness of plating is applied, the plating is separated from the master. The result is a *working alto,* that is, what is engraved or incised below the surface of the master plate now stands in relief above the surface of the working alto in reverse. Then, using the working alto in the plating tank, the process is repeated. This reverses the image to its original condition, and press plates are produced.

Still another method of plate making is to transfer the stamp design to a metal cylinder by photography, and the cylinder is then subjected to an etching process to produce a rotogravure cylinder.

Production Techniques

Equipment modernization is a continuing program at the Bureau of Engraving and Printing, which prints most U.S. postage stamps.

Today's postage stamp printing equipment includes:

Andreotti Rotogravure

This press can print on either gummed or ungummed rolls. It is capable of printing in seven colors, and can apply phosphor and deliver the finished printings in sheet or roll form. It can produce stamps at speeds up to 900 feet per minute.

Huck Nine Color

This press is capable of printing six direct intaglio colors and three indirect intaglio colors with one pass through the press. It is a web press capable of gumming, phosphoring, perforating and delivering the finished printings in sheet or roll form.

Cottrell Single Color

These presses are used to print single color stamps on a continuous web of ungummed paper. This equipment applies gum and phosphor to the stamps during the printing operation. These presses produce most of our regular postage stamp issues. They also have precanceling capabilities.

Giori Multicolor

Two of these presses are designed to operate with two printing plates while the third uses four plates. The Giori presses print on pregummed sheets of paper and print up to three colors with one pass through the press. A phosphor coating is later applied by the offset process. Many colorful commemorative issues are produced on the Giori presses, particularly those that combine the intaglio (engraved) impression printed over the offset underlay colors. Six offset (lithographing) presses are used to print background colors on some Giori-printed stamps.

Format of Plates

Postage stamps are produced in sheet, coil, and book form. Regular sheet stamps are usually printed from plates having 400 subjects and are divided into panes of 100 subjects. Coil stamps are produced from 360 and 432 subject plates, and book stamps from plates having 300, 360 and 400 subjects. Recent commemorative issues are produced in 200, 160, 128 subject formats. A new sheet format of 192 subjects was introduced in 1974 with the issuance of the Mineral Heritage stamps.

Perforating

Presently, the Huck 9-color press and the Andreotti gravure press are the only pieces of Bureau equipment capable of in-line perforating. Stamps produced on all other presses must be perforated separately. Coil stamps are perforated by equipment which reduces rolls of stamps into coils of 100, 500, and 3,000 stamps. For perforating stamps printed on the Giori presses, the Bureau uses an L-type perforator. Sheets are automatically fed into the machine, perforated in both directions, and delivered at the output end in a neat pile. Finally, the finished postage stamps are examined and packaged for delivery to the U.S. Postal Service sectional and first-class post offices across the country.

MINT SETS

1972, 1973 & 1974 Mint Sets each set contains all the commemorative and special stamps issued during the year, with acetate strips for mounting the stamps. Start your year-by-year collection in these bright, attractive folders that also give you the story behind each stamp, the designer, and other philatelic details.

Price $3.00 1972 Souvenir Mint Set
$3.00 1973 Souvenir Mint Set
$3.50 1974 Mint Set

STAMP COLLECTING KITS

U.S. Postal Service Stamp Collecting Kits (your choice of five different subjects) give you these four basic collecting tools:

> A 20 page album with a special theme.
>
> A 32 page booklet that tells you "The ABC's of Stamp Collecting."
>
> A selection of stamps to mount in the album in your kit.
>
> A packet of stamp hinges for mounting your stamps.

Just choose the kit or kits you like—World of Sports, Space, Animal Kingdom, Birds & Butterflies and Masterworks—and use the convenient attached order form for prompt service. Or write directly to: Philatelic Sales Division, Washington, D.C. 20265. *Price $2.00 each kit.*

Collecting Kit Binders keep your albums attractively handy, between bright, textured, toughwearing covers illustrated in full color. These sturdy, self-standing binders are 6″ x 9″. Three heavyduty ¾″ rings to hold up to 10 of your albums plus other inserts. *Price $2.00 each binder.*

215

HOW TO START
A STAMP CLUB

Historical records indicate that the first stamp club was the Société Philatelique de Paris which was organized in 1865. Since that time more and more stamp collectors have organized clubs devoted to the sharing of ideas, stamps and an enjoyable hobby. Being a member of a stamp club is a worthwhile way of learning more about stamps and collecting. If you would like to share your hobby with others, then why not join or form a community stamp club? If you are interested in forming a stamp club, here are some hints that could help make your club more successful and enjoyable.

GETTING MEMBERS

In order to find members for your club, it is important that you establish some form of publicity campaign. Try to publicize your club in as many different ways as possible, always remembering that your publicity should attract both younger and older collectors. Having members of different ages provides a diversity which is often the key to club success.

To help publicize your club to the younger collectors, ask the principals of your neighborhood schools to make announcements about it over the school's public address system. Also publicize your club through the use of the school's newspaper and bulletin boards.

If you're starting a stamp club in your school, you'll need a club sponsor—usually a teacher or the school's librarian. Club sponsors advise club members about such things as: organizing your club, planning club meetings, arranging field trips and explaining any special school policies which might affect your club. Finding a club sponsor isn't difficult. Ask the teachers in your school building —or you can ask your principal to help you find a sponsor.

Ask the managers of local stores, banks, restaurants and movie theaters if you may place club publicity posters in their business' windows. These posters should include such information as: when the club will meet, where the meeting will be held and how an interested person can obtain additional information. Try to make your publicity posters as colorful and informative as possible.

Another effective way to publicize your club is through the use of local newspapers and radio stations. Local newspapers are often willing to print announcements of club activities as a public service. Contact the newspaper's editor to determine if he will print free club announcements. Many local radio stations will make announcements of community activities at no charge. Contact the managers of your area's radio stations and find out if they will help publicize your club.

FINDING A PLACE TO MEET

The best meeting places are those which can be used for little or no cost and are conveniently located. Many stamp clubs hold their meetings in local schools, libraries, museums and churches. Other possible meeting places include the facilities of community youth organizations or the homes of club members.

ELECTING OFFICERS

The club's executive officers should be elected during the club's first official meeting. Begin by electing only the officers absolutely necessary for the club to function properly. Additional officers may be elected as they are needed from the club's expanding membership. It is extremely important that you encourage both younger and older members to accept leadership responsibilities within the organization.

ESTABLISHING CLUB RULES

The rules that govern club activities, members and officers should be

developed by the entire membership as early as possible. Many stamp clubs write a constitution or by-laws which can be duplicated and distributed to all members. Avoid making the rules too strict. Remember, your members want to learn and enjoy the hobby of stamp collecting and not be dominated by it.

KEEPING MEMBERS INFORMED

PLANNING CLUB ACTIVITIES

All of the club's membership should be involved in planning future meetings and activities. In this way you insure that the activities reflect the interests of the entire group. The planning of club activities should begin during the first club meeting. There are many types of activities that members enjoy; however, few members enjoy long business meetings, so try to keep them short.

Stamp clubs provide an opportunity for collectors to get together to trade, buy or sell stamps, and to exhibit collections. Often, guest speakers can be invited to provide informative lectures or to conduct a question and answer session. During these sessions a collector may learn the answer to many difficult hobby questions. Other enjoyable activities include the showing of films, conducting stamp auctions, participating in group discussions or staging stamp quiz shows. Stamp quiz shows usually resemble television quiz shows, however, only questions dealing with stamps and collecting are asked.

Keeping members informed of future meetings, activities, special events and important stamp news is a vital part of any club. Since this is so important, why not have your club consider publishing a newsletter? Many clubs issue a weekly or monthly newsletter to help keep their members informed. A club newsletter can be duplicated in a number of different ways and does not have to be elaborately designed. Many club newsletters consist of little more than a single piece of paper which has pertinent club information printed on the front and a calendar of meetings and special events on the back. Simple or elaborate, no matter how you make your club newsletter, remember that its primary purpose is to keep the members informed.

SUCCESS

These hints will help your club be successful. But real club success depends upon more than just helpful hints. The key to a successful stamp club lies in the interest and willingness of the members to share information and activities that unlock the wonders of the world of stamps.

FIRST-DAY COVERS

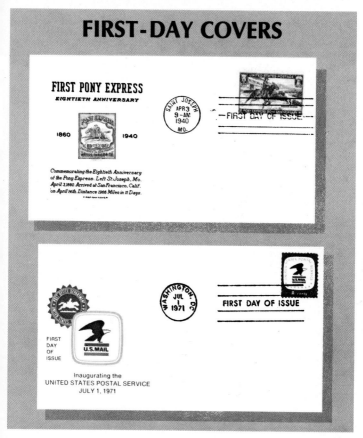

Collecting of first-day covers is a rapidly expanding part of philately. These covers are envelopes bearing a new stamp cancelled on the first-day of issue at the post office designated to conduct the first-day ceremonies.

For each new stamp or postal stationery issue, the Postal Service designates one post office where the item is first placed on sale. This post office generally is related to the subject being commemorated, and it is the only one permitted to sell the stamps on the first-day of issue. Other post offices place them on sale the following day.

The date and place of issue are announced through the press and on post office bulletin board posters. About six weeks prior to the issue date, collectors can send self-addressed plain or cacheted envelopes inside another envelope to "First Day Cover," care of the postmaster at the designated city together with the proper remittance for the stamps to be affixed.

The Postal Service does not provide cacheted envelopes (envelopes which carry a design or a cachet at the left of the envelope). These can be purchased from stamp dealers and some department stores or stationery stores.

The Postal Service services first-day covers as an accommodation only to collectors. For that reason, only a reasonable number—200 or less—will be serviced. Dealers and others requiring more than 200 covers should be present at the first-day city or make arrangements through private organizations which provide this service for a fee.

All requests for first-day covers must be postmarked by the day of issue. Covers submitted too late will be returned. Requests with improper remittances also will be returned.

Collectors who receive covers damaged in the mail should immediately return them to the designated post office for replacement.

The Postal Service makes every ef-

fort to provide quality and speedy first-day service, but the volume of requests sometimes causes delays. Between 400,-000 and 600,000 first-day covers are serviced on the average new issue. However, certain stamps are even more popular. The 10¢ Moon Landing Airmail Stamp had 8,700,000 first-day covers.

Elaborate local or state ceremonies are usually held on the first-day. One of the most widely seen ceremonies was a brief one conducted by astronaut David Scott on the moon, August 2, 1971, when he cancelled the twin stamps issued to mark a decade of space achievements.

SPECIALTY COLLECTING

Most people begin to collect stamps by purchasing new issues. In time, however, they begin to specialize in an area which opens new horizons of enjoyment. Stamp collecting is a personal hobby, and no two stamp collections are ever entirely alike. A collector should carefully and creatively explore each of the following areas to determine which specialties offer him the greatest satisfaction.

BLOCKS OF FOUR

Many collectors prefer to save blocks consisting of four mint stamps, since these are more plentiful than other blocks also described here.

PLATE BLOCKS

Plate block collecting is one of the oldest areas in U. S. stamp collecting. Plates used in the production of postage stamps possess serial numbers for identification. These appear on each corner of a sheet of stamps. After the sheet is cut into four panes for distribution, the plate number identifies which portion of the original sheet the pane occupied and by which plate it was printed. Known as plate blocks, these stamps with the serial number are eagerly collected. Because the length of effective use of printing plates does vary, some plates soon wear out. The relatively scarce panes printed by these short-lived plates are assiduously sought by plate block collectors.

BOOKLET PANES

Stamp booklets were first issued in 1898. On the average, only two new booklet panes are issued a year. Most philatelists collect entire unsevered panes or entire booklets (as sold in post offices).

The collecting of booklet panes or of plate, "ZIP", and "Mail Early" blocks is immensely popular because these collector's items are simple and easy to locate. All are available when issued at face value at most local post offices.

COVERS

Covers cancelled on the first day of issue of a postage stamp are collected enthusiastically by most philatelists. (See pp. 197-199.) In addition, many people collect anniversary, dedication, first flight, naval, space, and other types of covers.

"MR. ZIP" BLOCKS

One of the successful projects devised to increase postal efficiency is the Zone Improvement Plan, known as ZIP Code. This geographically keyed system of numbers helps postal clerks route the ever-increasing volume of mail more quickly. A "Mr. ZIP" cartoon with slogan was inaugurated with the Sam Houston Issue released January 10, 1964. The cartoon and slogan with adjoining block of four have since been readily collected.

"MAIL EARLY IN THE DAY" BLOCKS

The earlier in the day mail is deposited the faster it is processed. The slogan "MAIL EARLY IN THE DAY" was included in a margin of sheets of the 6¢ Flag and White House stamp released on January 24, 1968. This inscription appears on the selvage midway between the plate and ZIP blocks. Most philatelists collect the slogan in blocks of six stamps.

SOUVENIR CARDS

From 1938 to 1939 the Post Office Department Philatelic Truck toured the country distributing souvenir sheets which pictured the White House. These were the forerunners of modern souvenir cards. Now issued at philatelic exhibitions in which the government participates, souvenir cards bear reproductions of U. S. stamps which have been made postally invalid by enlargement or by alteration to remove denomination, country name, and reference to postage. This new aspect of collecting now has thousands of avid followers and is the most exciting innovation in many years.

With so many variations open to the U. S. collector, the stamp enthusiast works in a field of infinite possibilities in which to expand the pleasure and value of this hobby.

Mailgram...

A fast new communication service

Mailgram is a fast, new communications service provided jointly by the United States Postal Service and Western Union. Mailgrams are transmitted electronically over Western Union's computer-controlled communications network to terminal printers located in key postal installations throughout the continental United States. The Mailgram is received for delivery by regular letter carrier in the next business day's mail.

The service began in January of 1970 with a weekly volume of 35 messages being sent. Several hundred thousand Mailgrams are now being sent on a weekly basis.

Mailgrams may be sent in a variety of ways. Teleprinter subscribers may send Mailgrams directly via the Western Union computer center. High volume users may enter Mailgrams through computer-generated magnetic tape. Finally, the general public may send Mailgrams by calling, toll-free, Western Union's central telephone bureau or by going to a Western Union office.

Hey Kids!
You Can Get
All These
Stamp
Collecting
Kits By Mail!

BUILD A GREAT COLLECTION OF UNITED STATES POSTAL SERVICE STAMP COLLECTING KITS – OR GIVE THEM AS GIFTS!

Each kit contains genuine postage stamps; pre-folded hinges, 20-page illustrated stamp album, 32-page full-color illustrated booklet about the **ABC's of Stamp Collecting.**

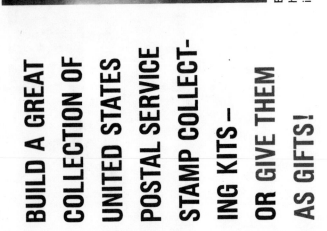

UNITED STATES PRESIDENTS AND VICE-PRESIDENTS

President	Term of Office	Vice-President
1. George Washington	Apr. 30, 1789 – Mar. 3, 1797	John Adams
2. John Adams	Mar. 4, 1797 – Mar. 3, 1801	Thomas Jefferson
3. Thomas Jefferson	Mar. 4, 1801 – Mar. 3, 1809	Aaron Burr (1881-05)
		George Clinton (1805-09)
4. James Madison	Mar. 4, 1809 – Mar. 3, 1817	George Clinton (1809-12)
		Elbridge Gerry (1813-14)
5. James Monroe	Mar. 4, 1817 – Mar. 3, 1825	Daniel Tompkins
6. John Quincy Adams	Mar. 4, 1825 – Mar. 3, 1829	John Calhoun
7. Andrew Jackson	Mar. 4, 1829 – Mar. 3, 1837	John Calhoun (1829-32)
		Martin Van Buren (1833-37)
8. Martin Van Buren	Mar. 4, 1837 – Mar. 3, 1841	Richard Johnson
9. William H. Harrison	Mar. 4, 1841 – Apr. 4, 1841	John Tyler
10. John Tyler	Apr. 6, 1841 – Mar. 3, 1845	— — —
11. James Knox Polk	Mar. 4, 1845 – Mar. 3, 1849	George Dallas
12. Zachary Taylor	Mar. 4, 1849 – Jul. 9, 1850	Millard Fillmore
13. Millard Fillmore	Jul. 10 1850 – Mar. 3, 1853	— — —
14. Franklin Pierce	Mar. 4, 1853 – Mar. 3, 1857	William King
15. James Buchanan	Mar. 4, 1857 – Mar. 3, 1861	John Breckinridge
16. Abraham Lincoln	Mar. 4, 1861 – Apr. 15, 1865	Hannibal Hamlin (1861-65)
		Andrew Johnson (1865)
17. Andrew Johnson	Apr.15, 1865 – Mar. 3, 1869	— — —
18. Ulysses Simpson Grant	Mar. 4, 1869 – Mar. 3, 1877	Schuyler Colfax (1869-73)
		Henry Wilson (1873-77)
19. Rutherford B. Hayes	Mar. 4, 1877 – Mar. 3, 1881	William Wheeler
20. James Abram Garfield	Mar. 4, 1881 – Sep. 19,1881	Chester Arthur
21. Chester Alan Arthur	Sep. 19, 1881 – Mar. 3, 1885	— — —
22. Grover Cleveland	Mar. 4, 1885 – Mar. 3, 1889	Thomas Hendricks
23. Benjamin Harrison	Mar. 4, 1889 – Mar. 3, 1893	Levi Morton
24. Grover Cleveland	Mar. 4, 1893 – Mar. 3, 1897	Adlai Stevenson
25. William McKinley	Mar. 4, 1897 – Sep. 14, 1901	Garret Hobart (1897-99)
		Theodore Roosevelt (1901)
26. Theodore Roosevelt	Sep. 14, 1901 – Mar. 3, 1909	— — —
		Charles Fairbanks (1905-09)
27. William Howard Taft	Mar. 4, 1909 – Mar. 3, 1913	James Sherman
28. Woodrow Wilson	Mar. 4, 1913 – Mar. 3, 1921	Thomas Marshall
29. Warren G. Harding	Mar. 4, 1921 – Aug. 2, 1923	Calvin Coolidge
30. Calvin Coolidge	Aug. 3, 1923 – Mar. 3, 1929	— — —
		Charles Dawes (1925-29)
31. Herbert Clark Hoover	Mar. 4, 1929 – Mar. 3, 1933	Charles Curtis
32. Franklin D. Roosevelt	Mar. 4, 1933 – Apr. 12, 1945	John Garner (1933-41)
		Henry Wallace (1941-45)
		Harry Truman (1945)
33. Harry S. Truman	Apr. 12, 1945 – Jan. 20, 1953	— — —
		Alben Barkley (1949-53)
34. Dwight D. Eisenhower	Jan. 20, 1953 – Jan. 20, 1961	Richard Nixon
35. John F. Kennedy	Jan. 20, 1961 – Nov. 22, 1963	Lyndon Johnson
36. Lyndon Baines Johnson	Nov. 22, 1963 – Jan. 20, 1969	— — —
		Hubert Humphrey (1965-69)
37. Richard Milhous Nixon	Jan. 20, 1969 – Aug. 9, 1974	Spiro Agnew (1969-73)
		Gerald Ford (1973-74)
38. Gerald R. Ford	Aug. 9, 1974 –	

POSTMASTERS GENERAL OF THE UNITED STATES

1789 Samuel Osgood, Mass.	1857 Aaron V. Brown, Tenn.	1885 Wm. F. Vilas, Wis.
1791 Timothy Pickering, Pa.	1859 Joseph Holt, Ky.	1888 Don M. Dickinson, Mich.
1795 Joseph Habersham, Ga.	1861 Horatio King, Maine	1889 John Wanamaker, Pa.
1801 Gideon Granger, Conn.	1861 Montgomery Blair, D. C.	1893 Wilson S. Bissell, N. Y.
1814 Return J. Meigs, Jr., Ohio	1864 William Dennison, Ohio	1895 William L. Wilson, W. Va.
1823 John McLean, Ohio	1866 Alexander W. Randall, Wis.	1897 James A. Gary, Md.
1829 William T. Barry, Ky.	1869 John A. J. Creswell, Md.	1898 Charles Emory Smith, Pa.
1835 Amos Kendall, Ky.	1874 Jas. W. Marshall, N. J.	1902 Henry C. Payne, Wis.
1840 John M. Niles, Conn.	1874 Marshall Jewell, Conn.	1904 Robert J. Wynne, Pa.
1841 Francis Granger, N. Y.	1876 James N. Tyner, Ind.	1905 Geo. B. Cortelyou, N. Y.
1841 Charles A. Wickliffe, Ky.	1877 David McK. Key, Tenn.	1907 Geo. von L. Meyer, Mass.
1845 Cave Johnson, Tenn.	1880 Horace Maynard, Tenn.	1909 Frank H. Hitchcock, Mass.
1849 Jacob Collamer, Vt.	1881 Thomas L. James, N. Y.	1913 Albert S. Burleson, Tex.
1850 Nathan K. Hall, N. Y.	1882 Timothy O. Howe, Wis.	1921 Will H. Hays, Ind.
1852 Samuel D. Hubbard, Conn.	1883 Walter Q. Gresham, Ind.	1922 Hubert Work, Colo.
1853 James Campbell, Pa.	1884 Frank Hatton, Iowa	1923 Harry S. New, Ind.

1929 Walter F. Brown, Ohio
1933 James A. Farley, N. Y.
1940 Frank C. Walker, Pa.
1945 Robert E. Hannegan, Mo.

1947 Jesse M. Donaldson, Ill.
1953 Arthur E. Summerfield, Mi.
1961 J. Edward Day, Calif.
1963 John A. Gronouski, Wis.

1965 Lawrence F. O'Brien, Mass.
1968 W. Marvin Watson, Tex.
1969 Winton M. Blount, Ala.
1972 Elmer T. Klassen, Mass.

THE FRANKLIN AND WASHINGTON DEFINITIVES OF 1908-22

Beginning in 1908 and continuing to 1922, all regular issues except 479-80 portrayed Washington or Franklin. Series showing Washington (as on Scott 332, 333) and Franklin (as on Scott 331, 414, 547) are as follows:

331-42, 422-3	Double line Wmk.	Perf. 12	462-78	Unwmkd.	Perf. 10
343-47	Double line Wmk.	Imperf.	481-85	Unwmkd.	Imperf.
348-56	Double line Wmk.	Coil Stamps	486-97	Unwmkd.	Coil Stamps
357-66	Bluish Paper	Perf. 12	498-518, 523-4	Unwmkd.	Perf. 11
374-82, 405-7,			519	Double line Wmk.	Perf. 11
414-21	Single line Wmk.	Perf. 12	525-530	Offset Printing	Perf. 11
383-4, 408-9, 459	Single line Wmk.	Imperf.	531-35	Offset Printing	Imperf.
385-96, 410-13,			536	Offset Printing	Perf. 12½
441-58	Single line Wmk.	Coil Stamps	538-41	Rotary Press	Perf. 11x10
424-40	Single line Wmk.	Perf. 10	542	Rotary Press	Perf. 10x11
460	Double line Wmk.	Perf. 10	543	Rotary Press	Perf. 10
461	Single line Wmk.	Perf. 11	544-46	Rotary Press	Perf. 11

The illustrated examples which follow will aid collectors in identifying various 2c and 3c issues of 1908-22 showing Washington, sia 333. Illustrations reproduced by permission of H. L. Lindquist.

Two Cent Types
Numerals in Lower Corners

Type I. There is one shading line in the first curve of the ribbon above the left "2" and one in the second curve of the ribbon above the right "2".

The bottom of the toga has a faint outline.

The top line of the toga rope, from the button to the front of the throat, is also very faint.

The shading lines at the face terminate in front of the ear with little or no joining, to form a lock of hair.

Used on both flat and rotary press printings.

Type Ia. The design characteristics are similar to type I except that all of the lines of the design are stronger.

The toga button, toga rope and rope shading lines are heavy. The latter characteristics are those of type II, which, however, occur only on impressions from rotary plates.

Used only on flat plates 10208 and 10209.

Type II. Shading lines in ribbons as on type I.

The toga button, rope, and rope shading lines are heavy.

The shading lines of the face at the lock of hair end in a strong vertical curved line.

Used on rotary press printings only.

Type III. Two lines of shading in the curves of the ribbons.

Other characteristics similar to type II.

Used on rotary press printings only.

Collectors are warned against copies of Type III (Nos. 455, 488, 492 and 540) which have had one line of shading scraped off to resemble Type II (Nos. 454, 487, 491 and 539).

Type IV. Top line of the toga rope is broken. The shading lines in the toga button are so arranged that the curving of the first and last form "ꓭꓷD".

The line of color in the left "2" is very thin and usually broken.

Used on offset printings only.

Type V. The top line of the toga is complete.

There are five vertical shading lines in the toga button.

The line of color in the left "2" is very thin and usually broken.

The shading dots on the nose and lip are as indicated on the diagram.

Used on offset printings only.

Type Va. Characteristics are the same as type V except in the shading dots of nose. The third row of dots from the bottom has four dots instead of six. The overall height of type Va is 1/3 mm. less than type V.

Used on offset printings only.

Type VI. General characteristics are the same as type V, except that the line of color in the left "2" is very heavy.

Used on offset printings only.

Type VII. The line of color in the left "2" is invariably continuous, clearly defined, and heavier than in type V or Va, but not as heavy as in type VI.

An additional vertical row of dots has been added to the upper lip.

Numerous additional dots have been added to the hair on top of the head.

Used on offset printings only.

227

Three Cent Types

Type I. The top line of the toga rope is weak and the rope shading lines are thin. The fifth line from the left is missing.

The line between the lips is thin.

Used on both flat plate and rotary press printings.

Type II. The top line of the toga rope is strong and the rope shading lines are heavy and complete.

The line between the lips is heavy.

Used on both flat plate and rotary press printings.

Type III. The top line of the toga rope is strong but the fifth shading line is missing as in type I.

Center shading line of the toga button consists of two dashes with a central dot.

The "P" and "O" of "POSTAGE" are separated by a line of color.

The frame line at the bottom of the vignette is complete.

Used on offset printings only.

Type IV. The shading lines of the toga rope are complete.

The second and fourth shading lines in the toga button are broken in the middle and the third line is continuous with a dot in the center.

The "P" and "O" of "POSTAGE" are joined.

The frame line at the bottom of the vignette is broken.

Used on offset printings only.

Two Cent Washington Types
of 1923-29 sia 554

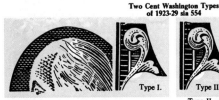

Type I — No heavy hair lines at top center of head. Outline of left acanthus scroll generally faint at top and toward base at left side.

Type II — The heavy hair lines at top center of head; two being outstanding in the white area. Outline of left acanthus scroll very strong and clearly defined at top (under left edge of lettered panel) and at lower curve (above and left of numeral oval).

Previous Contributors to U.S. Stamps & Stories

Tagging On United States Stamps

Two different luminescent qualities are found in U.S. postage stamps and postal stationery, they are fluorescence and phosphorescence. While all luminescent stamps glow when exposed to short wave ultraviolet (UV) light, only those with phosphorescent properties have a brief afterglow when the UV light is turned off. This afterglow is not affected by fluorescent materials sometimes found in the paper.

In August 1963 in Dayton, Ohio, the United States Post Office introduced mail handling equipment that automatically faces, cancels and sorts mail by sensing the UV light-activated afterglow from phosphorescent substances. The first stamps coated (tagged) with an invisible phosphorescent compound were the 8¢ carmine air mails (No. C64a). The compound used on air mail stamps glows in a range from orange-red to pink when exposed to short wave UV.

By June 1966, testing having proved the efficiency of the new equipment, all 8¢ air mails were phosphor tagged. By January 1967, all air mail stamps, regardless of denomination, were tagged with the orange-red glowing phosphor.

In further experimental tests, the City Mail Delivery commemoratives (1238) issued October 26, 1963 were tagged with a yellow-green glowing phosphor to distinguish surface mail from air mail. The 4¢ and 5¢ denominations of the regular issue (Nos. 1036b, 1213b, 1213c and 1229a) were also issued with the same green-glowing phosphor. From 1963 through 1965 limited quantities of the Christmas issues (Nos. 1240a, 1254a-1257a and 1276a) were tagged for continuing tests in the Dayton area.

On May 19, 1966 the testing of phosphor tagged stamps was expanded to the Cincinnati Postal Region. Additional denominations of regular issues, some postal stationery and a percentage of each commemorative issue were ordered tagged. After January 1, 1967 most regular issues through the 16¢, all commemoratives and additional items of postal stationery, were tagged. During 1973 higher denominations of regular postage were issued tagged.

Since there is no need to cancel mail bearing stamps precanceled by the Bureau of Engraving and Printing and, since precancel permit holders must post such mail already faced, Bureau precancels are not normally tagged. In some postal stationery the luminescent element is in the ink with which the stamp design is printed. On others, a vertical phosphorescent bar or panel has been placed to the left of the imprinted stamp.

Current stamps exist with the luminescent coating unintentionally omitted. As the coating compound used is usually invisible to the naked eye, the presence or absence of tagging is best determined by examining the stamps or postal stationery items under an ultraviolet lamp. CAUTION: Users of UV light must avoid prolonged exposure which can permanently damage the eyes. Wearing sunglasses or prescription eyeglasses while the light is being used helps screen the rays and provide some protection. One must never look directly into the ultraviolet light for any reason whatsoever.

A GLOSSARY of BASIC PHILATELIC TERMS

Bisect

Booklet Pane

Coils. These stamps are perforated on two sides only.

Cut Square

Approvals: Stamps sent to a collector for examination. Approvals must be bought or returned to the dealer within a specific time.

Bisect: Half of a stamp used to pay postage of half the face value of the original stamp. This variety must appear on its original cover with the cancellation or postmark covering the cut.

Block: An unsevered group of stamps at least two stamps wide and two stamps high.

Booklet Pane: A small pane of stamps especially printed and cut to be sold in booklets.

Cachet: A special handstamp or printed device on a cover to denote the special circumstances in which it was mailed.

Cancellation: A mark placed on a stamp by a postal authority to prevent its reuse.

Cancelled to Order (CTO): Stamps which are cancelled by the postal authorities without being sent through the mails. They are normally less desirable than stamps which have served their postal function.

Coils: Stamps issued in rolls for use in dispensers, affixing or vending machines.

Color Changeling: A stamp whose color has been changed, either accidentally or intentionally.

Commemoratives: Stamps which honor anniversaries, important people, or special events. Commemoratives are usually sold for a specific length of time.

Compound Perforations: A stamp with perforations of different sizes on different sides.

Condition: The state of a stamp in regard to centering, color, freshness, cancellation, and other related characteristics.

Cover: The entire wrapping or envelope in which a letter has been sent through the mail.

Cut Square: An envelope stamp cut out with a square margin.

Definitives: Regular issues of stamps as distinct from commemoratives.

Die: An engraving from which the plates for printing stamps can be made.

Encased Postage Stamps: Stamps inserted into small cases and circulated as currency.

Errors: Stamps with accidental mistakes in color, paper, inscription, watermark, etc. Errors also include bicolored stamps with inverted centers.

Essays: Designs submitted in stamp form but not accepted for issuance.

First Day Cover: A cover bearing a new stamp and cancelled with the first day of use, usually at an officially designated location.

Flat Press Stamps: Stamps printed on a flat bed press, as distinguished from a rotary press.

Freaks: Stamps which show conspicuous deviations from the normal caused by shifted perforations, heavy inking, color shifts, or similar accidents during production. Not errors.

Grill: Parallel rows of small pyramids impressed or embossed on the stamp in order to break the fibers of the paper so that the cancellation ink will soak in and make washing for reuse impossible.

Gum: The adhesive on the back of a stamp.

Hinges: Small strips of paper gummed on one side and used by collectors to mount their stamps.

Imperforate: Stamps without perforations. They must be separated with scissors and are usually collected in pairs to prove their authenticity.

India Paper: A soft, thin, silky appearing wove paper usually used for proof impressions.

Inverted Center: A stamp with the center printed upside down in relation to the rest of the design.

Laid Paper: A paper showing alternate light and dark parallel lines when held to the light or immersed in benzine.

Locals: Stamps issued for use in restricted areas either by governments or private carriers.

Margin: The border outside the printed design of a stamp, or the similar border of a pane of stamps.

Overprint: Any word, inscription, or device placed on a stamp to alter its use or locality, or to serve a special purpose.

Packet: A selection of stamps in a sealed envelope.

Pair: Two unsevered stamps.

Pane: A portion of the original sheet as cut for sale at the post office.

Part-Perforate: A stamp which has perforations on one, two or three sides.

Pen Cancel: A cancellation applied to the stamp with pen and ink.

Perforations: Line of small cuts or holes placed between two rows of stamps to facilitate separation.

Plate: The actual object from which the stamps are printed.

Plate Number Block: A block of stamps with sheet margin showing a plate number or numbers. Often it is known simply as a plate block.

Postal Stationery: Envelopes, postal cards, wrappers, etc. which had nonadhesive stamps embossed or printed on them.

Postmark: A mark struck upon envelopes, generally to indicate the name of the post office, date of mailing, etc.

Precancels: Stamps with cancellations applied before the mailing of the article on which they prepay postage.

Proofs: Trial printings of a stamp made from the original die or the plate.

Provisionals: Stamps issued prior to the regular issues or to meet a temporary shortage of regular stamps.

Reissue: An official printing of a stamp, or stamps, that had been discontinued.

Remainders: Stocks of stamps on hand after the issue has been discontinued.

Reprints: Impressions from the original plates, blocks, or stones taken after the issuance of the stamps to post offices has ceased and their postal use has been voided.

Revenue Stamps: Stamps issued for use in collecting special taxes on documents, proprietary articles, products, etc.

Imperforate Stamp

Perforated Stamp

Perforation Gauge
A device used to measure the number of perforations in a two centimeter area on the edge of a stamp.

Surcharge

Overprint

Tête-Bêche

Rotary Press Stamps: Stamps printed on a rotary type press from curved plates as compared to stamps printed from flat plates on a flat bed press. They will be slightly larger in one direction than flat press stamps.

Rouletting: Short consecutive cuts in the paper between rows of stamps to facilitate separation.

Se-tenant: An unsevered pair of stamps which differ in value, design, or surcharge.

Sheet: Complete unseparated group of stamps as originally printed.

Special Printings: Stamps of current design reissued, usually on a better grade of paper and in brilliant colors.

Stampless Cover: An envelope without stamps generally bearing a postmark and sometimes notations such as "Paid", "Paid 10", etc.

Straight Edge: The imperforate side of a stamp which is otherwise perforate.

Strip: Three or more unsevered stamps forming a vertical or horizontal row.

Surcharge: An overprint which alters or restates the face value or denomination of the stamp to which it is applied.

Tête-bêche: Stamps printed upside down in relation to each other.

Tied On: A stamp is "tied on" when the cancellation or postmark extends from the stamp to the envelope.

Topicals: Area of philately in which emphasis is on the subject portrayed on stamps rather than the stamps themselves.

Unused: A stamp with or without original gum which has no cancellation or other evidence of postal duty.

Used: A stamp which has done postal duty as evidenced by the cancellation.

Want List: A list of stamp numbers or philatelic items needed for a collection.

Watermark: A design or pattern incorporated into the paper during its manufacture.

Wove Paper: A paper of uniform texture throughout, showing no light or dark patterns when held to the light or immersed in benzine.

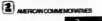

AMERICAN COMMEMORATIVES

FORT HARROD

Until the discovery of the Cumberland Gap, in 1750, Kentucky remained virtually unexplored, even by the Indians, who called it "the great meadow" for its beauty; "tomorrowland" for its promise; "the dark and bloody ground" for the many battles fought over it. After the discovery of the Gap, those hunters who ventured into "Kaintuck" returned calling it the closest thing to heaven. In the land-poor East, "Kentucky Fever" ran rampant. In the spring of 1774, James Harrod of Pennsylvania and a company of 32 men set out for Kentucky. They paddled canoes down the Ohio River and up the Kentucky River to the region called the Bluegrass. There, on a fertile plateau at the source of a large, pure stream they built Fort Harrod and began plotting out a town. Fort Harrod was started on June 16, 1774, and was the first permanent English-speaking settlement west of the Allegheny Mountains. Harrodsburg, the settlement built in and around the fort remained in a virtual state of Indian siege for nearly a decade. The founders' wives and children arrived in 1775 and Kentucky's first school was built within the fort. Kentucky's first industry—spinning and weaving—began in the cabin of Ann McGinty. By 1776, Harrodsburg held the first Kentucky physician's office and in 1777 Kentucky's first court convened there. In a blockhouse at Fort Harrod, General George Rogers Clark planned the campaign that led to the founding of Louisville and the capture of the Northwest Territory.

The stamp was designed by David K. Stone of Port Washington, New York. The associated vignettes printed from the original steel dies, were engraved from 1852 to 1879.

Stamps printed by the Bureau of Engraving and Printing, Washington, D.C.

Copyright 1974 American Bank Note Company

No. 34 in a series

June 15, 1974 / Printed in U.S.A.

. . . Use order blank
on pages 235-236

AMERICAN COMMEMORATIVE SERIES at $2.00 each

Series No.	Commemorative Issue	Quantity	Value
1	Wildlife		
2	Mail order		
3	Osteopathic Medicine		
4	Tom Sawyer		
5	Pharmacy		
6	Christmas 1972		
7	"Twas the Night before Christmas"		
8	Stamp Collecting		
9	Love		
10	Pamphleteer (Bicentennial Issue)		
11	George Gershwin		
12	Posting Broadside (Bicentennial Issue)		
13	Nicolaus Copernicus		
14	Postal People		
15	Harry S. Truman		
16	Post Rider (Bicentennial Issue)		
17	Boston Tea Party (Bicentennial Issue)		
18	Electronics		
19	Robinson Jeffers		
20	Lyndon B. Johnson		
21	Henry O. Tanner		
22	Willa Cather		
23	Drummer (Bicentennial Issue)		
24	Angus Cattle		
25	Christmas '73		
26	Needlepoint Noel		
27	Veterans		
28	Robert Frost		
29	Expo '74		
30	Horse Racing		

AMERICAN COMMEMORATIVE SERIES at $2.00 each

Series No.	Commemorative Issue	Quantity	Value
31	Skylab		
32	Universal Postal Union		
33	Mineral Heritage		
34	Fort Harrod		
35	Continental Congress		
36	Chautauqua		
37	Kansas Wheat		
38	Energy Conservation		
39	Legend of Sleepy Hollow		
40	Retarded Children		
41	Christmas Contemporary Currier & Ives		
42	Christmas Masterpiece Altarpiece		
Binder at $7.00 each			
Value of items ordered			
Postage and Handling charges			.50
Grand total			

PLEASE TYPE OR PRINT

_____

LAST NAME, FIRST NAME AND MIDDLE INITIAL

_____

STREET NO., STREET NAME OR P.O. BOX NO. ETC.

_____

CITY NAME   STATE   ZIP CODE

**Send your check or Postal Money Order with order form.
Do Not Send Cash.**

The United States Postal Service sells only commemoratives released during the past few years and current regular and special stamps and postal stationery.

Prices listed in this handbook are called "catalogue prices" by collectors and serve only as a guide to market prices for fine specimens when offered by an informed dealer to an informed buyer. They are taken from the 1975 Scott Catalogue whose editors have based these values on the current stamp market. Comments concerning them should be directed to the Scott Publishing Co.

The Scott numbering system for stamps is used in this book since it is the identification system used by most stamp dealers and collectors in the United States.

Note: When minimum price of a used stamp is fixed at 3 cents it reflects dealer's labor and service costs. The sum of these minimum prices does not properly indicate the value of an accumulation of stamps consisting only of cheaper stamps. Price of actual stamp sales are dependent upon supply and demand, changes in popularity, local custom, quality of the stamp itself and many other factors.

Souvenir Pages with First Day Cancellations

50¢ each plus the cost of affixed stamp

First day cancellation of each new stamp is affixed to an 8 x 11½ inch page suitable for framing or insertion in an album. Each page also has philatelic data and other information about the stamp and is printed in two colors.

Souvenir pages are available by subscription only and you can begin receiving yours by depositing $10.00 or more with your initial order. Once your subscription is received you will be given an account number and will be included in the next mailing. Every two or three months you will get pages with cancelled stamps issued the previous months, and the cost will be subtracted from your subscription deposit.* A renewal notice will be sent when your deposit is low. The delivery schedule depends on the number of issues released each month.

Gift subscriptions are also available—with a card announcing the gift sent to the recipient in the name of the giver.

To subscribe or make a gift subscription, send your check or Postal Money Order with the coupon on the next page—or write directly to the Philatelic Automatic Distribution Service, Philatelic Sales Division, Washington, D.C. 20265.

Guaranteed refund policy: Any subscriber can cancel their subscription on 30-day notice and receive a refund of the unused portion.

Here is your order form for subscribing to the Souvenir Page service. Just fill in the information requested below and send the completed form, along with your remittance, to: Philatelic Automatic Distribution Service, Philatelic Sales Division, Washington, D.C. 20265

PLEASE PRINT OR TYPE

LAST NAME, FIRST NAME & MIDDLE INITIAL OR FIRM NAME

STREET NO., STREET NAME OR P.O. BOX NO., ETC.

CITY NAME   STATE   ZIP CODE

SOUVENIR PAGES

AMOUNT OF DEPOSIT $_____

QUANTITY OF EACH PAGE REQUESTED   _____

Send your check or Postal Money Order with order form. Do Not Send Cash.

For your club or meeting . . .

A FILM THAT HIGHLIGHTS OUR NATION'S HISTORY & HERITAGE IN STAMPS

Qualified organizations may receive "Stamps—A Nation's Calling Cards" on a free loan. This 16mm color motion picture brings the audience the beauty and meaning found in postage stamps. Featuring the Apollo Eleven "Moon Landing" stamp, the film shows seldom seen processes, from the first hand-engraved impression of a single stamp through the steps that result in the final printing of millions.

    The 19 minute film brings to life numerous stamps that have become a part of our national tradition, with a mixture of creative photography and original music that will entertain anyone who uses a stamp—from the beginner to the advanced collector.

For free loan mail request to:

National Audio Visual Center (GSA), Washington, D. C. 20409
Include individual name, organization name, address, city, state, zip code.

Please indicate preferred and alternate dates.

240